RESISTING SECTARIANISM

RESISTING SECTARIANISM

Queer Activism in Postwar Lebanon

John Nagle and Tamirace Fakhoury

ZED

LONDON • NEW YORK • OXFORD • NEW DELHI • SYDNEY

Zed Books
Bloomsbury Publishing Plc
50 Bedford Square, London, WC1B 3DP, UK
1385 Broadway, New York, NY 10018, USA
29 Earlsfort Terrace, Dublin 2, Ireland

BLOOMSBURY and Zed Books are trademarks of Bloomsbury Publishing Plc

First published in Great Britain 2022

Cover design by Liron Gilenberg

A catalogue record for this book is available from the British Library.

A catalog record for this book is available from the Library of Congress.

ISBN: HB: 978-1-7869-9799-9
PB: 978-1-7869-9800-2
ePDF: 978-1-7869-9798-2
eBook: 978-1-7869-9796-8

Typeset by Newgen KnowledgeWorks Pvt. Ltd., Chennai, India

CONTENTS

FIGURES

TABLES

ACKNOWLEDGEMENTS

John Nagle would like to thank his former colleagues at the University of Aberdeen for help and advice in shaping this book project, particularly Bernie Hayes. At Queen's University, Belfast, John appreciates the School of Social Sciences, Education and Social Work for their help in allowing to complete this book. John gratefully acknowledges the support of the Leverhulme Trust for granting him a fellowship to carry out research for this book (Ref: 2017–616). John is eternally thankful for all the people who so generously gave up their time to patiently speak to him during research for this book. He sincerely hopes that he has not let them down. Finally, John expresses deep gratitude and love to Mary-Alice.

Tamirace Fakhoury wishes to thank the activists who made themselves available notwithstanding the ongoing protests and roadblocks in Lebanon and the ensuing Covid-19 pandemic. She would also like to thank Bassel Salloukh, Helle Malmwig, Carmen Geha, Rosita di Peri, Stu Cook, Omar Fakhoury and Fatme el Masri for inspiring discussions on protests, activism and postwar Lebanon. She is also grateful for the conversations and debates she has had with her students at the Lebanese American University. In particular, she would like to thank Christelle Barakat and Ayyad el Masri for their research insights. She also wishes to extend her warmest thanks to her family and friends who provided encouragement during the writing process despite the turmoil that Lebanon has experienced lately. She particularly wishes to thank Tala and Wael Fakhoury for their continuous support.

The authors thank Ken Barlow, Kim Walker, Olivia Dellow and Melanie Scagliarini for helping direct this book and for their patience in giving them time to complete it under trying conditions.

PREFACE

Same-sex relations and expressions of non-conforming gender are illegal in seventy-three jurisdictions worldwide as of 2020. LGBTQ activist groups have emerged in a number of these places with the objective of revoking criminalization, securing human rights for a persecuted population and transforming homophobic attitudes prevalent in their societies. Resistant states often respond by engaging in preventive strikes to halt the LGBTQ rights movement before it can gain significant traction (Human Rights Watch 2016). This backlash involves banning the promotion of homosexuality, and closing down the space for freedoms of expression, association, and peaceful assembly for activists (Ayoub 2016; Encarnación 2016; Nuñez-Mietz 2019).

How can activist movements create change in environments where they are subjected to state surveillance, harassment, violence and imprisonment? In these societies it is all but impossible for activists to work through formal political institutions to secure legislative and policy change within the various arms of the government. Public expressions of dissent and identity generate further vicious repercussions for activists and the LGBTQ population.

In this book we argue that activist movements have created significant advances in the teeth of a system that is closed and trenchantly hostile to LGBTQ rights. These changes rarely, if ever, come in the shape of new policies or legislation being rescinded. Instead of this, we draw the reader's attention to the complex, multidimensional and powerful forms through which activists effect positive change. LGBTQ movements do so by exposing loopholes in the legal system to render it inoperative in terms of penalizing individuals accused of conducting sex 'against the order of nature', through constructing new narratives of sexuality that destabilize the foundations of homophobic power, by navigating paths through informal institutions, and by forging intersectional alliances with other marginalized groups and across civil society. Most importantly, everyday politics (Tria Kerkvliet 2009) forms a big part of LGBTQ movements' action repertoires. Through subtle practices and acts, ranging from drawing graffiti to struggling with daily bureaucracies, they negotiate new imaginaries that contest official institutions and rethink governance. The various forms of everyday politics they engage in expose the failings of governments and resist oppressive structures.

Yet, as important as these modes of change are, we stress their contingency. It is unrealistic to claim that they possess permanency. They are instead revocable and unstable forms of progress, imbued with inherently impermanent qualities. In a cat-and-mouse game, the homophobic state is often willing to adapt to the creative tactics of LGBTQ activists in order to severely constrict the space that activists can operate within. At the same time, we show that assigning value to such modes of change cannot be reduced to tracking tangible policy outcomes. LGBTQ activists diffuse various forms of everyday resistance that instigate change from margin to centre and from periphery to the core.

We illuminate these issues in this book by focussing on LGBTQ activism in Lebanon. Queer activism in Lebanon has drawn significant scholarly attention, particularly since the first public queer movement in the Arab world emerged here (Moussawi 2017, 2018, 2020; Naber and Zaatari 2014). This book thus seeks to add to this literature. The case study of Lebanon is important for a number of reasons. First, it is here that the first above-ground LGBTQ activist group in the Arab world was formed. The Middle East is often portrayed as a region that is uniformly and virulently homophobic. Certainly, it can be argued that it is not a hospitable place for LGBTQ activism to flourish. Five of the ten states in the world that sanction the death penalty for homosexuality are in the Middle East. Most countries in the region endorse policies that criminalize non-conforming sexuality and/or place prohibitions on the freedom of expression and association for LGBTQ groups (Arab Foundation for Freedoms and Equality 2018). Such opposition to LGBTQ rights is often ascribed to conservative values supposedly inherent to the region. Homophobia, accordingly, results from these places lacking modernity. Yet, it is profoundly erroneous to suggest that the Middle East is a homogeneous space when it comes to sexuality. Same-sex relations have long been practiced and tacitly tolerated within specific configurations of class, gender and power. Nor is it the case that resistance to human rights for LGBTQ populations is simply down to cultural backwardness. It is instead more often driven by governments seeking to suck the oxygen from efforts to contest their vulnerable regimes (Human Rights Watch 2016). LGBTQ activists and populations provide convenient scapegoats for regimes to blame, for instigating a process of moral decay. Attacking LGBTQ movements also sends a signal to broader civil society that the government and its security forces are willing to deploy its coercive power to shut down the space for freedom of expression and assembly. Most importantly, through engaging in detail with activism in Lebanon we can track how activists have sought to craft movement tactics and strategies that resonate with the context they operate within. Thus, we emphasize the creativity and agency involved in activism outside of the space of the Global North. Rather than expressions of political imagination that are, as one activist explains, 'cut "n" paste' from the West, Lebanese activism engenders innovative and creative forms that challenge the idea that these movements are mere identikit copies of activism that diffuse in a unidirectional way from the Global North to the South.

Second, to understand the specific environment that activists work within, we argue that it is essential to engage with Lebanon's postwar sectarian system. Lebanon's sectarian system, designed to accommodate the main sects in political and public institutions, reproduces patriarchy and homophobia. In mainstream narratives and political manifestoes, Lebanon has often been hailed as one of the few democracies in the Middle East. Such accounts however overlook how the resiliency of sectarian politics is built on eroding the agency of ordinary citizens and anti-sectarian movements, namely feminist and queer movements.

Confronting the sectarian system is thus central to the activism of the Lebanese queer movement. One important way in which activists have done this is by building alliances with non-sectarian activists in Lebanon and with transnational grassroots actors such as migrants and refugees.

Third, by engaging with the Lebanese case, we show that queer activism takes on manifold forms that defy an *outness* versus *closetness* perspective or a binary logic of *visibility* versus *secrecy*. LGBTQ activists craft forms of dissent that flirt with an ambiguous politics of visibility, and that seek to decentre and recentre the periphery as the core. Transcending mere identity politics, their activism is geopolitical. To a large extent, it is about contesting the sectarian state and its attempts to exercise power over its territory, and over its citizens' bodies, pasts, lived realities and futures.

...

We have endeavoured to write this book in an accessible way. It draws on numerous conversations and interviews with activists, policymakers, and a range of people involved in shaping the LGBTQ movement and rights in Lebanon. As much as possible, we have tried to let these people speak for themselves. Rather than forming a coherent and unified narrative, the testimonies articulated by activists and others in this book reveal debate, ambiguity and even conflicting perspectives. They also illustrate the myriad ways and trajectories through which activists think about redesigning the postwar sectarian state, commonly framed as an assemblage of dysfunctional institutions captured by elite cartels and sectarian barons.

The structure of this book is as follows. Chapter 1 provides greater detail on the book's main themes, debates and arguments. In Chapter 2 we examine the various ways in which Lebanon's postwar sectarian system regulates and constructs sexuality. Chapter 3 focuses on the rise of the Lebanese LGBTQ activism, including the debates and divisions among activists about the direction of travel for the movement. Chapter 4 centres on activism designed to counter Article 534 of Lebanon's penal code, which criminalizes 'sex against the order of nature'. Chapter 5 turns to how activists articulate and negotiate the politics of visibility, particularly in terms of the media, cultural activities and linguistic activism. The impact of international actors – particularly funders from the Global North – is analysed in Chapter 6. In Chapter 7 we highlight the intersectional alliances that LGBTQ activists have formed within major waves of protest against the state's sectarian system since 2015. The role of LGBTQ activists in the 2019 October uprising framed as the thawra or revolution is discussed in detail. In Chapter 8 we conclude by exploring how queer activism in Lebanon presents an opportunity to reimagine the sectarian state beyond its frontiers.

Chapter 1

'NO HOMOPHOBIA, RACISM, SEXISM, CLASSISM'

Sunday afternoon in central Beirut permits a fleeting moment of relative calm as the weekday tumult generated by motorists fighting for space on gridlocked streets temporarily recedes. Sunday, for many Beirutis, is a time for a leisurely promenade with friends and family along the Corniche, a lengthy walkway that curves around Ras Beirut, the tip of the city's coastline. Yet, in a city absent of public transport networks and parks, and where many public services are failing, noisy expressions of citizen dissatisfaction against the state are not uncommon. Sunday afternoon, 25 April 2010, witnessed one such event as about five thousand people strode down the Corniche on their way to the Lebanese parliament in the nearby downtown area of Beirut in what was called a 'Secular Pride March'.

A group called Laïque Pride, 'a secular movement for citizenship', which started on Facebook, organized the protest. Organizers called for an end to the sectarian system that underpins Lebanon's postwar political and social order. During the march some protestors chanted 'What's Your Sect? None of Your Business.' One man held a fluorescent banner with a skull and crossbones proclaiming: 'Sectarianism: Danger'. At one point a parade participant held aloft a placard reading 'Queers for Secularism', while a small group unfurled the Rainbow Flag, the symbol of international LGBTQ pride, underneath which two women kissed.

The association of LGBTQ rights activism with a protest against Lebanon's sectarian system is no mere coincidence. Lebanon's postwar institutions, carefully crafted to accommodate the state's multiple sects, have specific consequences for the country's LGBTQ population. The sanctioning of homophobic violence and oppressive policies penalizing LGBTQ subjects is an unavoidable condition of the state's sectarian structure (Mikdashi 2014, 2018). LGBTQ activists recognize that they are required to confront Lebanon's sectarian system, specifically because it is patriarchal and requires compulsory heterosexuality (Naber and Zaatari 2014). In a manifesto published by activists, 'resisting sectarianism' is the main goal of the movement, since 'the biggest challenge to any form of social justice in Lebanon is the sectarian makeup of its society' (Meem 2010a: 15).

It is these issues that this book addresses. In this book we not only trace the impact – often pernicious but also contradictory – of the sectarian system for LGBTQ individuals; we further illuminate the varied and powerful tactics deployed by activists to demand rights within a system that is effectively closed to them. This project leads us to consider the variety of techniques used by activists to discredit the system by exposing its failings. To fully understand the relationship between Lebanon's postwar system and the struggle for LGBTQ rights, we emphasize the need for an intersectional approach.

'No homophobia, racism, sexism, classism'

Lebanon's sectarian system is legally enshrined in the state's constitution, which calls for a 'covenant of coexistence' between the various sects. This notion of sectarian pluralism institutionalizes a fragmentary vision of the state that assumes citizens' primary membership resides in supposedly self-evident sectarian groups (Joseph 1999; Salloukh et al. 2015). Yet, the legal fiction of sectarianism has created political realities that do not map onto social experiences. The belief that sectarian groups are homogenous entities obscures the diversity within; a suture runs through and across these groups along the seams of class, gender, sexuality and many other things beside. Individuals who identify with pluralistic political projects have been called Lebanon's 'hidden third' since they are not recognized in a system that prioritizes allegiance to sect-based communities (Farha 2019).

The system, by its nature, is paradoxically holistic and asymmetrical. Holistic in that it seeps into and captures all political and social issues and positions them as fundamental to the maintenance of the social and political order. At the same time, sectarianism distributes its effects unevenly across different social groups. It positions women as bearers of inferior rights with respect to men; LGBTQ people are violently excluded from rights; and sectarianism sustains inequalities among socio-economic classes. For many others, such as the millions of Syrian and Palestinian refugees and 'kafala' migrant workers[1] in Lebanon, the system consigns them to the status of non-citizens stripped of rights. Mariam, a Lebanese feminist and LGBTQ activist, explained to us over coffee in Badaro, a fashionable district of Beirut:

> If you want to look at the sectarian system, you have to look at it from an intersectional perspective. You have to look at in terms of how it effects your social class, your economic class, your race, your ability, your sexuality and if you look at that you will see how the layers are created.[2]

Intersectionality, Mariam argues, allows us to consider the multiple pinpoints through which Lebanon's sectarian system creates inequalities while simultaneously leaving itself open for contestation. While sex, gender and class represent the foundation of Lebanon's sectarian system, they also expose choke points where the sectarian structure is exposed and threatened. Struggles against racism, for class-based economic redistribution, gender equality, and rights for LGBTQ, refugees and migrant populations provide battle lines where it is possible to challenge the grammar that sustains sectarianism. In other words, Lebanon's sectarian system has been built through the exclusion of numerous groups; these groups have challenged their marginalized status thus contesting the very structure of the system. In a celebrated piece of graffiti that adorned a wall in Beirut's downtown area during protests against the state's sectarian leaders in 2015, the linkages between some of these issues were starkly illuminated: 'No Homophobia, Racism, Sexism, Classism' (see Figure 1.1). Since, as Naber and Zaatari (2014) note, sectarianism is founded on asymmetrical systems of gender, class, race, ethnicity,

Figure 1.1 Graffiti in the downtown district stating 'LGBTQ+ Rights' during the 2019 'thawra' protests

and sexuality, activism requires an intersectional approach that refuses to impose false binaries or hierarchies on a complex social reality.

Seeing the connections between struggles enables us to understand the multiple forms of inequity that shape sexuality in Lebanon and the cross-sectoral alliances LGBTQ activists have forged to resist the violences of the sectarian system. On this, an activist aptly told us that 'our vision is to chip at the system so that one day it all crumbles. This is our aim. Breaking the wall'.[3] Breaking the wall of the sectarian system is a collective action that requires what Chantal Mouffe (2000) calls 'chains of equivalence': various marginalized movements come together, often momentarily, to assemble creative political strategies to unveil inequality and reorder existing power relations. The groups in the chain each have their own distinct relation to the existing hegemony, and each group's experience and interests are irreducible to the others, while at the same time alliances are forged (see Purcell 2009).

Research on Lebanon's sectarian institutions emphasizes their resilience to any meaningful form of change. This claim is especially true when it comes to the system impeding non-sectarian groups that demand rights and services. Non-sectarian movements are groups that contain activists from all sections of society regardless of sect or ethnic background, which advance claims that transcend sect divisions (Clark and Salloukh 2013; Geha 2018; Nagle 2018a). The sectarian system is often presented as possessing the power to make non-sectarian movements invisible or as actors marginalized, co-opted, stripped of agency and disempowered (e.g. Kingston 2013). In short, as scholars correctly note, the system 'is deployed instrumentally by a sectarian/political elite bent on reproducing sectarian identities and obviating the emergence of alternative, trans-sectarian or non-sectarian, modes of political mobilization' (Salloukh et al. 2015: 2).

It is undoubtedly true that the system makes it extremely hard for non-sectarian groups to gain significant concessions from the state's institutions. Modest policy reforms have been leveraged with respect to women's rights in Lebanon despite the existence of major internationally supported feminist NGOs (Human Rights Watch 2015; Nadeem 2019; Nassif 2020). Even less is conceded to movements demanding better rights for migrant workers, refugees or for greater accountability on corruption. The same situation confronts movements demanding public services. Only a fraction of laws passed in the past decade relate to the citizenry's concerns in various domains such as health, water or employment, and parliamentary debates have dedicated more attention to issues regarding sectarian representation and security (see Atallah 2018; Geha 2018).

When it comes to LGBTQ rights, the system does not make it difficult for LGBTQ movements; it does everything in its power to ensure the state's LGBTQ population experiences their lack of rights and representation at all registers of state and society. Article 534 of Lebanon's penal code, which criminalizes 'sex against the order of nature' is directed at the LGBTQ population, and it carries a maximum one-year jail sentence (Helem 2008). Expressions of non-conforming gender identity are further prosecuted under several other articles regulating public morality and decency (Human Rights Watch 2019). Lebanese LGBTQ people confront 'discrimination in employment and arbitrary dismissal, to limited access to housing, health, and social services, to political and financial extortion' (Makarem 2011: 100). A report commissioned by activists noted that members of the LGBTQ population are 'periodically arrested, detained, and tortured by Lebanese security forces' (Gender and Sexuality Resource Centre 2015: 7).

Unfortunately, homophobia permeates the upper echelons of the state. Most political leaders of the many sectarian factions are publicly homophobic. Consider, for example, Hassan Nasrallah, the leader of Hezbollah, who declared in a major speech that 'homosexual relations defy logic, human nature and the human mind' (Issa 2017). In 2013, the then minister of internal affairs used the Arabic equivalent of 'faggots' to describe gay people in a TV interview. Five years later, a Lebanese delegation headed by the speaker of parliament was instrumental in voting down an international bill in Geneva for LGBTQ rights (Ministry of Information 2020).

The crude sentiments articulated by these leaders appear to broadly align with the views of a substantial section of the Lebanese public. In 2015, Lebanese activists published evidence from a survey that laid bare the nature of the citizenry's attitudes towards the LGBTQ population. The results made grim reading: 64.6 per cent stated that homosexuals should not be accepted into society; 85.1 per cent saw homosexuality as endangering the institution of the family; 65.6 per cent believed that laws against homosexuality were necessary (Gender & Sexuality Resource Centre 2015).

It is hardly surprising then that LGBTQ activists face major barriers in their efforts to claim rights. Lebanese LGBTQ rights groups are banned from formally registering as civil society organizations, which means they cannot open bank accounts to access funding from donors. As we shall detail throughout the book, the various arms of the state carry out a wide-range campaign of harassment, including arresting and detaining activists and censoring and closing down LGBTQ events.

Playing snakes and ladders

How can LGBTQ movements generate reform and rights within a sectarian system that is deliberately constructed with ossified properties rendering it resistant to practically any reform? In confronting the numerous obstacles placed in front of them, Lebanon's LGBTQ movement engenders creative ideas and practices to challenge their oppression and exclusion. In this book, we argue that LGBTQ movements stimulate potent and powerful forms of change. In so doing, we stress the importance of broadening our understanding of how social movements create the impetus for transformation in societies with a legacy of political violence and sectarian division. This requires us to accept that these movements rarely, if at all, create public policy reform since the formal state institutions are largely closed to the claims of activists.

A much richer and multidimensional analysis of change is essential to fully understand the impact of Lebanon's LGBTQ movement that takes into account the methods they deploy to render sectarian power inoperative and their capacity to contradict homophobic and patriarchal attitudes within society. LGBTQ activists work through informal institutions to make the day-to-day lives of their constituency more secure, they build alliances with human rights activists locally and internationally, and the movement crafts cultural practices to challenge homophobic stereotypes of LGBTQ people in the media. They also engage in forms of everyday activism such as wrestling with bureaucracies, criticizing employment discrimination, denouncing landlords who refuse to rent them property because of their sexual orientation or simply debating change in coffee shops and online fora. These daily practices, dispersed yet contentious, consolidate their presence as visible public actors.

While these achievements may not appear concrete or consequential in the same way as forcing the parliament to pass a new law or a public sector body to initiate formal statutory policies, they are nevertheless accumulative in their significance. Although activists have not been able to force the state to decriminalize homosexuality, they have successfully encouraged a number of judges – including within the military – not to sentence LGBTQ people on the basis of 'crimes against nature'. They have cooperated with psychologists and psychiatrists to declare that homosexuality is not a mental illness that requires reparative treatment. They have cooperated with health professionals to dissuade them from performing anal examinations – the so-called 'tests of shame' – against men and transpersons accused of being gay. While the Lebanese mainstream media once used pejorative epithets, such as 'faggots' and 'perverts', to describe the LGBTQ community, activists have worked with the media to encourage them to use more positive and acceptable terms in their reports.

Further achievements and progress may be identified. The LGBTQ movement has forged powerful networks with non-sectarian groups across Lebanon, including groups fighting for gender equality, rights for workers and refugees, and movements against corruption. These alliances now extend to the political sphere. In the 2018 national election all sixty-six candidates who formed part of the non-sectarian *Kallouna Watani* ('We Are National') movement endorsed the decriminalization of homosexuality. During the same election, one relatively notable sectarian party, the Kataeb, announced in their manifesto the plan to 'abrogat[e] all legal provisions that criminalize homosexuality' in the highly unlikely event that the party gains a government majority (Human Dignity Trust (2020). In addition, LGBTQ representatives and individuals are increasingly becoming visible in Lebanese culture. The Beiruti rock band Mashrou' Leila, which can rightly claim to be the most internationally famous group from the Middle East, are major advocates of LGBTQ rights, often articulated in their songs, and their lead singer is openly gay. In one campaign for a leading Lebanese restaurant chain, an online advertisement featured a lesbian couple while another advert for a different company used a trans* model. On a more social level, one activist noted that young people feel more confident 'coming out' these days compared to previous generations.

Beyond activism within and against the state, one of the most significant impacts of Lebanese LGBTQ activists in calling for rights is the internationalization of the movement. Internationalization encompasses regional and global dimensions for activists. At the level of the wider region, it is in Lebanon that the first public LGBTQ movement in the Middle East and North Africa (MENA) emerged. Since then, a wave of LGBTQ rights groups surfaced in Jordan, Tunisia, Egypt and Morocco. As an early riser, the Lebanese movement shares its accumulated knowledge and expertise with activists across the region in developing consciousness and movement-building tactics to deal with oppressive security forces, and long-term strategies for decriminalizing homosexuality. These regional networks provide a forum of ideas and practices to strengthen the movement (see Arab Foundation for Freedoms and Equality 2018).

At a broader scale, Lebanon's LGBTQ activist groups are positioned within the so-called 'global LGBTQ movement'. Lebanese activists often link their work to transnational LGBTQ campaigns. As the first public LGBTQ movement in the MENA region, Lebanese activism also attracted the attention of Global North funders and agencies seeking to work with local partners to disseminate LGBTQ rights across the region. LGBTQ activists are thus positioned as 'norm entrepreneurs', spreading LGBTQ rights across the Middle East. For the Lebanese LGBTQ movement, international agencies offer support and assistance in crucial ways. Beyond providing desperately needed financial support and resources, Global North actors allow the LGBTQ movement to upscale its activism to the international level. Since the local sectarian system is all but barred to activists, the movement animates international agencies to deploy their diplomatic offices and various forms of leverage against the Lebanese state in relation to LGBTQ rights. Some activists have also forged transnational alliances with anti-racist and migrant grassroots coalitions in the Middle East, Latin America and further afield. The intent is to anchor Lebanon's queer movement in a broader underground project that fights oppressive structures and injustices.

Successes and achievements are hard-won by the movement, yet such efforts are not unproblematic and without contestation. Activists cannot claim to have accomplished de jure rights for the LGBTQ population. Most of the gains mentioned above are provisional and revocable, often subject to swift and violent backlash. Activists must feel as if they are precariously positioned like pieces on a Snakes and Ladders board. Gradual and marginal progress is followed by sharp retreat when activists rub against the boundaries of what the state and sectarian factions are willing to accept. On this an activist wrote: 'We need to be very aware of the ramifications of all of our steps and to ensure that we understand the system and how far we can push, and push to the limit of that extent' (Choukeir and Poladoghly 2019).

There are also tricky questions on the precise nature of what constitutes positive change and progress. While some activists celebrate that a historically sectarian party like Kataeb now supports the decriminalization of homosexuality, another cohort displays equal amounts of scepticism about what they see as a cynical act of 'pinkwashing'. Similar debates surround the value of LGBTQ individuals being featured in advertisement campaigns and whether it represents a new politics of visibility and acceptance or mere 'queerbaiting', defined as 'using aspects of queer cultures or queer political support to signal hipness, coolness, political correctness, tolerance or open-mindedness' (Abraham 2019).

Perhaps the most problematical issue concerns the relationship that activists should build with Global North actors who support and fund LGBTQ rights in Lebanon. Activists rightly worry about their role in potentially importing Western notions of sexual identity and rights that are not sympathetic to local sensibilities and histories of sexuality. Lebanese activists are often accused by opponents of being little more than handmaidens of Western sexual imperialism, seeking to impose Western categories of sexuality as part of a concerted project of enforcing non-Arabic cultural norms and political values in the region (e.g. Massad 2007). Lebanese activists are acutely aware that these encounters between global human rights ideas and local practices may not always generate positive dynamics. Thus, while international funders press for decriminalization in Lebanon to instigate a 'norm cascade' across the MENA region, Lebanese activists recognize the necessity of tailoring campaigns to the local specificities of the environment they operate within, which is in itself profoundly shaped by the state's sectarian system. To an extent, a frictional relationship exists between the tactics used by local Lebanese activists and the aspirations and goals set out by global human rights promoters, such as the United Nations (UN), European Union (EU), and a host of Western states and their aid and development agencies.

'Sectarianism never makes a country happen'

In considering the multiple and complex forms through which Lebanese LGBTQ activists seek to effect change and realize rights, a question that follows is: What does this all add up to? What sort of change does this activism generate? To begin addressing this we look towards the burgeoning research on 'sexual citizenship'.

Two broad themes concerning sexual citizenship are of relevance. The first relates to how citizenship is historically grounded in assumptions about sexuality. Indeed, 'all citizenship is sexual citizenship, in that the foundational tenets of being a citizen are inflected by sexualities' (Bell and Binnie 2000: 10), specifically that heterosexuality is central to the logic of the nation state. It follows that the state has institutionalized heterosexuality as a precondition for citizenship and as the unspoken norm of membership and national belonging (Halperin 2012). In consequence, citizenship – as a set of civil, political and social rights – positions LGBTQ people as deviant and outside the bounds of citizenship. The second theme is concerned with forms of activism that challenge the ways in which sexual citizenship excludes and harms queer peoples.

The notion of sexual citizenship does not transfer easily to all environments. Sexual citizenship is often – though not exclusively – framed within the context of Western liberal democracies, especially in states where not only homosexuality is legalized but also where same-sex marriage and adoption rights have been secured. Demands for sexual citizenship, in this setting, is increasingly restricted to rights in the private sphere, thus reinforcing a neoliberal concept of individual rights founded on individual autonomy, domesticity and consumption (Duggan 2012; Halperin 2012; Ghaziani 2015).

In response, we need to take into account the 'geographies of sexual citizenship', which indicates how citizenship operates in a range of contexts and societies, particularly given its varied heterosexual connotations (Brown et al. 2010). Sexual geography also points to the fact that there are not only national differences in how sexual citizenship is practiced but also multiple forms of citizenship and non-citizenship *within* states and societies. This observation is particularly relevant when it comes to Lebanon. Here, it is perhaps better to think of the numerous dimensions of citizenship and how they overlap with sexuality.

While recognizing that all forms of national belonging are sustained by a 'civic myth' – myths that narrate who is and who is not eligible for citizenship – the dominant civic myth of Lebanon is grounded in sectarian pluralism (Joseph 1999). The civic myth of sectarian pluralism is that Lebanon is composed of a number of homogeneous sectarian groups that are simultaneously differentiated through their conflicting visions of state ownership. The aim of sectarian pluralism is to peacefully maintain the state's multicultural fabric through a bond of coexistence between the sects.

The sectarian system does not work to build a common or shared national identity; instead, it incentivizes individual citizens to locate belonging and affiliation within sectarian groups. Of course, it is too simplistic to claim that the Lebanese are imprisoned by sectarianism or manifestly wrong to ignore that individuals have many layers of identity, of which sect competes or sits alongside class, gender and geography. However, the upshot of all of this, as Rima, leading human rights activist and writer, admitted to us is that

> sectarianism never makes a country happen. It's the opposite of a country, because you keep thinking and conceiving yourself as just a member of a group, instead of thinking of yourself as a citizen in a country. And in order to have a strong state that respects people's rights, that protects people's dignities, it all starts with belonging to a country and that is one of the main ways in which sectarianism is affecting the protection of vulnerable groups.[4]

We should not view sectarian differences as natural or as products of ancient animosities between groups; the institutionalization of political and social identities is primarily a legacy of Lebanon's modern state formation, which is the result of Ottoman and French colonial divide and rule policies in the region. In contemporary Lebanon, an assemblage of formal and informal institutions and practices produce and reproduce sectarian politics and citizens at many registers of the state and society, ranging from government, communal elites, the public sector, to the media (Cammett 2014; Salloukh et al. 2015). Yet, the construction of sectarian pluralism can only be achieved through the production of gender and sexual inequalities. As Mikdashi (2018: 469) argues, 'Sectarian difference is dependent on, emergent with, and articulated together with sexual difference and the regulation of heteronormative reproductive sexuality.'

The work of anthropologist Suad Joseph (1997; 1999; 2000) is important here in tracing how sexual and sectarian citizenship is co-produced. Joseph argues that sectarian groups in Lebanon often resemble extended kinships, and membership in these sectarian networks is bound together in what she calls the 'kin contract': that one's obligations and loyalty is to the sectarian group above and beyond the state. For this reason, individuals in sectarian groups should not be understood as self-governing figures independent of others; selfhood is formed in relation to others within a group and linked to a relational notion of rights. Citizenship rights are sets of entitlements based on personal relationships with people who have access to desired resources and privileges. Thus, individuals do not go to the state for rights and resources but to their sectarian leaders – males who position themselves as the patriarchs and strongmen protectors of the group (Joseph 1999).

For Joseph, this relational sense of identity and rights is tightly linked to patriarchy – or what she terms 'patriarchal connectivity', a specific form of personhood linked with the state-building project in Lebanon (Joseph 1999). Patriarchal connectivity refers to how the sectarian system of imagining citizenship and rights is predisposed towards privileging the power of heterosexual males. All of this is intimately linked to the system of sectarian pluralism. Since the point of the sectarian system is to freeze the balance of power between the rival groups, it is necessary to ensure that the groups are viewed as homogeneous, and maintained as stable, unchanging cultures (Joseph 1999). In consequence, as we shall explore in Chapter 2, women are afforded differentiated and unequal citizenship rights in relation to men.

It is noticeable that Joseph does not specifically mention how LGBTQ individuals fit into the sectarian system. One can address this, of course, by acknowledging that they are simply proscribed and omitted – they have no official place at all. Yet all forms of omission are simultaneously revealing.

There are further dynamics that we need to attend to in order to understand how sexual citizenship is reproduced and contested in Lebanon. Lebanon's sectarian system sanctions the imposition of religion and religious leaders into public life. While religion is not intrinsically set in opposition to homosexuality, aspects of it can undoubtedly be constructed to frame non-heterosexual conduct as sinful and sexual 'deviants' to be punished or 'cured'. In Lebanon, fundamentalist religious authorities and groups – both Christian and Muslim – regularly intercede to demonize the LGBTQ population and put pressure on political leaders to resist any reform with respect to rights. Indeed, as Salloukh et al. (2015: 62) explain, 'Homosexuality is a symbolic challenge to the religious mores and patriarchal kin structures that support the sectarian system.'

In addition, the legacy of Lebanon's civil war (1975–90) created a class of warlords overseeing sectarian militias and their own personal fiefdoms. These warlords position themselves as both patriarchs of their sectarian communities and as political leaders ensconced in public life in the civil war's afterlife. A notable consequence of the power wielded by these figures is the militarization of Lebanese society, which itself is equally sustained by and reproduces forms of masculinity that legitimate homophobic violence.

More broadly, Rima pondered for a moment when asked if Lebanon's sectarian system impacted sexuality and gender. The legacy of sectarianism, she explained:

> is this culture of hate and of the rejection of the other that is different, it's what sectarianism is all about, and it's being extrapolated on other things, so if you're sectarian more or less there's a very big chance that you're going to be homophobic, that you're going to be racist, you're going to be sexist. It's all about rejecting the other: anyone that is different.

Yet, what precisely constitutes a progressive politics for Lebanese activists is a rarely agreed upon concept let alone policy goal. For anyone looking in from the outside, the issue of aims and goals for the Lebanese movement should be straightforward. Unlike activism in a number of so-called liberal Western states – which has achieved legal recognition of same-sex marriage and adoption rights – Lebanese LGBTQ people continue to be criminalized under a number of articles of Lebanon's penal system. Same-sex marriage is a dangerous and unwelcome ambition for Lebanese activists. Lebanese activists are understandably cautious of associating the movement's goals with same-sex marriage since many opponents of LGBTQ groups are apt to claim that decriminalization will set off an unstoppable and escalating set of demands inevitably leading to same-sex marriage and, in consequence, the very disintegration of society. Set within this context, rather than develop a movement concerned with bringing down the structures and institutions which sustain the heteronormative order, the bearings of some Lebanese activists are mostly oriented towards providing basic human rights and safety for a persecuted population.

At the same time, as we shall illuminate, Lebanese LGBTQ activism does not exist as a unified and coordinated movement representing a coherent and shared set of values and objectives. Deep fissures running through the movement mark activism. There have been divisions between gay men and lesbian women; socio-economic disparities within the LGBTQ population continue to conspire against the hope of an emergent collective consciousness needed to form a community. Such divisive dynamics are the inevitable result of the sectarian system, with its inbuilt properties driving gender and class inequalities. In consequence, the interests of gay men in the movement have tended to dominate at the expense of lesbians – thus delimiting an understanding of the specific ways in which sectarianism buttresses patriarchy. It is, furthermore, the 'queer unwanted' (Bell and Binnie 2004), individuals from working-class, transpeople or refugee backgrounds who are typically arrested, detained and tortured by the security forces and who find themselves in front of a judge. As Moussawi (2018) illuminates, middle-class and wealthy LGBTQ people are able to carve out a degree of protected space in their private lives that the state rarely intrudes into. In so doing, this has acted as a disincentive for many economically privileged LGBTQ individuals to become involved in a public movement.

At root, the various issues that activists differ on point back to debates about how to organize and how to confront the sectarian system. On one side is the argument that activists should engage with or find openings within the sectarian system so as to bring about change and rights. This form of activism involves the professionalization of the movement, especially via the setting up of formal NGOs – funded by Global North organizations – that advocate for human rights and services for the LGBTQ population. Critics of this strategy argue that NGOization depoliticizes the radical potential of social movements by redirecting its energies into service delivery and a narrow form of identitarian politics. On the other side, since the sectarian system is seen as legitimating sexual inequality, LGBTQ activists focus on a radical campaign of resistance against political sectarianism. Critics of this approach argue that it is toothless and incapable of dealing with the daily realities of oppression and violence and it overstretches the reach of the movement. These debates are played out in this book.

With regard to the existence of divisions, we pay attention to the intersectional effects of the sectarian system and the intersectional character of activism that has emerged in response. Intersectionality has become a major framework to understand the differences that lie within social categories and where these differences interact to generate systemic privilege and inequality (Cho, Crenshaw and McCall 2013; Collins and Bilge 2020). Thus, while there are clear inequalities between men and women, we need to bring in sex, ethnicity, race, class and ability, among many forms of social position, and show how they overlap and intersect to determine, in many cases, gradations of power and exclusion. The point of intersectionality is that it helps us understand the real-world consequences which determine the limits of life for people, ranging from their access to public services and employment to their daily experience of harassment and prejudice (Puar 2018).

Intersectionality, importantly, provides a tool to understand the dynamics of inequality and power in specific contexts. Concerning Lebanon, an intersectional approach is unavoidable when analysing the relationship between the sectarian system, gender and sexuality. Lebanon's sectarian system does not only politicize differences between sects but also constructs inequalities between social groups within and across sectarian formations. As noted earlier, political sectarianism deliberately constructs multiple inequalities along the lines of class, gender, sexuality, nationality and even race. For instance, as we will explore in Chapter 2, the system derives very acute effects and variances between women depending on the sect they are bureaucratically categorized as belonging to. When it comes to sexuality, the complexities of the sectarian system play out to create discrete but notable nuances of power, vulnerability and marginalization for LGBTQ people (Allouche 2017).

Intersectionality, beyond a way of analysing how sectarianism interacts with sexuality, is a form of practice that is used by activists to systemically interrogate and challenge the multiple points where the system reproduces itself. For this reason, LGBTQ activism in Lebanon has often been profoundly oriented towards the building of alliances and networks both within major waves of anti-sectarian mobilization and with numerous marginalized actors in Lebanon.

As powerful a paradigm of research and practice intersectionality is, some activists stress its limitations in the Lebanese context. As we show in Chapter 7, in a closed political system, intersectional coalition-building often forces queer activists to adjust and adapt to dominant activist projects in protest spaces. As they embrace and identify with multiple oppressions and cumulative understandings of identity, cutting across sect, race, gender and sexuality, they find it challenging to carve their own protest presence. They also find it difficult to deploy their own protest framings and slogans without alienating the crowds in Lebanon. What they need at times is to deepen conversations about how sexism deploys itself in their lived realities and to demonstrate explicitly how Lebanon's sectarian-based system subordinates them. Claiming intersectional narratives without getting to grips with the core of their struggle and capturing how their legal and social subordination unfolds may lead to a romanticized version of their bodies as sites celebrating 'solidarity', 'togetherness' and 'strength'.[5] A superficial approach to intersectionality might also lead to exposing the relationships between inequality without necessarily tackling the roots of dispossession. For example, adopting the queer cause in Lebanon's iconic protest spaces might only attend superficially to the various ways the system relegates them. The challenge for queer activists in Lebanon is to chart the trajectory of intersectionality as a political, economic and social project.

Power-sharing and sexuality

Writing about the relationship between Lebanon's sectarian system and sexuality invites us to place this within the wider context of postwar power-sharing. Lebanon's sectarian system is essentially given shape by the architecture of power-sharing (Hanf 2015; Nagle 2016a,b; Fakhoury 2019). Power-sharing has become one of the main institutional tools for ending conflict in a number of places around the world, ranging from Bosnia and Herzegovina, Iraq, Northern Ireland, Sudan and Macedonia (McCulloch 2014). It is currently suggested as a prescription for ongoing wars in Syria, Yemen and Iraq (Salloukh 2020). At root, power-sharing is based on the assumption that violent intrastate conflict occurs when groups, especially minority communities, are excluded from political power. Power-sharing seeks to remedy this situation by giving the main ethnic- or sect-based groups some form of guarantees of representation within government and even across the public sector, as well as group rights (McGarry and O'Leary 2006; McCulloch 2014).

It is fair to say that power-sharing invites trenchant debate among scholars and policymakers. Proponents argue that power-sharing provides the best opportunity to incentivize belligerent parties to exchange violence for peaceful inclusion within representative democracy (McGarry and O'Leary 2006; McCulloch 2014). More critical voices claim that power-sharing institutionalizes and even exacerbates ethnic and sectarian cleavages and further foments dysfunctional governance, rendering institutions prone to deadlock and periodic collapse (Horowitz 2014).

While these debates are well rehearsed, a growing body of research considers the consequences of power-sharing from another angle (Nagle 2016b, 2018a; Agarin, McCulloch and Murtagh 2018). That is, although power-sharing is predicated on including the main ethnic groups in conflict, it also at the same time risks being exclusionary. Power-sharing systems rarely, if at all, provide representation or rights to groups that are not necessarily defined in terms of ethnicity. Thus, provisions for gender equality, rights for migrant groups, and other non-sectarian groups, are typically overlooked by the architects of power-sharing systems. In justification, it could be argued that power-sharing arrangements are frequently hammered out under duress, often when communal violence is pervasive and there is a greater need for stability than performance. It is admittedly a difficult task for power-sharing structures to be truly inclusive, since this may risk overburdening the peace process when it is at its early and most fragile stage.

Despite these qualifications, a residual concern is that power-sharing is not only exclusionary, but more critically it generates deeply negative consequences for groups and issues not formally included. Feminist scholars, notably, have highlighted how power-sharing systems often regress the advancement of gender equality in the aftermath of intrastate conflict (Hayes and McAllister 2013; Geha 2019a; Byrne 2020). There are several overlapping factors that have been identified as accounting for this, including the extent to which power-sharing privileges ethnic and sectarian identities at the expense of all other forms of social struggle. Primarily, however, power-sharing rewards the hardliners of the respective ethnic groups, typically strongmen patriarchs, who have little interest in accommodating gender equality, whether it be in terms of fostering the representation of women in parliament and government, or in relation to reproductive rights. Lebanon, as we will highlight later, is particularly illustrative of how the power-sharing government, and particularly the Lebanese parliament, continues to have one of the lowest proportions of elected women in the world (Geha 2019a).

Given these anxieties concerning the relationship between power-sharing and gender it is surprising that very little is written about its effects on sexuality and queer rights (Nagle 2016, 2018b; Hayes and Nagle 2019). To an extent this is indicative of the fact that power-sharing arrangements are almost completely absent of any provisions to recognize LGBTQ rights. Yet, this is not to say that this omission means that power-sharing derives no consequences for questions of sexuality. At one level, power-sharing does not provide any openings for LGBTQ groups to mobilize for inclusion within government. The system is completely closed to such claims.

Beyond institutional openings for LGBTQ groups, power-sharing has key properties that can profoundly shape the lives of queer people. As noted above, power-sharing systems tend to empower ethnic- and sect-based leaders, almost exclusively male figures responsible for violence and intergroup acrimony. In some instances, these are leaders of groups who have deliberately targeted LGBTQ populations during wartime, often under the pretence of defending the morality of their community. It is not surprising, therefore, that the peacetime reinvention of warlords as legitimate political leaders carries the hazard of homophobia being entrenched in power-sharing. In addition, some power-sharing systems, such as Lebanon, are based on giving representation to sect-based groups. The self-proclaimed leaders of the political groups are often tied to religious organizations, particularly in terms of requiring support and legitimacy from religious authorities. These religious authorities typically express trenchant opposition to same-sex relations and non-normative gender identities, thus constricting the room for political elites to manoeuvre on LGBTQ rights.[6]

Understanding the complex relationship between power-sharing and sexuality is one of this book's main themes. Our intention, however, is not to simply present sectarian power-sharing systems as arrangements that completely eradicate the potentiality for queer movements to mobilize as social movements. Of course, as we shall detail, social movement activism can take the form of protest against power-sharing. This oppositional politics is commonly expressed via alliances and intersectional networks with actors across civil society who are marginalized and excluded by power-sharing (Naber and Zataari 2014). Activism in relation to power-sharing is not only expressed through the instruments of protest. Movements can engage with power-sharing. Yet, since the formal institutions of power-sharing are largely closed to queer movements, activists operate in the spaces and shadows formed by informal institutions. We allude here to activists building informal relationships with the judiciary, police and even politicians to establish procedures that give some degree of protection for LGBTQ people.

In examining queer activism, our book speaks to a broader set of research that addresses how non-sectarian movements mobilize, and demand rights and services within and against power-sharing (Carabelli 2018; Milan 2019). Such research challenges the perception that non-sectarian groups are either invisible or rendered as actors that are marginalized, co-opted, stripped of agency and disempowered by power-sharing. This book, thus, contributes to our understanding of the intertwining limitations and opportunities afforded by power-sharing and the forms of engagement created by non-ethnic movements in response.

'The crackdown is escalating'

Our intention in this book is to not only illuminate the struggles of LGBTQ activists but also further assess what, if any, change they have made in relation to rights, and to track how they have effected such a change. Many books on movement activism are written as exercises in ex post facto analysis; authors retrospectively identify the causal mechanisms that lead to a movement's success or failure. Such after-the-event analyses import a teleological dynamic to the policy outcomes of social movements. The highly contemporary nature of the research presented in this book makes it problematic for us to make grand claims with regards to the direction of travel of Lebanese LGBTQ activism. While we identify the complex, multilayered and yet constrained ways in which activists stimulate positive change, it would be remiss to declare that the accumulative effect of activism will inevitably lead to enduring rights for LGBTQ people in Lebanon.

Indeed, there is an assumption that a dynamic is driving global progress towards LGBTQ rights. Survey data from 1981 until 2008 shows that for the fifty-two countries with available data, approximately 67 per cent of them experienced an increase in the proportion of residents reporting that 'homosexuality' is always justified (Adamczyk and Liao 2019). In explaining why there is a progressive upswing in support of LGBTQ rights in many places, scholars point to the 'modernization' thesis. Adamczyk and Liao (2019), for example, argue that support for LGBTQ rights is dependent on the flourishing of the key attributes of modernization and liberalization: economic growth, democratization and secularization. In fact, LGBTQ rights and tolerance of sexual difference has become not only a signifier of modernity but it also constitutes the 'apex of Western exceptionalism'. Momin Rahman (2014: 121) argues that 'sexual exceptionalism is conjured as the marker of civilizational exceptionalism', which reinforces the ideals of progress and superiority supposedly inherent in the project of Western modernity.

International funders of activism in the Global South often see their mission as rolling out rights that have already been gained in the West (Rao 2014). In this framework, states are resistant to LGBTQ rights because they have not as yet achieved modernity. Homophobia is explained as a consequence of patterns of cultural conservatism and backwardness that remain deeply entrenched in some societies. These places are rendered as a 'living anachronism' (Nichols 2012: 54), stuck in the past, and thus requiring external help to develop into liberal pluralistic societies that are accepting of sexual diversity. In a trenchant analysis, Hakima Abbas (2012) argues:

> LGBTI issues have gained ground in the international arena as a barometer to determine who the 'good liberal' countries versus the 'bad backward' are. With racist undertones about the 'barbaric' and 'uncivilized', it has been written that the 'cultures' and 'traditions' of the Black and Brown peoples of the world have not yet been civilized enough to tolerate gay and lesbian people.

In the barometer of progress, states are ranked hierarchically in terms of their position with respect to LGBTQ rights. In an examination of the International Lesbian, Gay, Bisexual, Trans and Intersex Association (ILGA) usage of a traffic light system to determine a state's status in the spectrum of tolerance for LGBTQ rights, Rao (2014: 170) notes how this 'ranking impulse' reproduces a 'temporal narrative of sexual modernization'. Yet, since LGBTQ rights are classified as indicators of modernization, LGBTQ populations in homophobic states are 'interpreted as sexual subjects who already "embody" (some) elements of modernity'. For this reason, international actors are required to 'activate these populations so that they can begin a process of queer identity formation that will transform them … into important agents of modernization and development' (Klapeer 2018: 110).

Yet, there is a rather sad irony, at best, or hypocrisy at work here. Homophobic policies and influences were originally imposed during periods of Western imperialism. Laws penalizing homosexuality today in many countries are the direct result of colonial penal laws established in the nineteenth and early twentieth century. Indeed, Western administrators and observers once declared that fluid sexual relations and practices in non-Western places were the result of their pre-modern cultures (Dalacoura 2014). The shift against same-sex relations became associated with modernization. According to Afary (2009: 162–3), in the Middle East, '[the] notion of modernization now included the normalization of heterosexual eros and the abandonment of all homosexual practices and even inclinations'.

The assumption that rights will automatically flow from the Global North to the South generates major difficulties for activists in Lebanon. An LGBTQ activist wrote about how Western policymakers tended to promote 'Western' forms of activism and sexual development as a model for Lebanon and other countries to follow: 'The idea that LGBT liberation was a linear timeline, of which various nations and peoples were lagging behind a triumphant West, was deeply offensive' (Zeidan 2019). Recounting a conversation with policymakers in the United States, Hakim, a leading Lebanese activist, impressed on them that the idea of rights unalterably cascading downwards from the North is problematic for the Lebanese movement:

A lot of people especially in the West, especially donors are pushing 'policy, policy and engagement, let's get it out, let's talk', because emboldened by the rapid unfolding of what has been going on in the West, it's like a pack of cards, gay marriage is coming. But I always remind them that the gay lobby and movement in the West have been operating for years.[7]

Another activist, Hala, placed the issue in starker terms:

Why should I let somebody in Washington decide how I should create change because they went through this in the 1970s what we are going through now? They don't understand the language, the idioms, the culture – they don't talk to people.[8]

Rather than make bold predictions regarding the LGBTQ movement's long-term outcomes in the Middle East – that it follows in a simple undeviating fashion the trajectory of change that has been won for LGBTQ populations in parts of the Global North and Latin America – it is more important to recognize the shifting, contingent and insecure environment that Lebanese LGBTQ activists operate within.

To an extent, this apprehensive situation is a product of what Encarnación (2016) identifies as a current 'global reversal' of LGBTQ rights in a number of states across the world designed to intimidate the LGBTQ population and roll back gains in LGBTQ rights. As Nuñez-Mietz (2019) notes, many states deploy 'norm immunization', a strategy of creating legal barriers aimed at stymieing LGBTQ rights at root by targeting advocacy groups. In this, non-traditional sexual orientations or gender identities (SOGIs) are discursively constructed as an incompatible foreign norm that endangers the moral and cultural fabric of the nation, and thus represents an existential threat to the very security of the state. In making LGBTQ rights a security issue, states engage in legalized forms of 'hetero-protectionism' to defend the nation, including expanding judicial and extrajudicial powers to minimize the space for activism.[9]

While state elites may claim that the securitization of LGBTQ activists and population is justified in order to protect the nation from foreign vices and moral degeneracy, such discursive devices serve a more political purpose. There are different dimensions to the political opposition to LGBTQ rights. First, some autocratic states scapegoat LGBTQ populations as a way to consolidate power, to justify conservative policies and to distract the citizenry from other issues. Second, for other repressive regimes, clamping down on LGBTQ rights acts as a signal to the wider population of the leadership's willingness to crack down on political and civil liberties. Third, political opposition in many former European colonies is driven by elites seeking to purchase legitimacy by encouraging their populations to resist Western imperialism seen to be imposing itself in the form of LGBTQ rights. A Human Rights Watch (2016) report, on abuses against LGBTQ populations in former European colonies, summarizes:

> By closing the political space in which civic groups operate, autocrats are trying to suck the oxygen from organised efforts to challenge or even criticise their self-serving reign. ... An increasingly popular method to crack down on civil society is to target organizations of lesbian, gay, bisexual, and transgender (LGBT) people or those that advocate on their behalf. Some repressive governments claim, much like their calls to limit the right to seek foreign funding, that LGBT people are alien to their culture, an imposition from the West.

In Lebanon, these factors combine with an admixture of political expediency and opportunism to explain the opposition of LGBTQ rights by sectarian elites. Thus, while some figures have spoken against rights by alleging that it represents Western imperialism, others see such reform as a threat to the integrity of the sectarian system that they continue to prosper from. These same figures also condemn the LGBTQ movement as a convenient symbol to redirect attention away from their own manifold failings particularly evident in a weak state system riven by endemic sectarian division, widening socio-economic inequalities and increasing levels of poverty. On this point, Joey, an LGBTQ activist who deals with victims of homophobic violence on a daily basis, said: 'Our state is trying to do imaginary victories facing their failure on other levels. They are ready to target minorities and gay people as they are a catchy subject.'[10]

Thus, in mass demonstrations against the sectarian system, elites have publicly blamed LGBTQ activists for seeking to corrupt the youth of the nation. In being framed as a Western plot to weaken the moral fabric of Lebanon, General Security – the agency responsible for intelligence and national security – has been used to raid LGBTQ events. The idea that LGBTQ people in Lebanon constitute a security threat is evident in the fact that suspects are often detained in Hobeish station in Beirut, which was infamous as one of main sites where political prisoners were tortured and interrogated during the civil war. In sum, Mariam, a human rights worker and LGBTQ activist, who has been tracking the backlash has this to say:

> Definitely there is a crackdown on organizing in general, freedoms of assembly, freedoms of association, freedoms of expression. It is escalating and the crackdown on LGBT rights specifically is escalating and that's because it is easily weaponized as a political strategy to maintain the nation state and whatever idea of the Lebanese nation that people may have in some way by very easily saying that LGBT rights are against our morals because they are Western imports and once you let them in they are going to ruin the family and all we have is the social fabric of the family. We definitely see that the crackdown is escalating and it doesn't seem that it's going to get any better.[11]

Examples of backlash are found in abundance and to varying degrees of oppression. The state has deployed its powers to censor movies as part of the Beirut International Film Festival in 2016 purely because they contained themes and characters interpreted by the censors as sympathetic to LGBTQ people. While a number of judges refuse to sentence people under Article 534 and other morality laws directed at LGBTQ people, there has been an increase in number of arrests. In 2018 alone activists monitored thirty-five arrests and trials, including that of twenty-seven transwomen – a significant rise over a five-year period. In a move deliberately designed to target the LGBTQ population, the Telecommunications Ministry imposed a ban on Grindr – the gay dating app. Beirut Pride was shut down in 2018 by the general prosecutor of Beirut after the main Pride organizer was arrested and detained in a police cell by the vice squad. A few months later Lebanese General Security officers unlawfully shut down a conference on LGBTQ rights at a hotel in Beirut. In the following months General Security banned a group of foreign activists and academics that had attended the conference from re-entering Lebanon. In all, these incidents, a leading activist noted, form 'part of a bigger campaign and strategy to limit the spaces of the LGBT community' (Hall 2019). Rashida, a human rights worker and activist we spoke to, who had monitored all of these acts by the state against LGBTQ activists and people, noted that 'the more visible LGBT rights become to the fore in the political discourse the more backlash we are receiving'.[12] Samer, a senior activist, regretfully admitted that 'we are suffering from backlash of the LGBT rights movement of the West'.[13]

The forces of backlash and repression and the resultant vulnerability it creates seems from the outside to be compounded by the geopolitical context of the Middle East and North Africa. A number of states in the Middle East sponsor human rights violations against LGBTQ populations. Many governments in the region reject altogether the concepts of 'sexual orientation' and 'gender identity' (Human Rights Watch 2018a). Yet instead of framing the Middle East as a region uniformly governed by implacable patriarchy and homophobia, a more productive line of inquiry is to examine the potentialities, openings and opportunities for LGBTQ rights that exist in tension with definite social and political constraints.

It is in this contingent and ambivalent space – between progress and reversal –
that LGBTQ rights exist in Lebanon. It is this space that this book concentrates on.

What's in a name?

Neither of the authors of this book are members of the LGBTQ population.
We have not been subjected to or threatened with persecution, imprisonment,
harassment and the innumerable forms of violence and oppression that LGBTQ
individuals in Lebanon routinely endure. In so doing, we do not write with any
claim to being the authoritative voice of the LGBTQ experience in Lebanon. While
one of the authors – Tamirace Fakhoury – is Lebanese and works in Lebanon,
John Nagle is an academic from the Global North. It is thus necessary to take
into account the vital issue of power relations involved in researching and writing
sexuality and gender in the Middle East. Of utmost importance is to avoid quasi-
imperialist analyses. The sexual imperialist framework, as noted earlier, seeks to
impose Western ideas of sexuality and development as models for activists and
policymakers in the Middle East to adopt. Underlying such desires are neocolonial
notions of *liberating* MENA people from repressive political and social structures.
Such motivations often go hand in hand with analyses that present the Middle East
as uniformly homophobic and intolerant, containing little hope of change with
respect to LGBTQ rights.

The issue of terminology is one area in which neocolonial tendencies can
easily be perpetuated. The term 'sexual minorities' is notably problematic as it
assumes that heterosexuality is the dominant norm and majority. The concept of
'minority' and 'majority' sexualities suggests a fixity of these relative categories
that reinforces the idea of the status quo of the 'natural' social/sexual order.
Somewhat different concerns are directed at the use of 'LGBTQ'. As Richardson
explains, the term 'LGBTQ' risks omitting the differential experiences of social
exclusion and discrimination that often exist between gay men and lesbians.
Such anxiety is particularly relevant when it comes to LGBTQ rights activism
where lesbians become subsumed under the category 'gay', especially as rights
movements are associated historically with demands for the decriminalization
of male homosexual offences, such as anti-sodomy laws (see Richardson 2017).
These terminological concerns have enhanced importance in the context of
Lebanon where the sectarian system not only creates differences in citizenship of
lesbians and gay men, but also within women. These relationships of difference
and inequality have led to splits and a legacy of acrimony among some activists,
as we shall explore in Chapter 3.

There are additional problems associated with the descriptors 'sexual
minorities' and LGBTQ. These are culturally specific concepts that draw upon
Western assumptions and identity categories in relation to gender and sexuality,
concepts that may not translate directly in other languages or be meaningful
categories in other cultural contexts. As we shall see in Chapter 5, a key part of
activism in Lebanon is to challenge and change the Arabic terms that have been

used historically by the media and politicians to describe LGBTQ individuals. While recognizing that it is an imperfect term, in this book we continue to use 'LGBTQ'. 'LGBTQ' reflects the common deployment of this term by a number of activist groups when describing the constituency they represent and work for. We also occasionally use SOGI. SOGI is increasingly used by development agencies – such as the World Bank and the UN – due to its inclusivity; it embraces all forms of gender and sexual identity. Some activists in Lebanon use SOGI to describe their work.

These issues related to terminology expose questions about what constitutes sexuality in Lebanon. Terms such as 'LGBTQ' are typically used in the Global North to capture one's sexual identity. Yet it has long been noted that the idea that sexuality represents a signifier of intrinsic individual identity is essentially a Western construct that emerged through the interweaving of science and politics in the nineteenth century. It is a product of the way in which the constructions of the self and its location in modernity are understood. Homosexuality became constructed as a form of subjectivity by the subfields of psychiatry and sexology. In these new medical discourses, 'homosexuality' was a descriptor of a deviation from a developmental norm and thus had to be 'corrected' through interventionist forms of disciplinary power that served the good of the body politic (Foucault 1980). The rise of LGBTQ rights activism was to overturn the framing of homosexuality as a medical pathology by instead celebrating and demanding the recognition of sexual diversity as a key cornerstone of a liberal state.

This precept – that sexuality is an identity – does not necessarily travel well. It is often noted that people who engage in same-sex relations in the region do not necessarily see this as constituting a form of subjectivity. As Nasser-Edin, Abu-Assab and Greatrick (2018) note, the identity of categories of LGBTQ rarely map onto the experience of people in Lebanon who engage in same-sex relations and can instead appear to be alienating and insufficient labels. People may engage in same-sex practices but this does not necessarily mean that they have come 'out' and defined themselves as 'gay'. As one Western sociologist of sexuality notes with surprise of being in Beirut: 'Non-heterosexuals have not coalesced, whether purposefully or not, into identity-based public cultures' (Seidman 2012: 21). What matters instead are the types of relations, performances and forms of gender that are either permitted or severely sanctioned by the state. Thus, it is possible for privileged urban gay men and women to carve out a degree of autonomy, while transpersons, poor rural and urban men and women, refugees and sex workers constitute the groupings that experience an increased likelihood of being harassed and persecuted.

It would be remiss to suggest that sexuality in Lebanon is subject to local understandings that are somehow completely dissimilar to those in the West. The dynamics of colonialism, globalism and transnational activism collide to create complex sexual epistemologies in Lebanon that are neither purely 'local' nor 'Western'. These configurations of power and exclusion force activists to construct a movement that does not simply aim for the recognition of an LGBTQ identity. Yet what this may constitute is contested by activists and subject to numerous pressures, including those generated by international funders who seek to promote particular visions of sexuality.

A term that captures some of the dynamics of Lebanese sexual activism is 'queer'. Rather than an expression of a discrete, uniform mode of sexual identity, queer refers to those acts that disrupt, spoil and problematize sexuality so that it does not cohere into fixity and essentialist categories that sustain inequity. Many activists in Lebanon use 'queerness' as a way to describe their alienation from a sectarian system that reproduces patriarchy, racism, homophobia and class hierarchies. Queerness is also an invitation for all marginalized individuals and groups to come together and form alliances. Queer, as such, works towards imagining the intersections that exist between multiple struggles in society not only divided by sect but also by a much wider and deeper set of inequalities. This use of queerness echoes with what Muñoz (2009) calls 'Queer futurity'. Queer futurity, as a utopian project, is the construction of political imaginaries designed to dismantle systemic injustices while also constructing alternative visions of community based on interdependency, vulnerability and solidarity. It entails a recognition that dominant structures of power are not only profoundly complex but also reproduce multiple forms of inequality which require intersecting struggles based on including the most vulnerable members of present communities. Rana, a queer feminist activist, relates to us how identifying as queer has significant connotations for designing new political imaginaries. It allows Lebanese activists to position themselves within a historical underground movement that transcends the here and the now, stretching into the future and unravelling limitless possibilities as to how sectarianism can be undone.[14] In sum, we use both 'LGBTQ' and 'queer' as descriptors in this book, while recognizing the limitations of both to adequately capture the myriad political positions articulated by activists in this book.

Doing research

Here is a brief note on the methods used by the authors to collect the data for this book. The central form of data collection used by the authors results from simply talking and listening to people who in some way shape the narrative on LGBTQ rights in Lebanon. Activists, of course, represent the core community that we relied upon to generously give up their time and impart their knowledge and expertise to us. Since same-sex relations and non-normative gender is criminalized in Lebanon, resulting in the state harassment of activists, all interviews are anonymized. Yet, to humanize them, and because we want to tell a story from the rich narratives provided, activists have been given fictitious names. These activists are drawn from across the spectrum of the movement: directors of advocacy NGOs, current and former members of established networks and independent activists. We occasionally spoke to LGBTQ people who are not activists, such as the individuals who use the facilities and services provided by LGBTQ NGOs. The activists who speak in this book do not do so as part of a unified movement with a coherent and agreed-upon strategy. As we shall see, there are clear lines of difference between activists on a number of issues, and these disagreements are articulated in this book. It would be remiss, however, to caricature activism as a deeply fractured landscape. There are often moments of coalescence and intense expressions of solidarity, especially in response to another incident of harassment, violence and human rights abuse experienced by activists and members of the LGBTQ population.

In addition to LGBTQ activists, we have spoken to human rights advocates, LGBTQ allies in civil society, representatives of political parties, academics working on sexuality and gender in Lebanon and international actors involved in efforts to support LGBTQ groups in Lebanon. The information gleaned from these sources again illuminates the often-messy and multivalent field that constitutes LGBTQ activism in Lebanon.

In all, we have conducted more than seventy interviews. Nearly all of these have been conducted between 2014 and 2020, which gives the opportunity to show the development of activism over a period in Lebanon that has witnessed intense waves of contention by non-sectarian actors in the wake of the Arab Uprisings (2011–). Purposive sampling was used for the selection of interviewees in order to gain expertise that is rich with inside information-. Snowballing, in the form of word-of-mouth recommendations from interviewees, helped to expand the constituency of people we interviewed, though we by no means claim to be exhaustive in terms of coverage. Semi-formal interviews were conducted in a range of places, including cafes, bars, community centres and offices. A thematic approach was undertaken to identify key motifs regarding tactics and strategies, spaces used by activists and the perspectives narrated by other actors. We place this within a constructivist epistemology which focuses on understanding the social context in which individuals attach meaning to their social reality. This data is triangulated with extensive reports, social media sources and policy documents produced by activists, human rights groups and media outlets.

Chapter 2

'WE ARE HATED BY EVERYONE': SEXUALITY AND SECTARIANISM

Zain was a leading activist when the attack occurred. He had been going about his business in broad daylight on the streets of the Hamra, a busy thoroughfare of Beirut, when henchmen linked to a political movement subjected Zain to what he called a 'gay bashing'. The Hamra was thought to be a relatively secure area for LGBTQ people, a cosmopolitan district containing the main universities and numerous bars, some of which were known to be gay friendly and even owned. Yet, as Zain asked, 'How can you be safe in an unsafe environment'? The attackers left Zain battered and bleeding with no hope of calling for assistance from the police, who would more likely arrest him than his assailants. Recounting his beating at the hands of 'militiamen', Zain explained that 'the state forces itself through sect militias. This is the second layer of state enforcement, and what they do is they don't force the law, they force whatever morality they get out of the law'.[1]

The homophobic violence meted out to Zain illuminates some of the dynamics that drive the experience of LGBTQ people in postwar Lebanon. In particular, it reveals the dual nature of the Lebanese state, a bifurcated structure that is tightly bound in a mutually supportive relationship. On the one hand, Lebanon's sectarian system infiltrates 'every nook and cranny' (Salloukh et al. 2015: 3) of everyday Lebanese life. It dictates the shape of the government and how public sector jobs are doled out. It is manipulated by elites in the exercise of corruption and clientelism. It intrudes obtrusively into the private lives of the Lebanese in areas ranging from marriage to divorce and, in consequence, by sustaining patriarchy and homophobia. The system is maintained not only in terms of who is included but also who is excluded, such as the millions of refugees and migrant workers who are denied citizenship.

On the other hand, the state is also missing. 'Wayn al dawla?' ('Where is the state?') is a catchphrase commonly uttered by Lebanese people. It has attained cliché status, typically accompanied with an exasperated shrug of the shoulders and a wry grin. The phrase is summoned at practically any moment when the absence of the state is acutely felt: when the electricity cuts out according to a daily rota, when uncollected garbage accumulates on the streets or when yet another general election is indefinitely postponed. Where the state is absent, the sectarian networks try to step in to provide key services for their 'constituency', ranging from medical to energy and even, in the case of Zain, the policing of sexual morality on the streets.

Rather than existing in tension, the weak state and the strong sectarian system are tightly bound in a mutually supportive relationship. Importantly, they interact to impinge upon the daily existence of the LGBTQ population. The continuing criminalization of homosexuality and the daily acts of violent repression carried out by various arms of the state, including extrajudicial militias, all point back to the ongoing legacy of the postwar society and its sectarian structures. This means that the system operates in a way that cannot be avoided by LGBTQ activists campaigning for rights. The centrality of the sectarian system and weak state to our case study means that we too cannot evade confronting it.

The pie sharing system

Sectarianism is a word that has returned to the lips of scholars and policymakers (Haddad 2011; Abdo 2017; Hashemi and Postel 2017). As the Middle East moves from the so-called 'Arab Spring' to 'Arab Winter', the region is portrayed as undergoing a wave of vicious sectarian violence that is paradoxically ascribed to ancient, primordial hatreds. In his 2016 state of the union speech, US President Barak Obama (2016) proclaimed that 'the Middle East is going through a transformation that will play out for a generation, rooted in conflicts that date back millennia'. Yet rather than expressions of timeless, primal animosities, scholars have instead drawn attention to how sectarianism and ethnic identities are constructed and securitized through particular modes of modern state-building and via the manipulative strategies deployed by elites to hold onto power (see Makdisi 2000; Picard 2002; Traboulsi 2012; Salloukh et al. 2015; Darwich and Fakhoury 2017).

Lebanon's sectarian system, once seen as a model of stability in the Middle East, is now seen as a cautionary tale for many states undergoing political violence, particularly Iraq, Syria and Yemen. Lebanon's sectarian system can, depending on one's preference, go by the terms 'confessionalism', 'political sectarianism' (*al-ta'ifiyya al-siyasiyya*) or even, to use the expression deployed by social scientists, 'consociational power-sharing' (Picard 2002; Nagle and Clancy 2010; Traboulsi 2012; Hanf 2015; Salloukh et al. 2015; Nagle 2016a). Whatever the taxonomy preferred, Lebanon's sectarian system rests on a simple but yet controversial reasoning. This logic flows from an understanding of Lebanon as a permanently fractured state that accommodates many sectarian groups who hold mutually exclusive visions of identity and state ownership (Salibi 1990; Harris 2014). Conflict between sects is meant to occur when one group tries to dominate the state at the expense of the others. With the aim of ensuring the maintenance of peace and security, Lebanon's sectarian system gives guarantees of representation and rights for the various sects in government and across the public sector based on their presumed demographic size. In so doing, the sectarian system is supposed to solidify the balance of power between groups thereby safeguarding minorities from exclusion (Cammett 2014; Hanf 2015).

It would be entirely misleading, however, to characterize sects as homogeneous entities and any antagonistic group-based divisions as the natural expression of ancient hatreds. As political forms of identity, these sect-based groups are the product of long-term state-building processes spanning more than 150 years. In summary, sect divisions in Lebanon were first constructed and politicized in the twilight of the Ottoman Empire, subsequently reinforced under the French Mandate,[2] and then institutionally entrenched within the independent nation state from the 1940s onwards (Makdisi 2000; Harris 2014).

While the sectarian system is the result of historical dynamics, its current form is mostly an outcome of the civil war. The civil war (1975–90) ended with an estimated 170,000 deaths (*c.*2 per cent of the population), a million injured, 800,000 people leaving the country and 500,000 internally displaced (Picard 2002; Harris 2014). Rather than one single issue, the conflict went through a number of stages and invited the intervention of a large number of external states and actors, ranging from the Palestine Liberation Organization (PLO), the United States, Israel and Syria (Traboulsi 2012). For this reason, the war is often called 'the events'. The civil war was never simply sectarian in nature. It involved more than hundred parties, many of whom were divided on ideological rather than ethnic lines (Picard 2002).

Admittedly, the violence increasingly took on a sectarian character, 'characterized by wide-scale killing, rape, torture, arbitrary detention, and enforced disappearances, which caused a natural hardening effect on sectarian group identities. The war acted to practically erase "all memories of coexistence and common interests between the Lebanese"' (Traboulsi 2012: 38) as 'strategies of accommodation and avoidance were replaced by strategies of confrontation and radicalization' (Picard 2002: 153).

The civil war expedited the rise of the sectarian militias led by warlords who replaced much of the established pre-war political leaders with new powerful networks (Picard 2002; Cammett 2014). In the absence of a functioning state, the warlords nurtured forms of governance that covered their sectarian fiefdoms (Hanf 2015). The sectarian militias constructed their own spheres of civil society to distribute a wide portfolio of services for the communities they claimed to defend. Practically everything – ranging from medical care, education, refuse and postal collection, the supply of gas and electricity and even childcare – became subject to the purview of the sectarian militias (Cammett 2014). By providing basic services, the militias exploited the precarious situation to extend coercive control over their war-weary communities. At the same time, the militias maximized rents from the territories they controlled for their own personal enrichment. They taxed homeowners and levied customs duties on goods entering and leaving their enclaves. The warlords ran protection rackets to extort businesses and raised cash from the illegal trade in drugs and weapons. By the end of the war, the largest militia groups were operating as states within the state complete with their own social welfare departments, press and media outlets and powerful political parties proclaiming to defend the interests of particular sects (Rizkallah 2017).

The war formally ended with the Ta'if Agreement – also known as the National Document (*Wathiqat al-wifaq al-watani*) – a peace pact signed by the main parties in 1989 (Picard 2002; Hanf 2015). Ta'if essentially froze the new balance of power resulting from the war. The motto of Ta'if – 'no winner, no vanquished' – indicated that no group could dominate the state at the expense of any others, which is enshrined in the constitution through the principle of guaranteeing 'mutual coexistence' (*al 'aysh al-mushtarak*) between the sects (Traboulsi 2012).

To achieve this condition, Ta'if recalibrated the pre-war sectarian power-sharing system to reflect the new postwar realities. In terms of political institutions, the sectarian system automatically reserves seats and positions for the sectarian groups. At the executive level, the 'troika' positions of president, prime minister and the speaker of the house are allocated, respectively, to a Maronite Christian, Sunni Muslim and Shia Muslim. To ensure that Christian and Muslim sects are accorded equal representation in the government, a 50/50 quota system is applied to the cabinet positions and to the 128 seats in the national parliament (Salloukh et al. 2015; Nagle 2016a).[3] Indeed, as a scholar notes, 'The allocation of government posts by sect combined with the electoral system constitute and perpetuate sectarianism as the foundation of politics' (Cammett 2014: 64; see Table 2.1).

If that is not enough, the quota system is reproduced across the public sector. While only the highest-level civil servant jobs are supposed to be distributed according to sectarian quotas, the system rapidly expanded in the postwar era to infiltrate everything from entry-level positions to the boards of directors and vice-governors of independent state bodies (Salloukh 2019).

It is for this reason that Lebanon is unofficially endowed with the sobriquet 'the allotment state' (*'dawlat al-muhasasa'*) since all political and most public positions must be formulaically doled out to the rival sectarian groups. A Lebanese non-sectarian civil society activist more accurately labelled the system as one of 'pie sharing rather than power-sharing'. Pie sharing, however, attains a sinister meaning in the context of Lebanon's sectarian system. It alludes to how the various warlords exercise corruption, crony capitalism and clientelism to capture public resources and state institutions.

Table 2.1 Main Groups and Parties in Lebanon

Ethnoreligion	Size (%)	Main Political Parties
Christian	40.5	
Maronite	21	Kataeb, Free Patriotic Movement, Lebanese Forces
Greek Orthodox	8	
Greek Catholic	6.5	
Armenian	4	Armenian Revolutionary Federation
Muslim	54	
Sunni	27	Future Movement
Shia	27	Hezbollah, Amal
Druze	5.6	Progressive Socialist Party
Total	**99.1**	

Source: Lebanon Demographics Profile 2014 (see: http://www.indexmundi.com/lebanon/demographics_profile.html.)

Yet, it is not only in the institutional aspects of the state that the sectarian system holds its power; arguably, it is via informal institutions and practices that the system is able to reproduce itself. It is where the state is missing that the system becomes visible in the everyday lives of the Lebanese. As noted earlier, during the war the militias formed de facto states within the state, including developing their own administrative networks, civil societies and social services (Cammett 2014). They were able to achieve this by creating ethnically homogeneous, self-contained and exclusive spaces, which had the effect of maintaining communal solidarity and thus the local power of sectarian militias (Deeb and Harb 2013). The postwar hybrid paramilitary/political organizations that emerged from the militias continue to use these networks and resources to extend their political and economic power. Endemic state weaknesses are deliberately cultivated and maintained by sectarian elites so that goods and services are placed under their control. Sectarianism is renewed on a daily basis through the sectarian parties' provision of essential services and infrastructure, encompassing electricity, medical care, microcredit and even the construction of roads (Salloukh et al. 2015; Nucho 2016).

It is not only that the sectarian factions use these services as booty but these are also exploited to create cultures of dependency tightly binding communities with elites. The economically underprivileged, in particular, are compelled to seek sectarian patronage for a range of social services. In return for accessing services from the sectarian parties, individuals are expected to reciprocate by casting their ballot on election day and by generally providing unwavering support – or at least tacit consent – for 'their' communal leaders (Cammett 2014). This situation is facilitated by Lebanon's failing economy, characterized by galloping public debt, which has left a quarter of Lebanese living in poverty or deprivation and increasingly reliant on the informal sphere of sectarian networks (see Figure 2.1).

Rather than merely reflecting existing sectarian divisions, the weak state and strong sectarian system combine to elevate citizens as sectarian subjects above all other forms of social and political identity. Against this backdrop, a burgeoning literature has started to portray the so-called politics of weakness that the Lebanese state performs as a deliberate governance strategy (Fakhoury 2020). By performing liminality, the state constructs governance as a set of '(in)formal, contradictory and multiscalar powers' shaping lives on the ground (Carpi 2019: 83).

'The sectarian system divides our cause'

Sectarianism is recharged on a daily basis when individuals are forced to seek welfare and basic services from local sectarian leaders or when they apply for public jobs allocated according to sectarian quotas; it is made manifest through the threats of violence and rhetoric deployed by sectarian parties and in the divisive and emotive strategies they use to mobilize their constituency in electoral campaigns; it is relentlessly echoed in the commentary and content of the media channels owned by the sectarian parties.

Figure 2.1 Challenging urban contexts and illegal wires
Source: Photo credit – Stu Cook.

Sectarian groups and citizens are thus made and remade everyday via multiple institutions and ideologies. Sectarian identity and agency is not something that exists naturally; it is constructed and constantly refashioned to suit current political conditions.

This brings us to the question of how do power-sharing, sectarian systems – such as Lebanon – shape and control sexuality? In one sense, it could be easy to say that power-sharing has little to do with sexuality. As noted earlier, very rarely do power-sharing agreements specify provisions for LGBTQ rights or seek to include the voice of queer communities in any form. Yet, political and social systems that seek to accommodate and reproduce sectarian identities often place sexuality at its heart.

This overlap between sectarian divisions and the regulation of sexuality is captured by what Maginn and Ellison (2015, 2017) have termed 'sextarianism'. For Maginn and Ellison (2017: 809), 'sextarianism is a corollary of sectarianism'. In the context of power-sharing, specifically in Northern Ireland, 'sextarianism revolves around religious and patriarchal ideas, beliefs, practices and policies that stigmatize, physically harm, and criminalize members of sexual minority groups, and deny them their human and labour rights' (Maginn and Ellison 2015). The concept of 'sextarianism' thus alerts us to how societies riven by ethnic and sectarian polarization can generate deeply negative consequences for queer populations. A key reason for this relationship between sectarianism and the regulation of so-called sexuality, argue Maginn and Ellison (2017: 809), is because divided places seek to 'maintain the socially conservative, heteronormative and patriarchal status quo that buttresses polarization and antagonism'.

The concept of 'sextarianism' has been expertly developed by Maya Mikdashi to examine the case study of Lebanon. Mikdashi (2014, 2018) persuasively argues that sectarian identities can only be achieved through the construction of gender and sexual inequalities. Thus, states Mikdashi (2018: 445), 'sectarian citizens are reproduced through laws, bureaucracies and state practices that regulate sexuality, sexual difference, and gender'. This entwining of sectarianism and sexuality into the term 'sextarianism' allows us to see how the desire of maintaining communal pluralism is serviced.

It is in the control of gender where sextarianism is particularly acute. The construction of patriarchal sectarian groups is inextricably linked to what Suad Joseph (1997, 1999, 2000) called the myth of sectarian pluralism undergirding power-sharing: that Lebanon is made up of many homogeneous sectarian communities. For this reason, as Mikdashi argues (2018), gender differences underpin Lebanese citizenship. Indeed, the constitution defines 'the family' and not the individual as the basic unit of the state, thus inscribing the patriarchal family as the template for society. This idea of the family in Lebanon, notes Suad Joseph (1999, 2011), is inextricably linked to the concept of the sectarian group, imagined as types of families led by patriarchal leaders.

Indeed, the Lebanese legal system – enshrined in Article 9 of the constitution – is characterized by legal pluralism, which in effect grants a high degree of autonomy to the eighteen formally recognized sects over their internal matters, especially in religion and schooling (Mikdashi (2014, 2018). The sects follow separate laws regulating the personal status of their members, and each sect receives state funding to operate its own religious courts to adjudicate cases related to marriage, divorce, custody of children and inheritance (Human Rights Watch 2015).

The status laws, furthermore, legitimate cleavages and disparities among women – with women in some sects receiving better privileges than others in some areas. Mona, a feminist and LGBTQ activist, took time to explain to us how the sectarian system profoundly splits women along sectarian lines, thereby making it prohibitively difficult for feminist and queer women to engender a collective movement in which members begin to see their interests as women before the divisive impulses of sect affiliation. The activist, who was nominally born into a Christian sect, explained how 'sectarianism divides our demands':

> To take it back to the sectarian system and how this influences our movement. For example, I will tell you for women, because our civil status law is divided by religion, so if you are a Christian woman and you want to get divorced it is different to the process for a Muslim woman. And that is very dangerous because if you want to form one campaign on this issue it is impossible because there are different demands from different women. The sectarian system divides our cause and makes it impossible for us to cooperate together. They split our cause and it is very hard to remind women that we all have the same cause.[4]

In weaving together sectarian and sexual pluralism, gender is made into a security issue in Lebanon (Joseph 2011; Mikdashi 2018; Geha 2019a). Attempts to leverage even marginal reform for gender rights in the Lebanese parliament are blocked by the various sectarian factions on the premise that these rights threaten the civil peace. Sectarian elites tend to present themselves as guarantors of stability, using their prerogatives to impede any attempt to change the status quo (Geha 2019b).

It is hardly surprising that women are marginalized figures in formal politics. Despite being major protagonists in the civil war – as both combatants or peacemakers – the postwar era did not include room for women to demand greater equality. On this, an LGBTQ activist has written: 'Feminists who chose to introduce women's issues in supposedly progressive groups were told to form their own groups and leave politics to the men' (Makarem 2011: 101). The postwar institutions underwent a process of re-entrenching patriarchy. No woman was given a seat in the Ta'if negotiations or acted as signatory for the Agreement.[5]

Two decades after Ta'if, the inclusion of women in formal politics indicates only marginal progress at best. In fact, in terms of the MENA region Lebanon ranks as one of the lowest for women's political representation, with only Oman, Kuwait and Yemen having fewer women members of parliament. Nor, unlike a number of states across the MENA, such as Jordan, Morocco and Libya, has Lebanon introduced any measures to advance women's representation in politics, particularly via reserved quotas. Since granting women political suffrage in 1953, only seventeen women have been elected to parliament. Despite a record 86 women running for office during the 2018 parliament elections, only 6 of the 128 members elected were women, which ranks Lebanon 139th in the world for women's participation in government, and the vote share of women candidates rose only from a meagre 3 to 5 per cent (Geha 2019a; Nassif 2020).

To understand the poor electoral performance of women is to know that women's participation in formal politics is almost exclusively permitted through the prism of patriarchy and sectarianism. It is not too extreme to say that the system is rigged against female candidates. Lebanon's electoral law allows the political party leaders to make the lists of candidates and in which constituency each candidate will run. Although many political parties now have a quota reserved for female candidates on their lists, females are typically given marginal or even hopeless seats to contest. Joumana, a female candidate who ran as an independent in the 2018 election and almost won, explained:

> There are women who are candidates for seats that a party know that will never be won. They [the leaders] already have a projection of what's going to happen; they know which seats they have their eyes on. So in order for them to say, 'Look we did put women on the list to run but it's to no avail.' It means nothing with lists, they just choose the worst, most difficult seats and just give them to women.[6]

Women's participation in formal Lebanon politics is largely achieved in the context of 'political familism', a term used by Joseph (2011) to describe how political leadership in Lebanon is often continued through families. Leadership of political blocs is usually passed down from father to son. The presumption that sons will succeed their fathers as political leaders institutionalizes political familism within state institutions and promotes political patriarchy. On the rare occasions that women have assumed political leadership or have become parliamentarians it is often because they are wives, daughters or sisters of sectarian leaders and warlords.

Sectarianism has specific consequences for the state's LGBTQ population. It is no coincidence that Article 534 – which criminalizes 'unnatural sex' – was incorporated into the penal code to buttress the personal status laws underpinning the sectarian system. Rather than a reflection of local 'Arab' religious sensibilities towards sexuality, Article 534 and a number of other provisions related to 'public morality' need to be understood as the imposition of French colonial authority in Lebanon.[7]

'The custodians of chastity and honour'

The notion of the sectarian system seems to indicate the leading position assumed by religion in Lebanese life, thus adversely influencing people's attitudes towards sexuality. Certainly, rates of religious belief and attendance are high in Lebanon. Survey evidence indicates that 8 out of 10 Lebanese claim to pray on a daily basis while more than 60 per cent attend weekly religious services (see Hayes and Nagle 2016). Precisely how religion informs the Lebanese population's attitudes on homosexuality is indicated in a major survey conducted by LGBTQ activists (Nasr and Zeidan 2015). The results demonstrated that when it came to religious and moral opinions about homosexuality, public attitudes are largely negative.

Participants strongly agreed with statements such as 'I believe homosexuality is sinful' and 'Religious books condemn homosexuality'. The majority of respondents (81.3 per cent) also saw homosexuality as immoral, which suggests a strong correlation between religion and morality when it comes to sexuality. These results lend support to global research on attitudes, which consistently reveal that personal religious belief and the related wider religious culture impact negatively on the acceptance of LGBTQ rights (Poushter and Kent 2020). The higher the religiosity the lower the acceptance rate of homosexuality, and vice versa. Moreover, a body of research argues that the mainstream religious traditions have historically contributed to the oppression of LGBTQ people and have provided resistance to the advancement of LGBTQ rights both in the West and internationally.

In Lebanon, this situation is compounded by the demands of the sectarian system. Religion intrudes most evidently into the sectarian system via the personal status laws. It is here where religious leaders are empowered by being granted a high degree of control over their community's affairs. While very few religious leaders act as political representatives, neither can it be truthfully said that they are apolitical figures. The religious leaders of Sunnis and Maronites in Lebanon have historically played a significant role in brokering electoral and political deals, and in giving their blessing over the formation of governments. These religious authorities, moreover, 'perpetuate a sectarian system that inhibits social integration' (Henley 2016: 1). Religious leaders deploy their offices to frustrate any measures that promise all meaningful reform of the sectarian system. Most notably, clerics use their influence to block proposals for gender equality and in other areas, such as the debate on civil marriage, which featured the intervention of the Sunni Grand Mufti, who issued a *fatwa* declaring its proponents to be apostates (Massena 2020).

Activists recognize the overlap between the sectarian system, religion and homophobia. Hakim, a leading activist in Beirut, reflected on how the mutually reinforcing relationship between religious and political leaders stymies progressive politics:

> In terms of homophobia, the sectarian system also places a lot of emphasis on religion and on sect and on religious figures who play a very important job as backdrop viziers to all of these different leaders that we have. It is very difficult for any Lebanese leader across the board to govern and to maintain their influence without the support of the church or the sheiks, the fatwa, or of whatever. Unfortunately, these religious establishments are all incredibly homophobic and their lopsided influence on the policymaking process seeps through the decision-making process. It seeps through the way that politicians respond to the people that come to them with demands. So speaking to the Ministry of the Interior, for example, in regards to the torture that goes on in the Internal Security forces, it is practically impossible for me to imagine the minister of the interior going out and saying publicly as a Sunni or a Christian leader that you should protect and respect the rights of gay people.[8]

Maya, a human rights lawyer and political advisor to a leader of a sectarian party, agreed that religious authorities severely constrict the room for leaders to push for LGBTQ rights. For example, in 2019 a female parliamentarian who had positioned herself as liberal was part of a Lebanese delegation that voted against a resolution seeking to preserve the rights of the LGBTQ community at the assembly of the International Parliamentary Union (IPU) in Geneva. Maya noted that this female 'was pressurised by the religious figures in Lebanon, and she needed his [a religious leader] support to get more votes in Beirut. She was really lobbying against gay rights'.[9]

It is not altogether surprising then that religious groups and clerics in Lebanon have publically labelled non-heterosexuality as a heinous sin to be vehemently opposed. A report by LGBTQ activists noted that 'Lebanese religious authorities have been largely unanimous in their condemnation of homosexuals' (Nasr and Zeidan 2015: 8). Indeed, opposition to homosexuality represents a rare point of consensus for the various religious leaders in Lebanon. For example, the Committee for the Preservation of Moral Values, an umbrella grouping representing the main recognized sects in Lebanon, has called on the Lebanese to protect their children from 'satanic' homosexuality. Certainly, as Rabih, an LGBTQ activist noted with some weariness:

> We are hated by everybody, all of the sects. In a sectarian system, minorities always feel threatened. If Sunnis are against homosexuality Christians want to prove that they are against homosexuality too. There are figures trying to outdo each other.[10]

Lebanon suffers no shortage of examples of religious authorities – both Christian and Muslim – venting spleen against homosexuality. On the side of Islamic representatives, in 2003, for example, a leading Lebanese Shiite cleric, the Grand Ayatollah Sayyed Mohammed Hussein Fadlallah, emphasized the importance of the death penalty in pacifying society, including for homosexuality (Nasser 2003). Leading Sunni cleric Sheikh Bilal Doqmaq stated in 2013 that being 'gay should be considered a crime and have legal consequences in order for homosexuality, a shameful and horrific sin, not to spread' (El-Shenawi 2013). A more recent example of religious-led hostility was on display in the protests against an event for IDAHOT/Pride 2017, which brought together journalists, artists and doctors to discuss discrimination against the LGBTQ community. The Olama Organization, an extremist group of religious scholars with ties to Al-Nusra[11] and ISIS, issued warnings on its Facebook page for the minister of interior and the director general of the general security forces to cancel the talk, which they alleged was promoting homosexuality and drug use. The Olama Organization wrote on Facebook that, if the event was to go ahead, 'custodians of chastity and honor will flock from across Lebanon to prevent this conference from taking place' (see Beirut Pride 2017). The event was hastily cancelled.

Such statements are not empty threats. The experience was terrifying for the LGBTQ activists at the receiving end of intimidation. Fadi, an activist whose event was cancelled due to the Olama's threats, remembered the terror of that time when he felt that his life was under threat:

> The Olama called us wanting to know where we are located. We started getting a flood of calls and it was really terrifying. We locked ourselves in the centre and we left the centre at 12 at night. It was really scary. They were telling us that they were preparing to raid the place. They wanted to do a demonstration and attack those entering the event. It was a serious thing.[12]

In terms of Christian opposition, groups in Lebanon have called on their followers to 'pray against the threat of homosexuality'. Following an attack on LGBTQ individuals in a nightclub in a Christian district of Beirut, banners were hung across the street dispensing advice from the Old Testament, a Christian TV channel in Lebanon linked homosexuals with devil worshippers. The Maronite church, which is the largest of the Christian sects in Lebanon, takes full communion from the Pope and the Roman Catholic Church, which has historically deemed homosexuality as a crime against nature, an 'objective disorder'; a bodily expression of sin and evil that had to be disciplined. The Catechism of the Catholic Church presents 'homosexual acts as acts of grave depravity' (Vatican 2020). Christian groups in Lebanon – such as the Catholic Media Centre – have called on judges to apply the law in its strictest sense to prosecute LGBTQ people.

Yet, as worrying as the threat may be, we should avoid any simplistic explanation that homophobia is driven by any innate properties located inside the religions found across the region. To repeat such fallacies only contributes to the impasse between people on the extremes of the debate. Islam, in particular, is often framed as fundamentally incompatible with homosexuality. Such suspicions appear confirmed by the fact that thirty-one out of forty-seven Muslim-majority countries criminalize homosexuality and five of the ten states in the world that sanction the death penalty for homosexuality are majority Muslim (Iran, Mauritania, Saudi Arabia, Sudan, Yemen) (Human Rights Watch 2018a). These states justify such punitive measures in terms of Islamic Law, which is often perceived to be explicit in its condemnation of homosexuality (Siraj 2009). Islamic law is said to specify punishments for homosexuals, including one hundred lashes, stoning to death and being flung from a high tower followed by everlasting torment in hell (Whitaker 2011).

However, as Brian Whitaker (2011: 29) points out, 'It cannot be said that any universally agreed "Islamic punishment" for homosexual acts exists.' Tellingly, punishments for homosexuality in Islamic societies – prior to Western colonization – were less harsh than for adultery. Islam, instead, is historically noted for its relatively liberal attitudes towards sexuality, especially its 'freedom and openness to sexual play' (El Feki 2014: 11).

While the influence of religion is undeniably challenging for the LGBTQ population, it is not an insurmountable problem, especially since many religions do not have a consistent approach to same-sex relations. As Momin Rahman argues (2014), it is pointless to speak of a Muslim civilizational response to homosexuality, given the variety in historical, geographical, cultural formations of gender and sexuality. This diversity is exposed by the lack of concrete references to homosexuality in many holy books, which means that religious leaders' interpretations of these texts are profoundly shaped by prevailing cultural and social values (Siraj 2009; El Feki 2014). Indeed, Islamic scholars over the centuries developed a large body of legal rulings (*fiqh*) and lists of moral crimes (*kaba'ir* or 'enormities') to guide the interpretation of *shari'a* in a way that would be suitable and understandable to the context of their day (Epprecht 2013). This gives religious authorities and clerics some leeway to shift to a more tolerant view of LGBTQ people. For example, some notable conservative religious leaders across the MENA region (e.g. Rached Ghannouchi, head of the Tunisian Islamic Party, and Muqtada al-Sadr, leader of the Shiite militia in Iraq) have made statements in recent years asking their followers to be more tolerant of LGBTQ people. In relation to Christianity, despite the Catholic Church continuing to claim that 'homosexual acts are intrinsically disordered' (Vatican 2020), Pope Francis has publically articulated the need for greater societal tolerance for LGBTQ people.

These ambiguous and shifting interpretations of the relationship between religion and homosexuality provide openings for LGBTQ activists to challenge the premise that religion is naturally opposed to non-heterosexuality. Some activists here strive for what Khalid Duran (1993) calls a 'theological accommodation', where loopholes can be found in religious texts to permit same-sex relations. Islamic legal texts, particularly the Hadith, are noted for their obscurity and openness for different interpretations, especially since a number of variant readings have been approved as canonical. Rather than bound together by a single theological doctrine enforced by an authoritative structure, Islam more often resembles a contract between the individual and Allah (Epprecht 2013).

In this context, LGBTQ activists generate a range of responses to religious institutions and authorities which cannot be said to add up to a consistent or collective viewpoint. Some LGBTQ activists stress moderate, non-literalist forms of Islam that permit same-sex relations. Hakim, an activist introduced earlier, explained that across the Middle East, even in conservative countries like Saudi Arabia, 'homosexual sex is going on like you wouldn't believe, but no one identifies as gay. There is a suspension of religion sometimes and so much of what people do in these areas of the world is not mentioned in the Qu'ran or the Hadith anyway'.[13] Given these supposed theological 'gaps', some LGBTQ activists believe that their religious belief and sexuality can exist in simpatico. A collection of short stories by a queer women's group noted that not 'all queers are atheists' (Meem 2009: 3). These members write prolifically about subjects such as being 'a veiled queer woman, or about how their Christian faith and their faith in their activist work are alike and feed each other' (Meem 2010a: 3). LGBTQ activists also 'work on finding sheikhs, priests and other religious public figures who are at least tolerant towards homosexuality and don't want to kill or punish or "cure" gay people' (Meem 2010a: 13). Even when such figures may be found, Hakim explained that it was important for LGBTQ people not to believe that they can provide simple answers:

Our group has a public event on Islam and homosexuality – it was an Imam
who 'came out' and a hundred people came to this. There was a lot of people
who wanted to ask, 'Can I be Muslim and gay at the same time?' And of course
you had a lot of conservative and religious people who attacked us online. ...
Much to people's surprise, the Imam was not saying that you can be gay and
Muslim, he said this is what the Qu'ran says. ... He really pissed off a lot of
people who came along and thought that they were going to get an easy, cookie-
cutter solution to all of their acts.[14]

Rather than dismiss religion as homophobic some activists emphasize the
humanistic potential of these faiths, and the importance of human rights and
peace as central narratives to religious practice. These are values that the Lebanese
uphold and thus offer a window for activists to prise open in their attempts to
foster rights and protections for LGBTQ individuals.

While some LGBTQ activists engage with the power of religious belief and
leaders, a similar number take a more critical stance. The antagonism of these
activists is not necessarily directed at religion per se; their hostility is largely
reserved for the imposition of religion in the public sphere, most obviously evident
in the sectarian system. On this an LGBTQ leader wrote: 'What actually threatens
our rights is religious fundamentalism coupled with the interference of religious
leaders in the political and lawmaking process' (Azzi 2011a). Activists express
opposition through their support for the secular movement, including the Laique
Pride celebration mentioned in Chapter 1, which called for 'the non-interference
of the state in the citizen's religion and the non-interference of religion in the state's
affairs'. LGBTQ activists regularly took part in the now-defunct annual Laique Pride
demonstration, marching behind a banner announcing 'Queers for Secularism'. In
a blog post supporting Laique Pride, an LGBTQ leader argued: 'Secularism alone
does not guarantee women's rights or gay rights, but it establishes the healthy
context for us to open the debate' (Azzi 2011a).

Finally, and perhaps more problematically, it is wrong to assume that the
LGBTQ community is avowedly non-sectarian or unanimously opposed to
religion. Instead, to an extent, Lebanon's sectarian system reproduces itself
internally within the community. Hakim noted:

The way that sectarian politics works here is amazing, because sometimes it seeps
into the LGBT community itself, much less so than the rest of the country. To
be honest, you see a lot more bi-sectarian relationships among the community.
However, you also notice that there are a lot of LGBT people with a heightened
sense of confessional and religious belonging. They go to two churches, the gay
bar and the actual church. They are incredibly religious and of course they are all
products of their respective families and communities.[15]

Mona, a feminist activist, reflected on the power of the sectarian system to
normalize itself within the LGBTQ population: 'This is what sectarianism does to
us, we always think that our sect is better than the other.'[16]

'The fortress of resilience' in the masculinist state

In April 2013, a dozen Internal Security Forces (ISF) officers raided a nightclub in Dekwaneh, a suburb located to the north of Beirut, to arrest one transwoman and five men suspected of homosexuality. The local mayor had ordered the raid, accusing the nightclub of 'promoting prostitution, drugs and homosexuality' (see Moussawi 2018: 183). The arrestees were subjected to severe beatings by the ISF before being transported in car boots to the mayor's office. Here, the mayor ordered the suspects to undress so that he and the officers could determine their gender. The transwoman reported that the mayor called her a 'faggot' and 'half-woman and half-man' (see Öztop 2013; Allouche 2017).

The mayor initiated the raid, without first informing the public prosecutor, in contravention of the Code of Criminal Procedure. Neither were any of the arrestees transferred to the Morals Protection Bureau to face charges, as is supposed to be the case during arrests. In a subsequent TV interview, the mayor defended the use of extrajudicial means as necessary to cleanse his district of what he called 'moral perversions'. The mayor recounted his 'glorious' past as a militiaman during the civil war and described his district as a 'fortress of resilience. ... We fought battles and defended our land and honour, not to have people come here and engage in such practices in my municipality' (see Rizk and Makarem 2015: 102).

It is striking that the mayor made a connection between the deployment of sectarian violence carried out during the civil war and acts of terror against LGBTQ people in the present as essential measures to defend his community's safety, masculinity and reputation. The mayor's condemnation of LGBTQ people in his 'fortress' is, as two LGBTQ activists write, 'linked to the preservation of militarized masculinity and sectarian pride' (Rizk and Makarem 2015: 101–2). This connection is no accident or merely a by-product of local practices; sectarian and homophobic violence are co-produced. Cultures of militarized masculinity and sectarian antagonism travel hand in hand with ideologies and practices supporting oppression against LGBTQ peoples. The raid in Dekwaneh further exposes how, in the weak state, sectarian leaders can bypass state institutions to exercise vigilantism.

A rich body of research examines how gender and ethnic/sectarian violence are linked. It demonstrates that countries containing high levels of gender inequality have an increased probability of experiencing civil conflict (Caprioli 2005; Melander 2005). Yet, it is not necessary that the presence of gender inequality per se explains violence; feminist scholars, in part, explain this association in terms of societal norms that underpin inequality and which legitimate violence against women and LGBTQ people. Societies that permit gender- and sexual-based violence provide a template normalizing domination against ethnic and sectarian 'outgroups' (Enloe 2000). In this way, rather than illuminate manifestations of gender inequality – such as the absence of women in parliaments, or denying education to girls and young women – to explain conflict, analysis has begun to focus on how norms about masculinities and femininities which legitimate inequalities might also contribute to conflict and violence (Wright and Welsh 2014).

These norms are sustained by gender identities based on virulent forms of masculinity, especially those in which manhood is equated with toughness and where warlike attitudes among men are valourized (Duriesmith 2016). Such 'hypermasculinity' is particularly intense in so-called divided societies characterized by multiple ethnic/sectarian groups holding mutually exclusive visions of state ownership. In these places, 'masculine virtues' – such as honour, patriotism and bravery – are considered essential for the survival of the ethnic nation (Nagle 2003). With men cast as protectors of the ethnic nation, violence is justified as rightful defensive action (Myrttinen, Khattab and Naujoks 2017). During rounds of intercommunal violence, the respective militant factions come to represent an 'armed patriarchy' (McWilliams 1997). Scholars have coined the term 'fratriachy' – a fusion of 'patriarchy' and 'fraternity' – to describe fraternal and militaristic organizations that emerge during sectarian violence, which cultivate homosocial male bonding around militaristic masculine virtues (Myrttinen 2019). Hyper-(hetero)masculine identities are scripts that frame acceptable male conduct in ways that denigrate non-heterosexual people as non-patriotic or a threat to the very existence of the nation. As Nagel (2003: 160) notes: 'Standards for national conduct that reflect masculinized heteronormativity tend also to be homophobic, and thus are intolerant of sexual diversity, particularly homosexuality.'

These dynamics are evident in Lebanon's civil war and its continuing afterlife. The eruption of civil war in the 1970s saw the figure of the militiaman attain dominant status in Lebanon. Up to 300,000 men joined the various militias – illegal paramilitary organizations that acted as sectarian death squads (Khatib 2007; Haugbolle 2012). While the militias operated with ideas of Lebanese nationalism in some form, the militiaman effectively positioned himself as the protector of a particular sectarian community (Khatib 2007). In so doing, the militias fostered a culture of masculinity focusing 'on the responsibility of young men to defend the nation, sect, party or … mother's honor' (Haugbolle 2012: 128).

The conflict provided an opportunity for young men to escape and challenge the pre-war gerontocratic and patriarchal social order that placed power and resources in the hands of established sectarian elites who positioned themselves as patriarchs of communities. Myrttinen and his co-authors use the term 'thwarted masculinities' to capture the position of mainly young males who experience frustration at being unable to realize the goals of dominant forms of masculinity in their societies (Myrttinen, Khattab and Naujoks 2017). War thus provides opportunities for these men to attain the full status of manhood through acts of violence. Lebanese militiamen, as one novelist wrote, were youths 'who have broken down the door of conventional masculinity and entered manhood through the wide door of history' (Barakat 1995: 12). Ethnic nationalism and the neopatriarchal structures of the militia groups 'produced an ideological and emotional logic for the young men, who in time became fighters for "the cause"' (Haugbolle 2012: 128).

To what extent was sexuality embroiled in the conflict? The deliberate targeting of LGBTQ populations has become an increasingly visible dimension of political violence in intrastate conflict. In Colombia, paramilitary groups have used threats, torture, forced displacement and assassination against sexual and gender minority civilians (Payne 2016). Both pro- and anti-regime forces in the Syrian conflict subject LGBTQ people to extrajudicial executions. The organization known as Islamic State (also known as ISIS) has murdered more than fifty allegedly gay and gender non-conforming people in Iraq, Syria and Libya. In Iraq's civil war, another militia, the Mahdi Army, reportedly carried out a far-reaching campaign of extrajudicial executions, kidnappings and torture of men suspected of homosexual conduct, or of not conforming to masculine gender norms (Human Rights Watch 2018a).

The limited research considering homophobic violence during intrastate conflict indicates the varied motivations driving perpetrators, including those stemming from religious and cultural ideas about sexuality; the desire to eliminate (through forced displacement or assassination) individuals considered a threat to the purity and moral integrity of society; and as a demonstration of power, where the bodies of LGBTQ populations are used as a canvas on which armed groups inscribe their willingness to kill to dominate a territory (Payne 2016).

There is no compelling evidence that the militia factions intentionally used violence against LGBTQ people in Lebanon. Yet, the civil war belonged to a period when homophobic attacks were rarely acknowledged let alone recorded. This pervasive silencing has been retrospectively challenged to a degree. LGBTQ activists recounted stories of how at least one militia involved in the civil war decided to purge homosexual members and force them into exile. It is important to also acknowledge that LGBTQ people were not simply victims of political violence; activists have noted that 'instances of queer organizing and resistance were present as far back as the Lebanese civil war which began in 1975' (Arab Foundation for Freedoms and Equality 2018: 25).[17] Some evidence of homosexuality among the civil war militias has also been seized upon by activists as a sign that same-sex relations have not merely been invented in the last few years. One piece of graffiti discovered in a building used by militiamen during the civil war proclaimed: 'If my love for Gilbert is a crime, let history witness I am a dangerous criminal.' The militiaman – using the nom de guerre 'Tarzan' – scrawled the graffiti as a declaration of his sexual love for a militia leader called Gilbert. Youssef Haidar, the architect charged with transforming the building into a museum, said of Tarzan's declaration: 'His crime is being in love, being homosexual, and in love with Gilbert' (Akerman 2018).

The violent masculinity and patriarchy that became embedded in the civil war remains entrenched in the sectarian system and across the society that took shape in the postwar era. The masculinized memory of the militiaman remains a looming ghostly and tangibly violent presence. In many neighbourhoods across Beirut, murals, memorials and posters featuring the haunting images of martyrs – dead militiamen – look down on the local population, thereby serving as daily reminders of the sacrifice made by men to defend their community. The martyred militiaman is remembered within his sectarian community as standing for 'military-masculine virtues of strength and courage and is celebrated mnemonically in rituals of public commemoration' (Haugbolle 2012: 117).

In a broader sense, the political strength of Lebanese sectarian parties and leadership continues to be drawn from the masculinity of the political elite and their militias. Most obviously, the warlords responsible for administering mayhem and violence during the civil war are now reinvented as luminaries and leaders of peacetime political parties or groups. In many cases the male political leader, known as the 'za'im', acts as patriarch and decision maker on behalf of an entire sectarian community often in conjunction with religious leaders.[18] These male political leaders are often unelected figures who engage in dealmaking outside the formal institutions of the state, which leaves parliament and the government as largely irrelevant institutions. The male political leaders typically cast themselves as strongmen figures willing to summon military might to protect their group.

It is here where we see the strong sectarian system and the weak state reinforce each other to create overlapping forms of authority. In this sense, the main political parties in postwar Lebanon have not become detached from the militias. The sectarian parties, to various degrees, continue to host armed wings and auxiliaries. Hezbollah, for example, is by definition, a hybrid political-paramilitary organization, which runs for election while simultaneously retaining its extensive military apparatus for fighting internal and external foes. Thus, organizations are able to exert control over their districts and, in so doing, present themselves as the guardians of their communities' morality. An illuminating example of the militias acting as moral enforcers is evident in the actions of Hezbollah. Reports note that in districts controlled by Hezbollah its members often interrogate people they suspect to be gay before handing them over to the ISF. On one notable occasion, Hezbollah activists kidnapped five suspected gay men and then passed them to the police who duly arrested them (Meaker 2017).

While non-state actors can proclaim moral legitimacy as defenders of their communities from sexual perversion, state security forces are also a fragmented sector. Sectarian power-sharing politics permeates into the policing of sexuality in Lebanon. The formal security sector is characterized by multiple authorities and legal ambiguities stemming from the sectarian system, which makes oversight over security institutions difficult to operationalize. The Lebanese Armed Forces (LAF), General Security Forces and the ISF are sectors that are often sectarianized in Lebanon (Geha 2015). At times, depending on the control of these agencies, and the balance of power between elites, varying levels of surveillance and harassment are carried out against LGBTQ people. Rashida, who has been trying to monitor human rights abuses, admitted it made her task difficult:

It's ad hoc to the extent that it's confusing a lot of the time. Even within the security sectors themselves, so for example within General Security forces and Internal Security Forces have very different approaches towards transpeople or

LGBT people and LGBT rights. This depends on a lot of things, some of this is the power-sharing system, sectarianism, who is in power.[19]

The closet in the house of many mansions

As illustrated in the famous metaphor used by one historian, Lebanon's sectarian system is 'a house of many mansions' (Salibi 1990: 1). The many mansions symbolize the various religious sects uneasily cohabiting in the same small country, all articulating competing visions of the state's identity. To stretch the analogy further, it could be said that the house of many mansions sought to conceal the existence of more unwelcome residents, such as Palestinian refugees. When considering Lebanon's LGBTQ population – perhaps overextending the metaphor – they have been hidden in the house's closet.

Lebanon's LGBTQ population has never fit into the state's sectarian structures. To an extent, this is the consequence of a system that exists to accommodate sectarian interests to the point of complete exclusion of anything not defined as such. No room is permitted within the system for non-sectarian groups or expressions of political identity that cross-cut established sectarian divisions. Thus, for example, demands for gender equality or for workers' rights must be expressed through the prism of sectarian politics. One of the most significant factors underlying the hegemony of the sectarian system is in how it is presented by elites as 'normal' and as reflective of social and political realities.

Reducing political acts, groups of individuals and whole societies to the rubric of sectarianism not only elides the complexity of this force but it also reproduces what Pierre Bourdieu (2003) has called 'symbolic power'. Symbolic power is the imposition of categories of thought and perception upon social agents who, once they begin observing and evaluating the world in terms of those categories – and without necessarily being aware of the change in their perspective – perceive the existing social order as normal and just.

Sectarianism as symbolic power thus both *obscures* and *normalizes* profound processes of inequality and domination. The practice of sectarianism obscures the full range of social identities and political contestation that exists within individuals and groups that can expedite powerful modes of societal change. It also normalizes unequal power relations in a particular society by concealing how sectarianism works to maintain class, gender and sexual inequalities.

The task of many non-sectarian movements, such as LGBTQ activism, is to challenge both the normalcy of the sectarian system and its accumulative mechanisms that work to hide the existence of alternative forms of politics and identity. Yet, how is this possible in the teeth of a system that permits no access for LGBTQs demanding rights? On this point, Hakim somewhat ruefully noted how Lebanon's sectarian system does its best to close down any opportunity for change to occur:

The sectarian system in Lebanon is designed in a way with which to make it incredibly hard for change to happen and that renders it intrinsically homophobic, racist and patriarchal. The way that the system is entrenched has legitimized sectarianism in the minds of the Lebanese public as something legitimate, as matter of fact, that it exists, so it has unfortunately made a lot of mobilization for a lot of causes very problematic simply because it's a very easy card for Lebanese decision makers to exonerate their own positions and with which to rally support.[20]

Lebanon's political sectarianism is an edifice that refuses to countenance the existence of anyone or anything that does not adhere to its logic. The oppression and exclusion of the LGBTQ population is not an accidental outcome, but rather should be understood as an inbuilt property of the sectarian system. LGBTQ activists are of course acutely aware of the severe implications of the sectarian system for the state's LGBTQ population. A document by an activist group from 2010 declares:

> It is worth noting that all of the ... sects, parties, and coalitions between them strongly condemn homosexuality ... there is very little space for the protection or expansion of gay rights within the sectarian system in Lebanon. (Meem 2010a: 4)

In another section, the authors ask:

> How does one advocate for gay rights in Lebanon? Suppose the government did want to expand gay rights, how would they even do that? Any effort to reform laws and practices towards expansion of gay rights would have to negotiate independently with each religious community because ... any major political development in Lebanon requires the support of all the various sects. (Meem 2010a: 11)

Yet, the apparent, total victory of the sectarian system is incomplete. Such structures are never coherent, exhaustive or closed in the ways they are fantasized as being (Nagle 2016b). The weak state that sits alongside the sectarian system indicates how the overall system itself is infused with weaknesses and gaps that create openings and opportunities for resistance and the articulation of alternative forms of politics and rights. In Chapter 3, we begin to examine the emergence of LGBTQ activism in Lebanon.

Chapter 3

'THE LAW PROSECUTES THE WEAKEST': THE RISE OF THE LGBTQ MOVEMENT

Situated above a nightclub in Beirut, Helem's new community centre opened its doors in 2016. The centre is a refurbished apartment designed to provide a safe space and services for vulnerable users, and a focus for LGBTQ activism and community building. One room is a library hosting LGBTQ resources while another is called the 'chill out room', an area where members can talk or just sit alone and collect their thoughts. Shower facilities are available for all users, some of whom are homeless. Habib, the centre's manager, describes the space as 'a community centre but also an activism space. You have the advocacy programs, you have the capacity building programmes, you have the legal department, we have the documentation and reporting, and we have the community centre.'[1]

In the afternoon it is the kitchen that teems with activity. Habib – who has just arrived after an emergency call-out to deal with an LGBTQ person summarily evicted from their apartment – explains that food is an essential service provided by Helem: 'We call it "open lunch" – it is open for everyone. A lot of people who come to the centre are homeless and we provide food everyday.'

Many of the centre's users eating lunch are refugees fleeing the civil war, which is raging just a few kilometres away in neighbouring Syria. Habib explains that 'Helem plays a role in dealing with LGBT refugees from Syria. Most of the refugees that are coming to town [Beirut] are contacting Helem first because they know the name, because we are the first organization to deal with gay rights in the Middle East'. One of the Syrian users standing nearby – who we will call Hassan – begins to tell his story.

Since the start of the Syrian civil war in 2011 more than 1.5 million refugees have fled to Lebanon and most of them exist well below the poverty line. A 2014 report estimated that at least fifty thousand refugees in Lebanon were LGBTQ members who had suffered sexual violence in Syria (Heartland Alliance 2014). Syrian LGBTQ refugees are doubly marginalized in Lebanon as both refugees and LGBTQ people. As refugees, they are perceived as a burden on the local economy. In the summer of 2019, for instance, Lebanese refugees reported being summarily dismissed from their jobs as the result of a new government decree to prioritize Lebanese labour over foreign workers. As LGBTQ individuals, they are excluded, isolated and stigmatized due to their sexual orientation.

A report by the UN highlighted the levels of sexual harassment, assault and other forms of sexual- and gender-based violence, including rape, necessitating hospitalization or surgery in some cases, that LGBTQ refugees endure in Lebanon. The report continued to note that LGBTQ refugees 'are often fearful of reporting incidents of violence – including physical and sexual assault – to the authorities for fear of repercussions, including possible additional violence' (UN High Commissioner for Refugees 2017). A survey of 100 Syrian LGBTQ refugees confirmed the scale of violence and discrimination, with 56 per cent reporting having been physically assaulted in Lebanon, but only 7 per cent reported the crime to the authorities (Heartland Alliance 2014). There is even a specific Article (530) of the penal code for refugees, where they can be deported if they violate morality in Lebanon. Syrian LGBTQ refugees, thus, represent easy targets for the Lebanese state and various militia factions claiming that homosexuality is a foreign import (see Allouche 2017).

Hassan's story unfortunately affirms many of these facts. Hassan speaks about his experience as a gay Syrian refugee forced to flee Syria after a cousin threatened to kill him when it was discovered that he was gay. Hassan is an engineer by training, who plans to go to Canada to join his boyfriend who escaped a few months previously from the same small town they both grew up in. In Lebanon, Hassan's dreams of escape are frustrated by a more present violent reality. As a gay Syrian man living in Beirut for less than a year, Hassan could report numerous incidents of discrimination and abuse. Because Hassan is a Syrian refugee he is a non-citizen, prohibited from access to all of the accessories required to apply for jobs or even to gain access to the most basic services in Lebanon's sectarian system. Although he was an engineer and spoke good English, he explained 'it is forbidden by law for me to work here'. Hassan reflected on his limited options: 'I have two choices – to die or to work as an escort. In escort work they often have to have sex without a condom. It is not safe because of AIDS, but nobody cares. I don't want to go on the streets'.

Hassan told us of his wariness of Lebanon's security forces. The security forces, he continued, automatically checked Syrian males for evidence of homosexuality:

> If they know you are a Syrian guy, they [the security forces] ask for your phone, to look for pictures, for texts. It's much, much worse for Syrian refugees. I put my boyfriend's picture on my phone, so I know for sure if they caught me there is Law 534 and they would arrest me. If any Lebanese guy says 'he is gay', they will put me in jail. They don't care – they just see me as a Syrian refugee. I cannot stay here. I think they will send me back to Syria; I am afraid they will kill me. The international community doesn't care. I am human but where are my rights?[2]

As a refugee registered with United Nations High Commissioner for Refugees (UNHCR), the UN's agency for refugees, Hassan said he receives a monthly sum of $100, 'but the rent is a minimum $200, so how do I eat?' The 'open lunch' at Helem at least provided a daily meal for Hassan. To survive Hassan regularly frequents another LGBTQ NGO located in another district across the city. This NGO is one of the UNHCR's partners, delivering help and services for LGBTQ refugees. Here, Hassan receives training and psychological support.

Hassan's story illuminates the experiences typical of the people who visit Helem's community centre for help. His narrative also exposes the asymmetrical way that the forces of discrimination, violence, persecution and prejudice permeate the daily lives of LGBTQ population. Activists often affirm this observation, noting that refugees, transpeople and sex workers bear the brunt of the security forces' unwelcome attention and hostility. Wealthy and middle-class gay men, especially, have been able to carve out some form of autonomy that largely, though not entirely, protects them from harassment. The experiences of lesbian and queer women are also noticeably different from gay men, especially since, as we noted in Chapter 2, how the sectarian system creates both gender inequalities and internal cleavages among women. Indeed, as Hassan ruefully concluded from experience, 'the law prosecutes the weakest, not the strongest people'.[3]

These differences in the experiences of LGBTQ individuals present major problems for activists in relation to stimulating mobilization, of developing community consciousness – all of the attributes necessary for pursuing rights activism. In this chapter we address these issues confronting activists trying to create and form a movement and even creating a community in the context of the sectarian system and its uneven effects on the LGBTQ population. Towards this, we begin by following the story of Helem.

Helem: 'The dream'

Helem (*himaya lubnaniyya lil-mithliyinn*) is the Arabic acronym for 'Lebanese Protection for Gay People', and the word Helem in Arabic also means 'dream' (Helem 2008). A leading activist explained that Helem is 'the first LGBT organization not only in Lebanon but in the Arab World. It has set a template and an example for LGBT activism in the region'.[4] Helem is also an avowedly non-sectarian group. Helem, noted one activist, 'brings together all of these activists under one roof from different confessional backgrounds, different economic backgrounds, educational backgrounds'.[5]

Founded in Beirut, Helem emerged out of an established network of individuals blending socializing and activism. Khalil, a Helem activist who had been involved from the start, recounted that the network 'began as an underground movement online – people on IRC (Internet Relay Chat) started connecting'. Through making online 'virtual' connections, in 1998 members took the step of forming a group called 'Club Free' for people to informally meet in safe spaces, such as members' private residences. They first began meeting in the apartment of one of the members, as the group began to expand, before renting an apartment solely for their social meetings. Club Free eventually comprised around three hundred members (Helem 2008). A member of Club Free reminisced in an article that 'it was an underground group and you couldn't join unless you knew (at least two people in the organization), because there was this paranoia that the police would infiltrate' (Benoist 2015).

In essence, Club Free merged two streams of membership. In one, Club Free attracted people who saw the group primarily as an opportunity for socializing. In the other, a smaller group of members viewed Club Free as a stepping stone to stimulate an activist movement. This activism involved members who were already involved in radical non-sectarian and leftist politics in Lebanon.

Zain, an LGBTQ activist involved in Club Free, detailed the contradictions present in the group:

> On the one hand, we had the radical left, which was more or less very open on questions of sexuality and gender and was even too radical for some of the Club Free people. The organizing around the left led to a big debate on sexuality and gender, but the space was also open on a personal level, allowing men and women to speak about sexuality and gender and this was the only open space where a political debate was occurring. And then you had the crowd which was into the clubbing and was more of a social gathering. The two components intersected but were divided on class lines.[6]

A section within Club Free began increasingly to engage in what one member recalled to be 'subversive activism', which culminated in a radical LGBTQ film club and the 'Man is a Woman' film festival. The film festival attracted around 1,500 viewers over the course of seven days and led to debates on sexuality, gender identity and human rights.

The fear of persecution held by many LGBTQ individuals was brought home in 2002 when the Lebanese government released a draft for a new penal code, the first since 1943, which included an expansion of Article 534's remit. While the existing Article outlawed 'unnatural intercourse', the new draft changed the wording to 'unnatural sexual relations' (Makarem 2011).[7] The draft document contained a comment that the amendment was meant to include gays and lesbians, using the terms 'liwat' and 'souhaq' (both terms are used derogatorily to denote male-male and female-female sexual relations, respectively. See Chapter 5).

In response to the draft, a new movement called 'Hurriyat Khassa' (Personal Freedoms), comprising human rights activists and members of Club Free, campaigned to stop the draft not on the basis of sexual freedom but one of protecting the private sphere from the intrusion of the state. Following staunch opposition, the draft was sent back to the Administration and Judiciary Committee of the Lebanese Parliament, which eventually shelved it (Makarem 2011). The successful campaign to stop the draft law emboldened the activist wing of Club Free with the conviction that the moment was ripe for the emergence of an LGBTQ movement. The question, of course, concerned the precise course of action that the new activism should take.

In September 2004 five members of Club Free formed Helem and then set about obtaining support and advice from sympathetic lawyers, media figures and from international human rights organizations, such as the International Lesbian and Gay Association (ILGA) and Amnesty International. Thus, having announced their existence, Helem's activists initiated the task of crafting campaign strategies.

As an LGBTQ rights organization, a central focus for Helem's activism was decriminalizing homosexuality (Helem 2008). At the same time, Helem's activists positioned the movement within a much broader set of political projects. According to a founding member of Helem, the movement adopted 'an anti-sectarian, anti-racist, and anti-xenophobic position' (Makarem 2011: 105). While this reflected the political convictions and pre-existing activist networks of an influential cohort of Helem members, it was in essence a product of the fact that the left was a welcoming space. Zain, who is both a committed socialist and LGBTQ activist, remembered that 'the first time that we tried to organise politically the only space that was available was the "far left" and whatever civil society the left was connected to'. It was within this space that non-sectarian politics was prevalent. Zain remembered: 'We had to engage in the anti-sectarian movement so that you can reach a point where the system is eroded so you can bring about change. Anti-sectarianism is a very important part of the movement.'[8]

This alignment with radical politics set the template for the early stage of public activism. In 2004 LGBTQ members took an active part in the campaign against the invasion of Iraq, participating in the steering committee of the 'No War No Dictatorships' movement. In one demonstration LGBTQ activists publicly unfurled the Rainbow flag for the first time (Helem 2008).

As part of Helem's attempt to forge a place inside radical civil society, Helem participated in the 2005 Cedar Revolution, a social movement that drew in millions of Lebanese to demand the withdrawal of Syrian occupation after the assassination of Rafiq Al Hariri, the former prime minister of Lebanon. The Cedar Revolution is seen as an antecedent of the Arab Spring due to how people power and civil society came together in public spaces to successfully challenge authoritarian regimes (Knio 2005).[9]

Helem's activists were largely involved in the pro-democracy campaign aimed at ending the Syrian occupation. The participation of Helem's activists in the protests soon exposed the limits to which LGBTQ activism could be accommodated within broad-based civil society movements (Naber and Zaatari 2014). An LGBTQ activist involved in the Cedar Revolution recounted how both the March 8 and 14 alliances often displayed homophobia, including homophobic chants directed at political opponents, and were often outwardly hostile to LGBTQ activists. Zain reminisced: 'There was a spike of homophobia. There was a general atmosphere of xenophobia, hatred against Syrians, and this had a domino effect.' In one incident, LGBTQ activists were physically attacked in the 'Freedom Camp', a pro-democracy tent, and 'then they banned women and gays from sleeping in the Freedom Camp'. Zain, who was heavily involved in the protests, noted ruefully: 'The queers are always being accused of trying to sabotage the reform movement.'[10]

Helem's political activism found a more receptive audience a year later. In July 2006, Israel launched a ground and aerial attack on Lebanon. The attacks, which lasted thirty-three days, left more than one thousand dead and one million displaced, almost a sixth of the total population (Al-Harithy 2010). During the attacks, Helem became part of the organizing committee for Samidoun, a social welfare movement involved in the relief effort for the displaced. Helem's newly opened office in Beirut became an administrative centre to help coordinate assistance for refugees (Naber and Zaatari 2014). Through this work, Helem gained the unofficial and even official gratitude of many political parties and figures across Lebanon's sectarian divide – even including a certificate of recognition from Hezbollah, which once hung proudly in Helem's offices. Such acknowledgement, however, was short lasting. Elias, a former Helem activist involved in Smaidoun, recounted that Helem even received an award from some of the sectarian parties: 'We were accepted as Helem, as an LGBT group, because we were involved.' This support, however, did not last long:

> But after this they attack us. It is always like this. They use marginalized people during the war or the revolution. They use you and then after this you are not a priority and they won't change the law on LGBT rights. Even Hezbollah thanked us for what we were doing and now this year [2017] Nasrallah (the leader of Hezbollah) was talking publicly about gay men and he called us 'a perversion'. We were shocked.[11]

Reviewing the early days of Lebanese LGBTQ activism, a report by Helem noted that the movement's wide-ranging political activism resulted in the loss of a number of members 'who were not prepared to be openly associated with an LGBT organization'. As Helem became more politically vocal and visible, its membership declined from two hundred to forty.

As with all social movements that represent oppressed minorities, Helem needed to build a base of dedicated activists so that the movement can progress towards demanding rights. This riddle of how to stimulate and build collective action is a major area of social movement research. McAdam (1982) usefully introduced the concept of 'cognitive liberation', in which a body of individuals begin to formalize shared understandings of their situation as one of oppression and injustice, as a necessary first step in developing a movement to achieve rights. Movements, therefore, stoke the fires of community consciousness, to encourage individuals to see how unjust the system is so that they will demand rights.

The urgency of building a community of activists was not lost on Helem. Reflecting on the emergence of the LGBTQ movement, Hakim explained that 'it is very difficult for me to conceive of a LGBT community in Lebanon much less a LGBT movement'. For many individuals, Hakim ruefully concluded, their priority is not to be activists, but to 'have fun and laugh'. 'There is nothing communal about it', Hakim explained:

> The community itself here is divided and leaderless and undisciplined and who knows who might come up and bring it together, who knows if it even can

be brought together. It's not just on sectarian lines; it's also on economic and political lines.[12]

The exercise of community building, of constructing a sense of 'we-ness' – a shared and cohesive identity among LGBTQ people – was thus fundamental to the ambition to gain rights, but such feelings of belonging were somehow missing. Why then has there been this absence of community among Lebanese LGBTQ people and how have activists tried constructing a shared identity and political consciousness to sustain mobilization?

The most obvious factor militating against the development of a political community is the fear of harassment and violence meted out by state and non-state actors. Helem reported that in the years following its formation, many associates left the movement 'for fear of reprisal' (Helem 2008). And reprisals against Helem did indeed come swiftly.

Almost immediately on its foundation Helem rubbed against the boundaries of what the state would permit. In 2004 Helem – as all Lebanese civil society organizations are required to do – submitted a formal notification of its existence as an NGO to the Ministry of the Interior (MOI), which as per custom then registers applicant groups. Although the MOI never officially rejected the application, neither did it issue Helem with a licence and registration number (Helem 2008). When Helem's activists visited the MOI to enquire about the progress of its file, they were told that the application was 'shameful' and had been permanently shelved. Habib, the activist introduced at the beginning of the chapter, explained the negative implication of Helem lacking formal MOI notification:

> In 2004 we asked for registration – we applied as an LGBT rights NGO. We didn't get accepted but we didn't get refused. We do not have a legal identity so you cannot open a bank account – we have been without a bank account for twelve years. This is the major problem for Helem, because you need core funds and project funds, and the core funders, 95 per cent of the time, won't give resources to organizations that do not have a bank account.[13]

Neither did it take long for the security forces to direct their unwanted attention towards Helem. Shortly after Helem completed its first IDAHO[14] celebration in 2005, the police raided Helem's office and seized the group's computers. A rumour followed that the police found drugs in the office – opponents of LGBTQ rights in Lebanon often allege that homosexuality and drug abuse are linked and even satanic worship is somehow associated. Helem members also noted the presence of what they strongly suspected to be undercover police officers infiltrating meetings (Helem 2008). Local politicians also used the opportunity to fire cheap shots at Helem. Although Helem's office was located in a cosmopolitan district close to the major universities and a hub for the city's nightlife, the residential demographic is largely Sunni. An elected member of Beirut city council filed a complaint against Helem, accusing them of 'endangering society and public morality'.

'Where the state freaks out'

While the very real threat of persecution and violence stopped individuals from associating themselves with the movement, it is important to consider the asymmetrical effects of harassment on the LGBTQ population. As Moussawi (2018) argues, understandings of sexuality in Lebanon are shaped by complex assemblages of gender and power. Same-sex relations may be tacitly sanctioned by the state – both the formal arms of the security forces and 'informal' militia networks – as long as they do not violate gender norms and they are restricted to affluent people in the private sphere. Expressions of sexuality that do not cohere to these boundaries are ruthlessly penalized by the various arms of the security forces and the state. Rural or working-class men, transpeople, Syrian refugees, men who do not conform to nationalist and masculinist identities and queer women who do not follow gender norms also have an increased risk of being subject to surveillance and violence. These sexual boundaries that determine what is tacitly permitted and what is subject to violent proscription have consequences for the development of activist building. These dynamics of inclusion/exclusion are illuminated in the production and erasure of queerspaces in Beirut.

We can begin by looking at the gay bars and clubs that emerged within the more cosmopolitan and liberal districts of Beirut and its environs, which ran parallel to Helem's embryonic activism. Commercial queerspaces emerged in Beirut within districts undergoing gentrification, including Badaro, Gemmayze, Mar Mikhael and the Hamra. Beirut's commercial queerspaces are largely concentrated in a few select places – bars, a yacht club pool and a nightclub called 'Acid' – which was said to be the first openly gay club in the Middle East. Rather than definable 'gayberhoods', commercial queerspaces are better described as positioned within a spectrum of spaces. Some are located within 'Queer friendly neighbourhoods' (Gorman-Murray and Waitt 2009), localities that have a heterosexual majority in commercial and residential terms but where LGBTQ businesses and people are tolerated. Alongside these, there are liminal Queerspaces: cafes and bars which are not expressly 'gay' but where LGBTQ people are welcomed (Moussawi 2015, 2018). All commercial queerspaces are what we call 'contingently tolerated spaces', since they are never completely safe havens. The emergence of these commercial queerspaces in the early 2000s onwards quickly drew the attention of Western journalists, penning accounts of Beirut as 'the 'gay paradise' of the Middle East. In one infamous travel guide to Beirut in the *New York Times*, the city was portrayed as the 'Provincetown of the Middle East', a place of sexual licence in relation to the rest of the MENA region (Healy 2009). The report suggested that the authorities appeared indifferent to these spaces.

These spaces are remarkable since they were rarely subject to scrutiny or harassment by the security forces and the morality police infamous for their violent intimidation of LGBTQ people. The degree of licence given to these bars and nightclubs drew the attention of a few Western journalists, who after a night of partying in some of these spots wrote accounts of Beirut as 'Gayrouth', the 'gay paradise' of the Middle East (Reid-Smith 2012). Indeed, many of these spaces are now referenced in international gay travel guides and blogs.

The relative sovereignty afforded to these gay bars and clubs underscored the degree to which they were spaces reserved for economic elites, a group that the state rarely interferes with. For example, the entrance charge for many clubs and parties exceed $30, a cost markedly beyond the economic means of many Lebanese. An activist recounted: 'These clubs were extremely exclusive; they would not let anybody in!'[15] Indeed, as a leading Helem activist asked in a blog:

> Is this freedom accessible to everyone? Definitely not. To enjoy this freedom, you need to be able to afford it. LGBT individuals and even heterosexual women from lower economical classes do not have the luxury to live alone in Beirut, or go to bars every day. (Azzi 2011b)

These places, which catered to young professionals and the wealthy, provided little interest to the homophobic state and its surveillance apparatuses. This, of course, begs the question: Why did the state permit or at least overlook the existence of LGBTQ spaces?

Part of the answer lies in the fact that these spaces were not obviously 'flaunting' an LGBTQ identity. It would be more accurate instead to say that these were places that attracted an LGBTQ clientele, who recognized that the locations afforded some safety. This point is important as it demonstrated that the state could tacitly accept or more likely ignore LGBTQ spaces as long as they were not visibly 'gay' or perceived in any way as a threat to 'morality'. Fadi, an independent activist, explained that there appears to be even a tacit consent for the existence of a certain type of LGBTQ population and identity in Lebanon, which gives the appearance of freedom to some privileged LGBTQ people. He concluded:

> The government is giving us a certain kind of space to exist. As long as it's not known to be gay, there's no illegal behaviour going on inside, there is no sex and there are no drugs, you can go there. But outside don't ask for your rights. You find that most of the community think they are living their freedom, but they are not. They are just living in this bubble.[16]

On this, Moussawi (2018: 184) explains that 'having access to gay-friendly spaces and LGBTQ networks in Beirut requires having economic, cultural, and social capital'. More crucially, the security forces are wary of taking on middle-class and moneyed individuals. Wealth and class in Lebanon, like everywhere else, provide a degree of immunity from the sectarian state. Wealthy citizens do not pay taxes but they can pay bribes to police officers. Affluence endows you with the vital commodity of *wasta*: connections to key people in authority or with power who are able to leverage their power to overcome formal rules. For those LGBTQ individuals who possess high amounts of *wasta* they can use this to evade arbitrary detention, harassment and abuse at checkpoints. Money and connections in Lebanon, like so many places, elevates some individuals beyond the law (see Naber and Zaatari 2014: 103–4). Fadi admitted: 'It's bad to perceive it this way, but it exists: if you have connections you are protected.'[17] A human rights worker and activist concluded that privilege 'plays out in every single aspect of LGBTQ people's lives: class, power, family connections and *wasta* in a country like this goes a really long way to the extent that they can even transcend some of the violence and the discrimination that any other person might experience'.[18]

Yet, a more complete answer needs to consider that rather than existing outside the system LGBTQ spaces were incorporated into the logic of the sectarian and weak state. Thus, some of the bars and nightclubs are located within the fiefdoms of the militias and are required to pay 'protection' to these groups, including having militiamen providing 'security' at the doors. On the one occasion the security forces raided a bar, a writer noted that it was carried out 'in order to gather the club owner's bribes that were perhaps late that month' rather than owing to any homophobic impulse (X 2017).

While it is not possible to gain entrance into the sectarian system for LGBTQ rights, it is possible for the movement to play by the rules of the game. This rule playing can be seen in further important aspects. The premise underlying sectarian pluralism is that each of the officially recognized sects is granted autonomy over their own internal communal affairs. In this framework, the various groups in Lebanon are deeply wary of interfering in the internal cultural matters of neighbouring groups as this would be contrary to the spirit of peaceful coexistence. The principle of communal autonomy means that most Lebanese avoid intruding too far into an individual's or group's private affairs. This has consequences for LGBTQ people: while there is state harassment of LGBTQ people in the public sphere, LGBTQ people can be tolerated as long as they remain private (see Nagle 2018b). However, the private sphere is only accessible to privileged LGBTQ members. While bars and clubs provide a key part of a limited sphere of cultural autonomy, Hakim explained it also extends to the private lives of a few people:

> This country is small, it's divided, gay people still crave invisibility and they crave being in a place where they have some measure of privacy. And it is very difficult if you stay in your traditional communities, so there are a lot of people who can move and who can afford it, start over and live a double life. They can seek refuge in another part of town to escape discrimination.[19]

Zain, a radical activist, had noted that the emergence of what he described as 'commercial queerspaces' seemed to coincide with a concerted programme of social cleansing of aspects of LGBTQ life deemed insalubrious by the state. To an extent this was a consequence, the activist continued, of the rampant postwar reconstruction of parts of Beirut – 'the process of the gentrification of queerspaces has been the harshest. Beirut today does not have any non-commercial queerspaces, which it had before'.[20] It's not clear if any part of the process of gentrification should be viewed as a conspiracy purposely designed to eradicate non-commercial queerspaces; nevertheless areas around Beirut's coastal line, once renowned among the LGBTQ population for hosting relatively private 'cruising' spots, have undergone extensive privatization.

More tangible evidence of a deliberate campaign of intimidation against what the state defined as the 'queer unwanted' (Bell and Binnie 2004) became apparent in two outrages. The first of these was a raid by ISF members against a cinema that screened gay sex movies (Moussawi 2015: 600). This cinema, located in an Armenian neighbourhood, was known to serve a working-class clientele. The ISF arrested thirty-six individuals, who were then transferred to Hobeish police station where they were tortured and subjected to anal examinations (BBC 2012). The second involved another raid by the ISF, this time against a sauna in Beirut. The ISF arrested twenty-seven people: twelve employees, many of whom were Syrian refugees, and fifteen customers, in addition to the owner of the bathhouse. The public prosecutor in Beirut used his powers to charge the arrestees with a range of criminal offences (LebMASH 2014a). These incidents demonstrate what Zain described as 'a vicious circle of spaces opening up and closing down'.[21]

A dual and unequal gay Beirut had arisen. On the one side exists a relatively protected and autonomous private sphere of bars and clubs, while on the other are increasingly shrinking spaces subject to state surveillance and violence. Zain simply noted: 'It is fine if you are gay in a controlled middle-class environment like a middle-class bar. But it is not fine if you are outside of these spaces because you will not be protected.' Zain explained that those arrested, such as the men arrested at a 'gay' cinema', were the 'lower class that don't find space in other LGBT spaces and parties that are becoming too expensive for them; it's always the poor, lower social economic classes that are persecuted'.[22] Another activist noted that this idea of state accepting while simultaneously denigrating certain renditions of acceptable homosexuality was confirmed in their interactions with a police representative, who distinguished between 'the respectable gays who are from good families and go to respectable places, and the rabble who don't go to such places and who might have sex in the street and are poor' (Benoist 2015).

The existence of bars and clubs in Beirut unmolested by the state generates a debate about how they can be harnessed for rights-based activism. For one group of activists these spaces needed to be protected as they were in some cases owned by LGBTQ individuals, and they represented a potential focal point for the building of community identity and activism. Hakim, a leading activist reflected on the need for 'real spaces' rather than virtual ones. Yet, he continued, while these spaces represented something of a 'gay ghetto' in Beirut that are 'incredibly expensive, exclusive and hyperconservative', they had at least the potential to provide the basis for community building in the same way that gay enclaves had done in the United States and elsewhere:

The good thing about those enclaves in the United States, in Europe and wherever, is that you can have a lot of gay people move into a neighbourhood.

Some people open up a barber shop, some people open up a supermarket, some open whatever, and all of a sudden you have a community that satisfies the needs more or less.[23]

Habib, a former manager of one of the bars, explained that more than providing a focal point for community building the gay establishments were doing their best to protect the people. They were providing safe spaces for people. Ali confirmed this: 'There is a small space, a safe haven, and you have war all around you.'

Yet, for other activists, the bars represented the commodification and depoliticization of activism. On this, Zain recounted his and other activists' resistance to the commercialization process:

There were moneyed people who thought that there were privileges from having such spaces and thought that if we start opposing the state the state might hit you. And you always have to deal with this type of balance – confronting injustice could lead to a backlash.[24]

In a more forceful critique, Zain viewed these spaces as – wittingly or not – complicit with state-led social cleansing of queerspaces. The bars only permit respectable and acceptable versions of LGBTQ identity in order to gain some degree of tolerance from the state. It was not only that the bars and clubs were exclusivist in relation to class but they also marginalized visible expressions of sexuality that were non-normative:

This whole emphasis on cleanliness – that this is the only way that you will get state acceptance. This whole idea of cleaning up the queerspaces to be safe and then the state will say, 'Oh, ok, now we accept you.' A bar can agree to be gay friendly and have all gay staff, but they are not supposed to act gay. If they don't look the typical gay man look, they don't get into the bars. Long hair sometimes doesn't allow you to get into the gay bars. The problem is that these middle-class gay men keep their privileges, they have to do this, they have to kick everyone out else, clean out the space to be accepted and tolerated by the state, because they are the ones who need the state's tolerance. Normally the poor don't care about state tolerance, they know that even if the state tolerates you because you are gay, they will not tolerate you because you are poor.[25]

Norms and performances related to gender and masculinity are reinforced through processes of exclusion. Zain noted that there is a 'fear of transgressing gender norms within the gay community'.[26] He noted that 'the policing in this area focuses on clean up: they focus on transgenders and gay men don't matter'. Ali, a young activist, pointed out that many men are wary of being seen as 'effeminate':

If you are masculine, you are likely to be exonerated by the state of any sexual act. Homophobia is expressed more on a gendered level. It is not really a fear of sexual relations; it is more a fear of breaking a gender role and this is where the state freaks out.[27]

The comparative freedom for LGBTQ bars and clubs provided a problem for activists. Rather than provide a base for the emergence of an LGBTQ community and a social movement, these private and exclusivist spaces acted as a disincentive to many LGBTQ people becoming involved in public activism. Hakim explained that LGBTQ activists 'aren't those that have, they are the have nots':

> This country has created quite ironically a very difficult position for gay rights to advance because of the relative comfort that you have here. If you ask a gay man here, they would say, 'Why do I want go down and protest and attract attention to what is a perfectly comfortable and good situation that I have? I have the bars and the clubs that I need. I have the relative tolerance that I need. Why do you want to go and play with the hornets' nest?' This is unfortunately really, really difficult to capitalize on when you want to mobilize people to do social change because they don't want anything to change.[28]

Hakim continued arguing that the situation incentivized many relatively comfortable gay men from joining the movement, who instead tended to remain 'incredibly private and very low key':

> It is possible if you have access to resources and contacts to exist as a gay person in Lebanon and to be fine. You have got your gay bars; the police don't arrest you, they arrest Syrian refugees, transpeople, sex workers and drug users, the invisible part of the country that we work with, so there is no impetus for people to go down onto the street and protest.[29]

Activist debates about the bars and clubs echo distinctions between 'good' and 'bad' sexual citizenship. Good and bad sexual citizenship is used to describe how states regulate sexuality in ways that construe some practices and relations as legitimate and good, while others are decreed unacceptable and bad (see Richardson 2017). To a considerable extent the difference between good and bad sexual citizenship historically maps onto heterosexual and non-heterosexual identities and practices. Good sexual citizens are seen to belong to the community of value, whose sexual behaviour conforms to traditional gender norms, intimacy and monogamy. Non-heterosexuals, alternatively, are constituted as holding sexual acts, behaviours, identities defined by the state as deviant, thus meaning that LGBTQ individuals are liable to forfeit their status as full citizens (Bell and Binnie 2004).

Writing about the LGBTQ rights movement in the United States, Steven Seidman argues that rather than challenge the sexual norms and forms of social regulation associated with the good sexual citizen, it instead narrowed the agenda to assimilation, meaning equality and integration, leaving in consequence the dominant sexual norms in place (Seidman 2004). In this sense, good and bad sexual citizenship is not only a marker of difference between heteronormativity and non-heteronormativity, but also a way of internally cleaving LGBTQ communities. Good sexual citizenship for some rights-based LGBTQ movements involves becoming compliant with heteronormative identities, with an emphasis on respectability and privacy, thus casting non-heteronormative sexualities outside the bounds of political and social integration (Ghaziani 2015).

Good and bad citizenship has been extended by some scholars, especially in the United States, through the concept of 'homonormativity' to critique a particular strand of LGBTQ rights claims (Duggan 2012). This is an activism that sustains dominant heteronormative institutions through 'the construction of an acceptable homosexuality ... specifically, gender conformity' (Rosenfeld 2009: 621), since these are the values and identities which our society rewards as legitimate and meriting rights. Homonormativity secures privilege for affluent and gender-normative gays and lesbians based on adherence to dominant cultural constructions of gender, while marginalizing the needs of working-class LGBTQ people, lesbians, people of colour and transgender individuals, who are cast as deviant and a threat to the moral order of society (Stryker 2008: 146–7). At its most politically inactive, homonormativity restricts LGBTQ rights to a narrow neoliberal framework in which rights are fundamentally protected in the private sphere while leaving the public sphere untouched.

To extend these concepts of good and bad sexual citizenship, and homonormativity, to Beirut, we can see that the state makes distinctions between expressions of sexuality that are implicitly tolerated and those that are proscribed. Commercial queerspaces are tacitly incorporated into the neoliberal and sectarian state, while at the same time spaces and people deemed transgressive to the moral order are violently erased. These binaries between tolerable and intolerable queerspaces are contingent and the state reserves the right to withdraw acceptance at any point. Affluent gay people with *wasta* – connections – can exist as long as they do not transgress dominant norms of masculinity. The 'Queer unwanted' (Bell and Binnie 2004) – transpeople, refugees, sex workers and working-class queer members – forfeit their right to sexual citizenship. Through the exercise of good and bad sexual citizenship, those with privilege can enjoy the benefits of homonormativity (Halperin 2012: 441). The existence of some commercial queerspaces provides safe havens for the privileged. Yet, safe havens do not always stimulate community activism. They can also be spaces that prohibit the formation of collective consciousness and community identity required for a movement to develop. Safe havens, contingently at best, give security only to a privileged few.

In an environment where certain configurations of sexuality, class and power are tolerated or criminalized, activists inevitably confront questions on how to build an inclusive movement. Here, we turn to two questions: first, whether the movement should develop as a radical protest organization that is both anti-sectarian and situated within leftist politics or a more narrowly defined professional, LGBTQ rights NGO; second, the extent to which movements become exclusionary rather than inclusive, particularly in regards to gender.

'The radical aspect of civil society has been shut down'

Helem's emergence involved the movement positioning itself within radical political projects in Lebanon. At the same time, Helem also began to increase its profile as an LGBTQ rights group. Indeed, Helem has described itself as a 'rights-based organization that focuses on advocating and lobbying for the legal and social rights of people with alternative sexuality' (Helem 2008: 4). One of the main ways in which Helem became a rights-based organization was through its consolidation as a professional NGO advocacy organization, funded by international actors (see **Chapter 6**). This funding enabled some activists to become full-time professional NGO workers, which is particularly important since, as Hakim noted, 'very few people, including myself, can do this fulltime, can do this as a career'.[30] The ability to become a professional NGO further endowed Helem with legitimacy – it was now not only recognized by international agencies, but it also could now claim to serve a definable LGBTQ community that had specific needs. Thus, once constituted as a professional NGO, the funding model Helem was positioned within incentivized the organization to exclusively dedicate its support to the LGBTQ population. Central to this process of becoming an NGO was Helem's role as distributor of services to the LGBTQ community. These services involve – among many things – HIV testing, medical support, legal casework, clinical management for rape cases and psychosocial help.

For a number of activists Helem's development as a professional NGO is an unavoidable but necessary step to assist a vulnerable LGBTQ population in the context of a weak state. LGBTQ NGOs have become front-line as a result of the Lebanese state increasingly shrinking from its role in providing basic public goods, which are now devolved to the realm of civil society. Hakim argued:

> Because of the absence of the state, a lot of civil society organizations have filled in the gap of where the state ought to be in terms of services, especially, in terms of health, in terms of social support, in terms of education. So civil society I would argue has never been more important. Because without it there would have been a much more acute collapse, especially among rural and disenfranchised communities that we work with. If it wasn't for organizations like Helem, sex workers, trans population, sexually active people, would not have any place to go to even for a simple HIV test.[31]

Helem's identity as a professional NGO focused primarily on service delivery and rights; this enabled it to act as the legitimate representative of a beleaguered LGBTQ community. It moreover helped construct the very idea that the LGBTQ population – until then hidden – existed as an identifiable community with a definable identity and clear set of requirements. At the same time, through this, Helem risked NGOization.

NGOization refers to the process through which social movement activism geared at the social and political transformation of sectarian and authoritarian

regimes have instead been directed to professional NGOs limited to advocacy work
and services. NGOization is seen as driven by the almost complete withdrawal of the
state in many parts of the MENA region from investment in the public sector, which
has resulted in a severe deterioration of social and economic rights, rising rates of
unemployment and declining social welfare support. Professional NGOs have taken
up the role of service providers in the absence of a functioning state, and they are
funded by international actors who see civil society as an instrument for advancing
democratization and human rights in the region (Choudry and Kapoor 2013).

Lebanese LGBTQ activists acutely feel the pressure to undergo NGOization,
especially as it provides some financial security for them to operate. More critical
voices within the movement, however, view NGOization as directing activism
away from radical politics, such as anti-sectarianism, and towards the depoliticized
sphere of service provision. It was not only that NGOization closed down the
space to contest the sectarian system, but also the development into rights-based
NGOs had the potential to reproduce the logic of the system. These issues are
perhaps most evident in relation to how the LGBTQ movement became entwined
within clientelism. Zain, a former Helem activist, who noted his opposition to
NGOization argued:

> Our movement is sectarian in the sense that it is sucked into the clientelistic
> system and it has an impact from funding and donors and they are a very big
> factor in what happens. The radical aspect of civil society has been shut down.
> I think that it has been co-opted by the system. It's the Lebanese system, it's not
> just the government, the administration, it's not just the warlords and elites; it's
> the actual nature of the state.[32]

Lebanon's clientelistic system is indeed central to the operation of the sectarian
system. In Lebanon, clientelism usually refers to how individual citizens, in order
to access many social services and even jobs, have little option than to go through
the powerful sectarian leaders rather than the state. The sphere of civil society
represents the main instrument through which the clientelistic system works on a
daily basis. The main sectarian factions host civil society wings which are responsible
for producing and distributing social services for their constituency. Research has
shown how these sectarianized civil society networks are primary providers of up
to 60 per cent of basic health and education services in Lebanon (Cammett 2014).
At the same time, the clientelisic system has rapidly expanded in the postwar era to
severely constrict anti- and non-sectarian movements from following a programme
of social and political transformation or even critiquing the sectarian system. The
sectarian factions engage in strategies to weaken and even co-opt non-sectarian
movements. The systemic incentives of the power-sharing regime are tilted in a
way that encourages non-sectarian activists to operate within the confines of the
system, often by working with sectarian leaders. As Clark and Salloukh (2013: 732)
argue, in Lebanon most civil associations 'are used as tools to reinforce the clientist
and sectarian status quo'. The net result of this is that the logic of power-sharing

has 'both precluded the emergence of cross-sectarian, interest-based identities and sabotaged direct attempts to challenge the sectarian system'.

It is clear that the LGBTQ NGOs are not clients of the sectarian parties, who are on the whole deeply homophobic. The point is that NGOization has forced the movement to play by the rules of the system, characterized by clientelistic behaviour and service provision in the context of a weak state. Moreover, it incentivizes NGOs to function as depoliticized organizations that work on behalf of a narrowly defined constituency rather than building alliances with a range of groups across society.

The process of NGOization drew heated debate among activists. Hakim recounted the nature of the discussions that were waged within the group:

> Some people were saying, 'No, we are not single issue people and we can't lead single issue lives and you can't tell me that poverty is an issue that is not affecting the LGBT issue, because it is', and so people were saying that we need to fight it. Other people were saying that there are other people fighting it and we are the only group that have the resources to address these other LGBT-specific issues, which is also valid.[33]

Former Helem board members wrote from the perspective of the radical wing of the movement:

> The rift in the LGBT movement ... manifested around a leftist membership that called for political engagement and the opening of the organization's doors to refugees, on one end, and the more identitarian membership that called for an exclusive focus on gay rights as the ceiling for engagement. (Rizk and Makarem 2015: 13)

At times, the debate veered towards outright conflict. Habib, a Helem activist, remembered:

> People wanted Helem to go as a leftist movement, which I think is ridiculous. When you are an organization that is defending LGBT rights you don't care for one perspective of the people and leave the others. You don't treat LGBT people who are rich as capitalistic whatever. Your main goal is to protect the LGBT community. If you want to put politics before help, that is ridiculous, that is discrimination.[34]

Excluding and incorporating gender

Debates about NGOization and clientelism generate further questions about gender inclusivity/exclusivity. Helem contained a cohort of feminist activists – 'Helem Girls'. Helem Girls took on a proactive role within Helem, particularly in terms of devising campaigns, writing policy documents and voicing the concerns and aims of lesbians within the movement.

Despite the existence of women activists in the movement, Helem quickly became identified as a movement dominated by the interests of men. To some extent this situation was a by-product of Helem's rising profile as an LGBTQ rights NGO. This form of activism was supported by international funders, especially from the Global North, who sought to export into Lebanon the modes of gay rights activism historically dominant in the West, which was oriented to the needs of gay men since criminalization tended to target sodomy charges rather than lesbianism. In fact, the sexuality of queer women is not acknowledged by Lebanese law in the sense that legally there is nothing which says sex can happen without a penis (Arab Foundation for Freedoms and Equality 2018: 22). This emphasis on providing support primarily for gay men was given added urgency by Helem's advocacy work providing support in relation to HIV AIDs. Helem became partners with public health bodies in leading the testing for HIV AIDS (Helem 2008).

While a focus on these issues is unquestionably important, it carried obvious risks of sidelining the needs of queer women and others. An article by two female activists provides a flavour of these concerns: 'LGBT activisms led by middle-class gay men tend to isolate the struggles of migrants, women, trans, workers … especially once they are able to lobby for wider recognition …. such as in the Beiruti context' (Al-Ali and Sayegh 2019: 249). This claim – that Helem essentially became a masculine movement – was also put forward by two activists, including the former executive director of Helem. For them, Helem reproduced a 'hegemonic masculinity', a movement founded on a 'respectable, middle-class, educated and professionalized masculinity' (Rizk and Makarem 2015: 103). Hegemonic masculinity, in the context of LGBTQ activism in Lebanon, refers to the presentation of gay men as unthreatening to the sectarian state as a precondition to demanding rights.

For a former female member of Helem, the group's emphasis on masculinity led to a situation in which the movement acted to 'reproduce patriarchal structures among many members of Helem', particularly in terms of sanctioning what she called 'non-normative versions of femininity' (El Hage 2012: 50). Hakim admitted in retrospect that male activists had not sufficiently understood the specific needs of queer women in the movement, which had left a legacy of a fractured and acrimonious sphere of activism:

> You've got a very big problem between gay men and lesbian women, which is really a great pity because our list of allies is thin. The last thing that you want is people to be wasting their energy and time clawing at each other across gay and lesbian lines instead of working together. I don't think that gay men understand that lesbians are women, and women already in the Middle East have to deal with a lot more. Lesbian women also feel that they don't have enough voice or that they don't have enough representation and unfortunately it translates into a zero-sum game, where we can't have a movement that has everyone together, so let's have a lesbian movement.[35]

The departure of Helem Girls from Helem led to the eventual creation of new queer women's movements. Hakim admitted that 'a lot of queer women's movements are a lot more active and lot more vocal [compared to men]' in Lebanon

> because as women they are much more discriminated against as women and as lesbians, because of the way that the system is, because of domestic violence, the right to give your children nationality, because of misogyny across the board, you name it.[36]

The most notable of these activist groups was Meem. Formed in 2008, Meem was set up to engage in feminist and queer politics. Rather than position itself as an identitarian movement focused exclusively on rights for gay women, Meem's activists utilized the post-identity term 'queer' to situate their politics, which can be seen as a refusal of fixed identity-based approaches to gender and sexuality. As part of its mission, Meem's (2010a: 12) activists variously described the group as a 'grassroots movement where women are empowered' and as a 'social justice movement' that mobilizes to contest the existence of oppression against gay women and bisexuals by targeting political sectarianism.

Meem differed from Helem by introducing a more intersectional analysis and approach to LGBTQ activism, especially in relation to exposing the complex range of effects generated by the sectarian system. In a document produced by Meem activists, the writers explain how 'queer women and transgender persons in Lebanon face multiple layers of discrimination: sexism, classism, homophobia, racism and sectarianism'. In so doing, Meem actively constructed 'alliances with local women's and human rights movements, with leftist political parties and progressive thinkers' (Meem 2010a: 15).

Meem was also profoundly opposed to the sectarian system. Rather than pursue public visibility for this, Meem prioritized empowerment and a safe space for lesbians. Meem's 'resistance to patriarchy and sectarianism' begins as 'an underground community' (2010a: 9). Through remaining initially underground and thus relatively invisible, Meem sought to create a movement deliberately designed to encompass and transcend sectarian divisions. Meem requested its members to 'leave their religions at the door' (Meem 2010a: 9). Meem made non-sectarianism to be a defining feature of the group's identity. Activists wrote that Meem's 'very existence as a diverse yet united community – one of the rare few in Lebanon – is in itself a challenge to the sectarianism endemic in Lebanese society and politics' (Meem 2010a: 9). Located within this dissident public culture, sexual difference is also articulated as a challenge to the separateness of sectarian identity mandated by the sectarian system.

Meem's activism lasted only a few years. Rather than a cohesive and unified social movement, Meem was more an umbrella for a relatively loose and diverse network of activists concentrated around promoting inclusive LGBTQ politics. Meem did not develop into a public activist movement that used protest tactics to confront the authorities or even outlined specific campaigns. Yet, it would be remiss to overlook the significant legacy left behind by Meem on LGBTQ activism.

Meem successfully placed a gendered and feminist analysis at the core of LGBTQ activism. At the same time, Meem expanded and deepened an intersectional perspective, which illuminated the multiple forms through which the sectarian system generates inequalities that impact on sex, gender, class and ethnicity among many aspects. Meem's lasting importance is also evident in its refusal to subscribe to the template of a fully funded professional, rights-based NGO. Meem's alternative model of grassroots and 'invisible' activism endowed the group with a degree of flexibility, including a license to pursue radical politics.

Meem's activism resembled what the social movement theorist Alberto Melucci (1996) has identified as networks composed of a multiplicity of groups that are dispersed, fragmented and submerged in everyday life and that act as cultural laboratories – experimenting with new cultural models, forms of relationships and alternative perceptions and meanings of the world. The submerged networks function as a system of exchanges in which individuals and information circulate. Thus, rather than a traditional movement that seeks to use street protests, Meem's focus was on solidarity, community consciousness and network building designed to engender new ways of understanding and confronting the systemic ways that Lebanon's sectarian system reproduces violent inequalities. In this sense, Meem's politics is 'prefigurative', an expression of queer futurity – an attempt to embody in the movement itself the kind of society they want to bring about by developing counterhegemonic institutions and modes of interaction that embody the desired transformation (Van de Sande 2013).

While Meem represented a largely underground and submerged network of activists and members, it nevertheless provided the foundation for subsequent LGBTQ activist groups willing to be publicly visible and active. An important example of this emergent activism can be found in Nasawiya, formed in 2010, and whose membership overlapped with Meem. Nasawiya described itself as a 'feminist collective' containing 270 independent activists. Dina, a former member, recounted that the 'feminist collective in Beirut' is 'a collective co-operative rather than a funding-based organization. It is a co-operative of women; it is a safe space for women; it is based on economic and social solidarity for women'.[37]

In its literature, Nasawiya, like Meem, emphasized the importance of intersectionality as central to its thinking and activities. Its members called for collaboration with all marginalized groups to 'recreate a world free from sexism, and all other forms of exploitations and discriminations that collaborate with it: classism, heterosexism, racism, capitalism, etc'. On its website, Nasawiya (2012) elaborated on the character of its activism:

> We strive to not only be a movement of educated and privileged women, but a movement by and for the single mothers, the refugees, the disabled, the sex workers, the migrant workers, the people of non-conforming gender identities and non-conforming sexualities, etc. We understand that we have been taught to believe that we do not have much in common, but having been united in marginalization, we can make an effort to unite in seeking a change in ourselves and in our society.

Nasawiya's commitment to intersectional feminist politics demonstrated a strong family resemblance to Meem. The correspondence between Nasawiya and Meem was further evident in terms of organizational structure. Both movements eschewed the formalized and professional structure of NGOs preferred by Helem in favour of a more flexible, inclusive and non-hierarchical form. A Nasawiya activist wrote in detail to describe the importance of the group's structure:

> Nasawiya is a loose organization within the women's movement that had made the conscious choice to avoid 'NGOization' and professionalization in order to allow the maximum of independence [for] its members within their initiative, thus enabling a wider independence for the organization as a whole. (El Hage 2012: 50)

Nasawiya (2012) outlined a programme of campaigns, initiatives and training for activists, such as the campaign – 'Ghayreh 3adtik: Feminist Tools for Change' – which provided 'training program for women on how to use a feminist analysis to bring about change … by undertaking legal reform, grassroots pressure, building a community, raising awareness, creating support groups, or running for public office'. Nasawiya's difference from Meem was additionally evident in the movement's willingness to take part in public protests and street demonstrations. Some of these demonstrations saw Nasawiya inserted within broad-based anti-sectarian movements, such as the Laique Pride protest mentioned at the beginning of Chapter 1, in which Nasawiya took part as a feminist bloc. As a feminist social movement, Nasawiya also organized events for International Women's Day, including a 'Take Back the Night March' to protest against sexual harassment and as a call for safe streets for women.

'Under one roof'?

Helem emerged as the first above-ground LGBTQ movement in the Arab world. Yet rather than represent a homogeneous movement and community with unified beliefs and goals, Helem quickly became riven by numerous cleavages that ultimately fractured the group. These fracture lines appeared to be caused initially by debates among activists on whether the movement should be a professional, rights-based NGO or whether it should be a grassroots political project allied to and intersecting with a range of radical and oppressed groups. Helem's rupture was further expedited by questions relating to incorporating gender. In addition, the rapid emergence and subsequent spotlight placed on Helem exposed a number of cross-pressures buffeting the group. Hakim, a Helem activist from the outset of the movement, provided more detail:

> People forget that when Helem was established in 2004 – and you bring together all of these activists under one roof from different confessional backgrounds, different economic backgrounds, educational backgrounds and political

backgrounds – it was an experiment that nobody knew what to expect. And all of these issues came up that was observable for the first time in the modern Middle East, stuff like misogyny in the LGBT community, stuff like the question of Palestine, the question of queer activism and how it fits, a question of priorities, a question of resources, all of this stuff came bubbling to the fore. Then there was Helem in Beirut, filled in this little space with people who didn't know by and large what the hell they were doing. And this is a small place and personalities matter, so personal clashes between people, in this case personal problems between prominent members and senior members at the time of the formation of the organization led to a massive, massive effect on the movement as a whole.[38]

Somewhat inevitably, all of these tensions led to the hiatus of Helem. In its place emerged a number of LGBTQ NGOs, including the Arab Foundation for Freedoms and Equality, MOSAIC, Proud Lebanon, MARSA and the Organization for Sexual Education (OSE), many of which are led by former Helem activists. The abundance of foreign donors supporting LGBTQ groups in Lebanon has encouraged a proliferation of professionalized civil society organizations each providing niche services for the LGBTQ community. At present, a number of LGBTQ NGOs in Lebanon have forged a network in which activists meet once a month to ensure that they do not duplicate applications for funding. The net effect of the increase of LGBTQ project funders has expedited a situation in which LGBTQ groups are primarily directed towards working on projects that have clearly defined goals and primarily include service provision. For example, Simon, a former Helem activist who left the organization to set up an NGO, explained that 'we have an emphasis in service provision and capacity building … we are working on issues to do with torture, child protections, human rights, HIV testing, mental health'.[39] Fadi, who led another NGO, stated that 'we are trying to empower LGBTQ people from local regions, tackling LGBTQ health or tackling advocacy'.[40] Other NGOs, for example, work on helping Syrian LGBTQ refugees, providing help with sexual health and education. There are many other activists who refuse to go down the road of NGOization and prefer to remain independent, radical activists who form part of intersectional and anti-sectarian politics in Lebanon.

Helem re-emerged in 2016. Hakim explained that the movement underwent 'splintering into 5 or 6 organizations that now do different things and concentrate on different populations', such as refugees, health, HIV, gender, transpersons, education and training. This meant that 'part of Helem's restructuring was to figure out where it fits into this new topography'.[41] Helem has six full-time staff and about three hundred active members who help run its many programs, from movie nights to sexual health workshops and classes on knowing your rights in case of arrest. Helem's return is marked by the groups' outward commitment to addressing some of the issues that created so much friction among activists. Helem now forefronts gender equality in its mission. Habib, the manager of the community centre, reflects on this: 'When Helem restarted there were no women. Gay men and transwomen were here but lesbian women were not really here, so we need to do something about this. I do not accept to be a manager of a place where there is a lack of equilibrium.'[42]

These efforts to build unity while recognizing diversity are, of course, not easy. Activist groups are always riven by internal tensions, fragmentary processes which can at times disrupt organizing and collective action. Such divisions can weaken the capacity of the movement to effect change, transformation and to realize key objectives.

In Chapter 4, we turn to analyse the strategies and tactics used by the LGBTQ movement aimed at achieving rights and change in postwar Lebanon. Given the limited institutional openings for activists to pursue LGBTQ rights, the chapter argues that it is necessary to broaden our understanding of social movement impacts in Lebanon from the viewpoint of policy domain to also include the process through which movements can, in certain instances, render sectarian power inoperative and increase their capacity to foment wider attitudinal transformation.

Chapter 4

'WHAT KIND OF RELATIONSHIP CAN BE CONSIDERED CONTRARY TO NATURE?': CONTESTING CRIMINALIZATION

On the evening of Friday, 29 February 2008, a police patrol stopped to inspect two young men in a car parked at the side of a coastal road in a town north of Beirut (International Commission of Jurists 2012). The police officers proceeded to arrest the men and the security forces eventually charged the suspects under Article 534 of Lebanon's penal code, which criminalizes 'sex against the order of nature'. If found guilty, suspects are liable to imprisonment for a maximum of one year and a fine of up to $663. Under Lebanon's electoral law, anyone sentenced on the basis of Article 534 has the right to vote taken away, even if they are not imprisoned. In many cases, arrestees lose their jobs when the police inform their employees that they are being prosecuted under 534.

Yet, while the case of the two males reached the law courts, the presiding judge threw it out. Since then, on at least six occasions, various Lebanese judges have rejected prosecutions brought forward under Article 534, and on each occasion increasingly narrowing the legal underpinning of 534. Rather than see these failed prosecutions as the product of judges' individual whims, it is better to understand them as the result of templates formulated and disseminated by LGBTQ rights activists.

These models, in turn, reveal important insights into the strategies deployed by LGBTQ activists in their struggle to secure rights. Activists generate knowledge and practice designed to fashion change in the context of a sectarian system purposely designed to withstand reform in LGBTQ rights. Change, however, does not come in the form of forcing the state to create binding policies, such as agreeing to decriminalize homosexuality; there is little or no opening in the system to permit tangible and enduring statutory and legislative reform. Activists are instead forced to create activism that operates through informal institutions and processes, or which exposes legal ambiguities that can be seized upon to claim rights.

In this chapter we examine the campaign by LGBTQ activists in relation to Article 534. While activists work on many issues, Article 534 represents a structure that exercises much of the movement's focus. The effects of Article 534 permeate into all spheres of life for the LGBTQ population. It permits the use of interrogation and torture by the security forces against suspects; it sanctions the use of pejorative terms to describe LGBTQ people; and it creates an environment in which many LGBTQ people feel and are excluded from society. For these reasons, activism against 534 encompasses a wide spectrum of forms, ranging from legal procedures to promoting modes of visibility of LGBTQ populations, and generating new discourses to frame LGBTQ experience. LGBTQ activism in relation to Article 534 also importantly requires activists to often work behind the scenes, informally with key stakeholders and decision makers to secure some degree of protection for vulnerable LGBTQ people.

'Sex against the order of nature'

Challenging Article 534 provided a major stimulus for the emergence of LGBTQ rights activism in Lebanon. For these activists, it was clear that the criminalization of LGBTQ people needed to be confronted in order to gain basic rights that could be built upon. Article 534, at its most basic, strips LGBTQ individuals of the right to access any protections afforded to the citizenry by the state. For this reason, LGBTQ people experience the malevolent properties of Article 534 in a highly personal way.

Let us begin by considering the process through which suspects are arrested and detained according to 534. The various arms of the security force are not required to catch suspects *en flagrante delicto* in order to carry out an arrest. All that is needed is some form of suspicion that an individual or group of individuals is LGBTQ. This, of course, endows the security forces with a high degree of scope to harass anyone they identify as 'deviant'. In some cases, where the security forces have not been able to accrue sufficient evidence to prosecute individuals suspected of being drug dealers, or even taking drugs, they have instead changed the allegation to one of homosexuality since the threshold for proof is demonstrably lower. This tactic, an activist explained, is 'plus plus – it's drugs and then they discover that they are gay'.[1] On one occasion, an activist recounted, an LGBTQ volunteer went to the police station because his driver's licence was found to be out of date and ended up being detained for four days under 534. Arrests are often justified on the basis of an individual holding what the officers determine to be a non-normative physical appearance and even mannerism. Transwomen, especially where their identity does not correspond to the gender stated on their personal registry card, are particularly vulnerable to arrest (Human Rights Watch 2019). Another common way for arrests to be made occurs when the police respond to tip offs and allegations from various sources. Activists have noted at least two instances when parents reported their sons to the police.

One of the problematic issues is that it is not necessarily a single article that is applied to LGBTQ people. An array of articles related to debauchery, morality, prostitution, distributing pornographic material and even 'masquerading' are deployed against LGBTQ individuals.[2] Given the various articles that can be used by different arms of the security forces – often working independently of each other – to harass the LGBTQ population, it is difficult for activist and human rights organizations to keep consistent data on arrest figures. This situation is compounded by the fact that the security forces are not required to invoke any specific article when detaining suspects. Maya, a human rights worker and activist engaged in monitoring abuses of LGBTQ people, explained that on many occasions people who have been arrested or detained do not know what they are being charged for since 'a lot of the time it's not in writing'. She continued:

> It's often something about sodomy, something about morality, so it's not specifically under a certain law. But [for the security forces] it's 'if we see this act, we have this suspicion that this is immoral and now we are going to charge you with whatever is in front of us'. A lot of the time it is unfounded; it doesn't have any legal basis at all.[3]

Suspects arrested under 534 or any associated article are typically detained at a police station (though in many cases they may be transported to prisons in different parts of the state). Here they can expect to endure interrogation and torture supposedly designed to extract evidence and a confession. The process often begins with the interrogators combing through the suspects' mobile phones in order to find any sign of what they constitute to be proof. Proof is a rather nebulous property for interrogators and prosecutors and can be anything from images found on the phone to Grindr – the gay dating app – being seen or even chat histories. Of particular interest to the interrogators is the suspect's contact list. The police will use the list as a basis to question and arrest a fresh batch of suspects. At this point, many suspects confess because the police lie by telling them that all they need to do in order to secure a release is they confess their crime. A young activist called Wassim told us that one of the first things he learnt from older activists is when the ISF arrest you, 'throw away your phone, anywhere, but get rid of it'.[4] Many activist groups provide information for LGBTQ people, including foldaway pamphlets, explaining what action they should take in the event of being arrested. Nevertheless, since the Lebanese Code of Criminal Procedure does not guarantee that suspects will have access to lawyers during the investigation stage of proceedings, this gives police a broad mandate in collecting 'evidence' (Helem 2017a).

Regardless of whether or not they confess, suspects will often be exposed to a wide range of torture methods. Some of the torture may be loosely described as psychological or what one activist termed 'moral torture' – for instance, the police incorrectly telling suspects that they have tested HIV positive. Mostly, the torture methods involve physical violence, including sexual violence. So common are the methods used by the torturers that they have gained their own labels to distinguish them. The act of tying the suspects upside down and striking the soles of their feet with batons and whips is called 'al-farrouj' ('the chicken'), whereas forcing the suspect to walk on their hands and knees while being kicked or struck is known as 'al-watwat' ('the bat'). Suspects have also reported being flogged with an electrical cable (called the 'Sudan'), being handcuffed in bathrooms for long periods, stripped naked and having cold water poured on them (Chamas 2015). It is typical for the police to confiscate or deny suspects access to food and water as well as their medication.

Hakim, a Helem activist, has been at the forefront of tracking cases of detention and torture in Lebanon. He explained how the process often worked:

> It's about the ISF security officer suspecting that someone is gay and then arresting them based on that suspicion, and then going illegally through their phone and their personal belongings to find any sort of damaging evidence. When they do, they of course arrest everyone else they can find using these mechanisms and then what you have is the systematic use of torture and adaptive torture whereby they learn what works and doesn't work.[5]

It should be noted here that in many instances cases never get to court. This is not so much a result of a lack of evidence handed to the prosecutors, but because the arresting officers blackmail suspects. It is known that off-duty ISF officers purposely entice gay men in order to blackmail them. A young activist explained that a man initiated contact with him through a gay dating site. The man turned out to be an off-duty ISF officer who threatened to expose the activist unless he paid a bribe. The activist refused to do so since he had already come out to his family and friends.[6] In desperation, however, many arrestees pay bribes rather than suffer the humiliation, ostracism and imprisonment associated with public prosecution and shame. Some relatively privileged suspects can rely on *wasta* – the system of personal and familial connections – that allows well-connected people to use their influence to get a case dropped (see Chapter 3). In many cases, suspects simply remain in pretrial detention for extended periods of time, way beyond what is legally permitted, where their cases are not monitored since they are often denied the right to make a phone call.

In sum, the pernicious effects of 534 ensure that the LGBTQ population is not only divested of its rights, but it also creates a situation in which many of them live in daily fear of harassment, persecution and humiliation. Thus, in order to secure rights for Lebanese LGBTQ individuals, activists recognized that they would need to craft a broad-based campaign to contest 534.

'You can't run for elections to get to parliament'

The most direct way that activists could achieve de jure decriminalization is by securing legislative change wrought through Lebanon's parliamentary system. This process entails activists submitting a bill to repeal 534, which would then need to work its way slowly through the various levels of parliament and government. Such a bill would first have to go to the speaker of the house, who, if they do not use their prerogative to block it, would then send it to the parliamentary committee. Once approved at this stage, it then goes to two committees (administration and justice and human rights committees), who both need to agree to the bill before it goes to the parliament to vote on, where it would need a two-thirds majority to become legislation.[7]

Even if activists were to draft and submit a bill for decriminalization, its likelihood of success is negligible. Various forces interact to guarantee that such a bill would inevitably fail. At a very broad level, the legislative system is set up in a way to block any type of reform or thwart new policies from being passed that are not from sectarian parties and vested sectarian interests. New laws have either stalled in the parliament or calls for reform fail to gain traction. Indeed, as one scholar (Kingston 2013: 1) notes of the efforts of non-sectarian movements, at best they have forged 'preliminary institutional reforms and policy successes', mostly 'within the lower levels or trenches of the bureaucracy'. These changes have been 'difficult to sustain and have failed to translate into fundamental changes in institutional practice let alone shifts in the dominant patterns of state-society relations in postwar Lebanon' (Kingston 2013: 1). The weak state, marked by the evisceration of public services and dysfunctional power-sharing institutions, means that it is practically a futile exercise for non-sectarian groups to try and access formal institutions to leverage policy and legislative reform. In fact, when it comes to issues associated with gender and sexuality, legislative reform tends towards increasing conservatism.[8]

More specifically for LGBTQ rights, the system is even more tightly closed. At present, only one relatively small sectarian party – the Kataeb – has declared its public support for decriminalization. The party lost two of its five seats. In the same election, all sixty-six candidates who formed part of the non-sectarian *Kallouna Watani* ('We are National') movement endorsed the decriminalization of homosexuality. None, however, were elected (Rowell 2018). Nearly all of the major sectarian parties are outwardly homophobic and their political representatives will not publicly court LGBTQ issues or activists, save to denounce them. The intractability of the parliamentary system is starkly illuminated by the fact that in order for a draft bill for decriminalization to get off the ground, it needs the support of the speaker of the house, Nabih Berri, who in 2019 led the Lebanese delegation and reportedly played an active role in rallying support for the opposition to vote against a resolution seeking to preserve the rights of the LGBTQ community at the 139th assembly of the International Parliamentary Union (IPU) within the UN (Ministry of Information 2020).

Given the nature of the system, many LGBTQ activists, therefore, do not see the point of trying to engage with the legislative process. Zain, a former Helem activist, explained that 'the formal process is not open; it is closed to LGBTs':

> Even if you want to go inside the institutions, you can't because there is no formal democratic process that is clear for anyone willing to defend rights based on this process. You can't run for elections to get to parliament or link up with one of the militias or one of the tycoons.[9]

Hakim provided a blunter prognostication for the struggle to remove Article 534 from the legislature:

I can't imagine in my lifetime the Lebanese parliament sitting and discussing whether they should keep, remove or augment 534. I don't imagine a single Lebanese parliamentarian pushing that amendment through anytime soon. It is nearly impossible to find a Lebanese leader, decision maker, influencer, who cares in the slightest about their political future to adopt this cause, or to come out in favour or in support for it.[10]

Despite these obvious structural institutional barriers, LGBTQ activists have not completely abandoned making headway into the system. A lot of the time the engagement is unofficial and not in public view. For example, some activists have invited and received some political representatives and senior advisors to their centres and have even discussed LGBTQ rights reform with them. One activist, Fadi, has appealed for support from some political parties for decriminalization. He explained that he has been working with representatives of political groups informally. He had even, in conjunction with a sympathetic political advisor, 'drafted a law for decriminalizing homosexuality. We drafted the law, we shared the draft and we are now looking for comments from the political parties'.[11]

A key issue here, however, is how to frame any prospective draft law for decriminalization so that it may build some momentum. Mariam, an advisor for a leader of one of the traditional sectarian parties, had been approached by Fadi as someone who was known to be sympathetic to human rights. Mariam explained that any prospective draft law would have to steer away from discussions about religion, such as how homosexuality is not incompatible with religion. Mariam continued:

You have to talk about it from a human rights perspective, from the perspective of the UN's declaration of non-discrimination. You don't talk about rights; you talk about non-discrimination. This would be acceptable to many MPs, and they may sympathize with your cause even if they don't go all the way with it, but it would at least neutralize some of them when they come and tell you, 'Oh you want marriage rights, you want to adopt kids?' You are not going to ask them for rights, you are asking for non-discrimination, you are asking for people not to be put in jail based on their sexual and gender identity and in the constitution itself it says that discrimination is prohibited, so this is law. If you are going into a religious discussion, whether religion allows it or not [homosexuality], you are going to lose on that basis.[12]

At present, however, few activists believe that decriminalization is a realistic objective. There is instead a fear that pursuing such a route would more likely cause a backlash, which would reverse any momentum that the LGBTQ rights movement has built up. On this point, Maya explained that few activists were committed – as the situation stands – to advance claims for decriminalization:

Now the consensus among the coalition on LGBT rights in Lebanon is that the primary focus is on protection and awareness and it's not necessarily changing legislation, just because it can backfire. Until we can actually guarantee the support of different political blocs in an effective way where they can champion these causes, then we can start talking about challenging legislation from within the parliament. But for now of course legislation is very important and it's on everyone's radar all of the time but to go this route at this moment may lead to a backlash specifically as the crackdown is only increasing, the more visible LGBT rights become to the fore in the political discourse the more backlash they are receiving, so it is not necessarily the most supportive environment right now for legislative change.[13]

Destituent resistance and shatara

The closure of the formal political institutional system to demands for LGBTQ rights compel activists to find other routes to effecting change. This involves activists working to expose loopholes in the law, ambiguities and contradictions to render, in some instances, homophobic and sectarian power and practices inoperative. But because these gains rarely, if ever, translate into formal policies, it means that any progress is revocable and subject to violent backlash and reversal by the various arms of the sectarian state.

This form of political activism comes close to what the Italian philosopher Giorgio Agamben (1998, 2014) calls 'destituent' power or resistance. 'Destituent' resistance does not necessarily aim to replace existing structures of governance or even laws; it is instead 'a force that, in its very constitution, deactivates the governmental machine' (Agamben 2014: 65). Destituent resistance is the type of activities that make governmental apparatuses inoperative by evading, nullifying and rendering powerless the practices and techniques mobilized by authority. Destituent resistance opens up new ways of turning techniques of government so that they are unable to efficiently execute what they originally aimed to do. Through the deployment of destituent power, social movements not only ensure that dysfunctionality is caused to the system's ways of governing but they also aim to be in some way ungovernable. Destituent acts of resistance are not obviously intended to oppose the institution. Rather than 'lead a frontal attack against it; the gesture neutralises it, empties it of its substance, it takes a step aside and watches the institution expire' (Invisible Committee 2017: 48).

Destituent resistance resembles somewhat the act of 'shatara'. For the anthropologist Ghassan Hage (2018: 91), shatara is a 'quintessential Lebanese ethos'. At its most basic definition, it describes a certain level of cunning and craftiness to get what one wants. Shatara refers to creatively beating the system when it is set up to defeat you. It means taking advantage of the weaknesses of the formal institutions by dexterously working through and manipulating the informal ones, such as finding loopholes and gaps in them. Shatara is to be skilful at manoeuvring oneself inside and outside existing structures and regulations by making the system work for you or at least against itself. Shatara overlaps with Agamben's notion of destituent resistance in the sense that activists use astute tactics to manipulate, evade and nullify the homophobic system. The system may still stand, but it is at least – momentarily perhaps – made inoperable and even weakened.

Hakim captured some of these dynamics when recounting a conversation with 'Western donors'. The donors, the activist described, were 'pushing policy, policy and engagement, let's get it out, let's talk', since this is how the LGBTQ movement had supposedly developed and achieved its rights, including decriminalization, in the Global North. Such activism was purposely designed to secure the support of key legislators, which eventually translated into policy change at the level of the state government. Hakim responded to the donor by explaining that Lebanon 'is not a country based on administration and laws; it's based on connections and craftiness and families and nepotism'. To create change for the LGBTQ population, Hakim explained, it is necessary for the movement to reflect upon the nature of the system in Lebanon:

> If we're going to make things better for LGBT people we have two choices: either we start to create a society similar to the West so that we can follow the trajectory of Western LGBT activists in making things better, or we can actually sit and observe the way things are done here and ask ourselves, 'Can something be done within this sort of reality that is here?' If the system here, and the way it works, the relationships and the mechanisms that make it operate are really inefficient, there may be a way whereby we can make things better in the short term, because you have a responsibility to save people who are being killed and hurt.[14]

Hakim continued to outline in more detail what activism may look like in the context of Lebanon. Here he noted how the system can be manipulated because it relies on personal rather than impersonal power. While impersonal power may be understood to be characteristic of strong state institutions, which, in its ideal type, refers to invisible, rule-bound bureaucracies that adhere to blind neutrality and sameness in treatment for all citizens, personal power refers to state institutions in which individuals and relationships between people are important. Thus, while Lebanon is renowned for its bureaucracy and red tape in regards to the state, these systems are easily overcome if one has the right connections. This situation is particularly true when considering how many individuals access key social services – especially health and education – through their personal contacts with sectarian leaders. While it is not possible for LGBTQ activists to build links with sectarian elites to work for rights, the idea of cultivating personal relationships with key figures in institutions is important. Hakim drew from his own personal experience:

> We are working around the clock in order to make things better, particularly with the judiciary and the Internal Security Forces, so we create some sort of an understanding, not necessarily a law, but a procedure, an understanding, a relationship. In a way, things work this way here sometimes, They don't all have to be codified in a very systematic way. Sometimes it means reaching out

and having a conversation with the head of a certain bureau somewhere who can make things a lot easier; they may not necessarily be official, they may not necessarily be legal, but you have done a huge service to people.[15]

Activists often remarked upon this process of manoeuvring and outsmarting the Lebanese system. For example, Fadi, an activist from another LGBTQ group, justified the work of his organization by explaining how 'we are making an impact on the society in a very diplomatic way, because of all of the sectarian divisions, you cannot just try to shock the system with politics. You need to find your way within the system'.[16]

Perhaps a good example of how activists may deploy destituent resistance and shatara is by gaining an official state permit that recognizes their existence as a civil society NGO. As noted in Chapter 3, LGBTQ groups in Lebanon, such as Helem, have failed in their application to be registered by the Ministry of the Interior, which means they cannot set up a bank account to receive funding. Fadi noted with some relish how they manipulated the bureaucratic system to receive a permit:

> We play with the words in the application because we know if you mention 'LGBT' you will not get a permit. We didn't mention LGBT. We can open up a bank account and everybody knows about us, everyone knows that we are LGBT. We get into the system the Lebanese way. We turn it around. On our permit it says we are a non-profit civil society group trying to spread democracy and infrastructure, socially and economically, and to empower society. So we have the right to do workshops, training, we can do small projects to help vulnerable populations, for women, to work for citizenship and democracy.[17]

Destituent resistance can be exercised in other ways. The dysfunctionality of the state, characterized by fragile institutions and a power-sharing system either on the point of breakdown or in abeyance, provides opportunities for the LGBTQ movement. Zain noted that the state 'leaves all the gaps':

> Sometimes there are complete gaps where the state does not have the capacity to be in because it does not function like this, and this is what allows Helem to operate. It allows you to have a gay film festival on films banned in Lebanon and the state saying no to it later and not being able to do anything about it.[18]

In Ghassan Hage's (2018) work on how ordinary citizens cope with failing public institutions in Lebanon, he argues that the partial absence of the state – or at least any serious centralized planning – fosters more than just a lack. It also offers an opportunity to imagine alternative ways of being and conducting politics. This space is not simply to be understood as positive or progressive – one in which the sectarian state is transformed through its disappearance. For Hage (2018: 94), such spaces that exist 'outside-the-law' permit, in some circumstances, what he calls a 'negotiated being': a mode of sociality, a skill and an affirmation of a desire to coexist with others differently. In this sense, LGBTQ activism, in the context of fragile institutions, is not always about being recognized by the state, but about being left unmolested by the authorities. It is an affirmation of difference that does not necessarily seek acceptance from the sectarian state. Of course, this also suggests a degree of passivity by activists in relation to challenging homophobic power and norms that radiate outwards from the state. More directly challenging to homophobic institutions is an activism that seeks to deactivate and make inoperable the power of 534.

'The republic of shame'

On 8 May 2012 an episode of the popular investigative TV show 'Anta Hurr' ('You Are Free') aired on Murr TV (MTV), a mainstream broadcaster. The episode featured an undercover report from an adult all-male movie theatre in Tripoli, Lebanon's second largest city. The report used images from a secret camera, which appeared to show men engaging in sex acts. In other shots, the faces of the customers could be clearly seen and potentially made identifiable to viewers. The reporter filming the videos also tried to entrap some of cinemagoers by inviting them into the bathroom for sex. In his report, the show's presenter – Joe Maalouf – labelled the cinemagoers 'shazoz', a pejorative epithet roughly translating into 'perverts'/'faggots', which is commonly used to describe LGBTQ people (see Chapter 5). Maalouf concluded his tirade by calling on the police and the local sectarian leaders to shut down 'such places', which he alleged afforded a 'safe haven' for prostitution and for men to lure and drug innocent teenagers (Awadalla 2012; Mandour 2013; Allouche 2017).

While the report represented the culmination of a concerted campaign waged by the show against the LGBTQ population, the cinema in Tripoli closed without notice a day after the episode aired. Then on 28 July, the vice squad of the ISF raided a movie theatre after another undercover report by Maalouf on cinemas showing 'gay porn'. The theatre – known as the Cinema Plaza – was located in Bourj Hammoud, a predominantly working-class neighbourhood of Beirut. Here, the ISF arrested thirty-six men, who were transferred across town to Hobeish police station to be subjected to anal examinations by forensic doctors under the orders of the police prosecutors (LebMASH 2014a).

Anal examinations are reportedly used in at least eight countries in which consensual same-sex conduct is criminalized. These tests can be used against men often arrested on unrelated charges but then suspected of being gay. Anal examinations typically involve medical professionals working on behalf of the police to find 'proof' of homosexuality. In Lebanon, forensic doctors have performed the examination by inserting an egg-shaped metal object into the anus of the accused, with the purpose of determining whether the tone of the anal sphincter or the shape of the anus demonstrates the individual has engaged in anal sex (Human Rights Watch 2012).

The use of anal examinations to establish homosexuality relies on junk science and the medical community has long since rejected them as useless. In a BBC report, the head of the Lebanese Association for Forensic Science, who had been conducting examinations since the 1990s, admitted that the 'tests prove absolutely nothing. Their scientific value is nil' (BBC 2012). These uncontrolled examinations – typically conducted at police stations rather than in hospitals – are instead more likely to place the victims at risk for infections such as Human Papilloma Virus (HPV) and Hepatitis. Rather than deriving from any medical logic, the tests should be categorized as forms of torture, a method designed to extract pain, humiliation and a confession from those subjected to it. For this reason, the examinations violate the Convention against Torture and the International Covenant on Civil and Political Rights, while Human Rights Watch classifies them as a form of sexual assault. The UN Committee against Torture declared that the examinations 'have no medical justification and cannot be consented to fully' (UNHCR 2016).

The arrests and anal examinations of the men in the Cinema Plaza stimulated a powerful response from activists. While this activism did not lead to the termination of 534, it did result in key aspects of it being rendered unworkable. The campaign illuminated the multilayered tactics activists could harness to effect positive change.

To begin with, activists demonstrated that the media could be used to orchestrate public opinion in favour of basic rights for LGBTQ people. Just three days after the arrests of the thirty-six Cinema Plaza men, a report was shown as an introduction to the main news on LBCI, a rival broadcaster to MTV. In a powerful intersectional analysis, the report made a connection between the anal examinations of the men and an oppressive and incompetent sectarian state that failed to provide major services and rights for its citizenry:

> We are living under the 'republic of shame' since its apparatuses do not waver over subjecting detainees to virginity and homosexuality tests. … In that same republic of shame, officials threaten to inflict collective punishment on the Lebanese people by depriving them of electricity. (see Mandour 2013)

The report concluded with an interview with a leading Helem activist, the first occasion an LGBTQ activist featured on the TV news. The report went viral on social media and also garnered favourable comment from sections of the print media. In response, MTV, the station responsible for the campaign against the cinemas, proudly announced that it had been always known for supporting sexual freedoms and 'marginalized' homosexuals.

The positive report on LGBTQ rights by LBCI was the product of activists establishing key relationships with broadcasters and media executives sympathetic to human rights causes. In this particular case, the head of the news department at the LBCI TV station was known to be a vehement supporter of rights- and class-based struggles. His brother, furthermore, is a lawyer-activist who is the co-founder and executive director of The Legal Agenda, an organization renowned for its legal work in defence of LGBTQ people. Hakim, who had been deeply involved in building relationships with the media, remembered:

We noticed that when there was a very high-profile case when they closed down a cinema with gay people and thirty-six people were arrested and tortured. So on one show on one of the channels, MTV, the host [Joe Maalouf] was responsible for that arrest because he publicly called out for the Lebanese to go out and arrest them. On the other channel, where the news section is run by a very socially conscious person, they decided to say for the first time, 'This is an outrage, where are the rights of gay people in Lebanon?' He actually said that on the 8 o'clock news that everyone watches, and the subsequent day, of course, MTV said, 'No, we are with gay people.'[19]

LBCI's report also validated the importance of activists building a network of sympathetic stakeholders in key institutions that can use their influence to expedite some degree of progress for LGBTQ rights. This network building largely involves, as noted earlier, the cultivation of informal personal relationships rather than with bureaucratic and formal institutions.

We can further see evidence of this form of activism in terms of lobbying stakeholders involved in anal examinations. In particular, LGBTQ activists began to work with and even have health professionals as activists within the movement. These health professionals used their influence to pressure the Lebanese Order of Physicians to call on their members to end the practice of anal examinations. A statement by the head of the Lebanese Order of Physicians on 8 August 2012 requested that the examinations be terminated since they were medically and scientifically invalid in establishing homosexuality and that they constitute a form of torture. The statement further added that the examinations violated Article 30 of the Lebanese law on medical ethics, which prohibits doctors from engaging in harmful practices. Further success appeared to have been won when justice minister wrote to the prosecutor general, urging him 'to halt random rectal examination procedures, after the issue was raised by human rights organizations' (Human Rights Watch 2012). The prosecutor general subsequently issued a memorandum on the examinations.

Yet, these directives on anal examinations also revealed the contingent and ambiguous position of LGBTQ rights. Activists discovered a copy of the memorandum sent by the prosecutor general, which, far from banning the anal examinations, stated that anal examinations could continue 'with the consent of the accused, according to standard medical procedures, and in a manner that does not cause significant harm' (Human Rights Watch 2012). The directive added that if the accused refused to consent to the examination, he should be informed that his refusal 'constitutes proof of the crime'. Rather than signal a complete ban on anal examinations, LebMASH, an NGO that deals with the sexual and reproductive health of the LGBTQ population, discovered in 2014 that at least one forensic physician in Lebanon had conducted anal tests on several individuals to determine their sexual orientation (LebMASH 2014a). In fact, the memorandum was more notable for being infused with gaps and omissions given that it made no reference to the practice of vaginal examinations used against women.

Thus, any change that activists have made in regards to anal examinations is provisional and has the potential for reversal. Hakim, who has been a central figure in gaining this 'concession', realizes that such gains are contingent:

> The only tangible policy change that we were able to create, which is temporary because it's non-binding, so it might change at any point, is getting the Beirut Syndicate of Doctors to ban rectal exams and to get the Ministry of Justice to issue a memo, not a ruling, to the prosecuting general and heads of police bureaus and police stations saying that you are not allowed to do this test anymore. But, nuance, they said that you are not allowed to do this examination; they didn't say that you are not allowed to arrest people arbitrarily, they didn't say that you can't detain someone because you think they are gay, they didn't say that you are allowed to break the law and look into people's phones. They mentioned that you shouldn't do a rectal examination because that doesn't prove a person's sexuality, but they didn't mention that they do vaginal examinations to prove virginity which were also part of the problem. But still the fact that it wasn't even mentioned goes to show that there is a great deal of resistance in order to condemn these actions and a great deal of work needs to be done to even get the most obvious of concessions from the system, changes or amendments.[20]

'If a tree is giving unusual fruits'

While lacking permanency and riddled with incompleteness, the success gained in relation to anal examination sheds light on the model of activism used to confront 534. This model of activism does not obviously claim to be about decriminalization; it instead focuses more on making certain structural features of 534 inoperative. The template additionally focuses on the importance of establishing and fostering relationships with powerful individuals and decision makers within key organizations who can use their authority to generate some form of positive change for LGBTQ rights.

The power of this template can be witnessed in terms of activism devised to challenge the notion of 'nature' that sustains 534. Let us consider first the way in which homosexuality in Lebanon, as it is in many other countries, is historically understood to be a disease or mental disorder and thus an abomination of nature which needs to be cured. This diagnosis of homosexuality as deriving from some form of psychological and psychiatric aetiology has led to the practice in Lebanon of 'Sexual Orientation Change' performed by a number of psychologists and psychiatrists, particularly the use of 'conversion' or 'reparative therapy' intended to 'cure' gay people. Indeed, a 2009 survey of the Lebanese medical profession showed that the vast majority classified homosexuality as a disease that requires either medical or psychological treatment (El Feki 2014: 256). The idea that homosexuality is a medical abnormality thus legitimates the rubric of 534's depiction of homosexuality as unnatural. In some cases, individuals sentenced under 534 have been forced to undergo conversion treatment as an alternative to imprisonment.

LGBTQ activists mobilized to make inoperable this medical claim of nature. The activists achieved this objective through their work with influential Lebanese psychologists and psychiatrists. A case in point is the Lebanese Psychiatric Society (LPS) and the Lebanese Psychology Association (LPA) coming together in 2013 to declare that 'homosexuality is not a mental disorder and does not need to be treated' (Sandels 2013). In its official statement, the LPS declared that it had been inspired to act in response to reports 'about arrests and abuse of homosexuals in Lebanon' (Sandels 2013). Both the LPS and LPA called on its members to stop engaging in harmful 'gay conversion' therapies designed to 'cure' LGBTQ people (LebMASH 2016). The LPS, which is part of the Lebanese Order of Physicians, a professional syndicate with legal powers, has also stated that it refers any of its members who use 'reparative therapy' to the ethics committee for punishment.

The fingerprints of LGBTQ activism in this process are clearly evident. Joey, a Helem activist, explained that one of the major successes of the movement is 'the psychologists and the psychiatrists denying that homosexuality is a disease, it cannot be cured'.[21] Indeed, Helem organized a joint press conference between the LPS and LPA to announce their position in 2013. In November 2015, the LPS extended its support for the LGBTQ population by 'demand[ing] that the article 534 of the Lebanese penal code that prosecutes homosexual activities be abolished' (LebMASH 2016).

For activists the significance of the statements by the LPS and the LPA can be understood as extending to weaken the logic undergirding 534. If the legality of 534 rests on the premise that homosexuality is unnatural, the declaration by medical professionals that it is not a medical disorder negates the legitimacy of criminalization. Why then, asked an activist, are the security forces 'charging a person, if he's not doing anything wrong or unnatural, so what is the point of 534?' (LebMASH 2014b).

The law courts represent a major arena of LGBTQ activism against 534. This legal activism is not directly intended to achieve decriminalization; the aim is to make 534 inoperative by ensuring that prosecutions under 534 cannot be successful. As noted at the beginning of the chapter, on at least six occasions since 2009, judges have decided to throw out cases brought forward by the state under 534.

These rulings are largely the result of LGBTQ activism. Activists have used their connections within Lebanon's legal profession to form working relationships with lawyers and judges, specifically in connection to dealing with cases prosecuted under the remit of 534. Helem, for example, has its own legal activist team, who have developed models for legal professionals to use to protect the rights of LGBTQ activists arrested, tortured and prosecuted by the security forces. Some LGBTQ NGOs also provide information cards and foldout leaflets that outline in detail rights that LGBTQ people can demand in the event of them being detained. LGBTQ activists also collaborate with key allies to create and apply activist models, such as The Legal Agenda – a Beirut-based NGO that works on protecting the interests of marginalized groups. These models are disseminated and refined via various fora.

Workshops that bring together LGBTQ activists and legal professionals represent an important sphere for rights activism. LGBTQ activists explain that these workshops are aimed at cultivating relationships with judges who are not necessarily sympathetic to LGBTQ rights. Fadi, an activist, who had organized a workshop between judges who were either in favour or against LGBTQ rights, mentioned how it illuminated a range of perspectives:

> We had a fight between the judges. Some said if there is a law for LGBTs then there is a crime and some said if there isn't a law then there isn't a crime. All of the judges were saying we will not implement it [534] if it is not done in private but if it is in public. We are not necessarily changing all of their minds but we are contributing to change in a different way.[22]

Another activist, Yasin, recounted a conversation she had with a female judge on the issue of LGBTQ rights, which indicated some degree of basic support for decriminalization:

> I was talking to a judge and she said, 'I don't mind homosexuals being homosexuals but I just would never support them having families in Lebanon and having children.' But this to me was very interesting: a judge aged fifty-five in a sectarian system and she is saying to me, 'Look I don't mind people being the way they want to be, I just don't want them to have children because I do not want to change our culture.' It's ok. This is enough for me. Now if she has a case of two gay men she is not going to put them in jail because she believes they have a right to have sex and just to let them be.[23]

These workshops provide a forum for activists and legal professionals to discuss and eventually formulate strategies that endow judges with the power to reject prosecutions advanced on the basis of Article 534. It is worth reviewing a few of the cases in which judges have thrown out cases. Through so doing we can see the incremental development of the judgements used, which have the effect of increasingly winnowing the legal opportunities for prosecutors to successfully win cases brought forward according to 534.

Judges have commonly used two particular reasons to reject 534 prosecutions: lack of evidence and the legal basis of 'nature'. In regards to evidence, judges have simply been able to dismiss cases since the prosecution's case typically provides little or circumstantial evidence, often collected through torture. In one case in 2009, against two young males mentioned at the beginning of the chapter, the presiding judge quickly issued a decision 'to stop all investigations against the two defendants in application of Article 534 due to the absence of any felony' since the prosecution's case failed to demonstrate that sexual activity had occurred (International Commission of Jurists 2012).

Let us turn in depth to the legal basis of 'nature' which underpins 534. This has been systematically questioned and rejected by a number of judges. In the 2009 case noted above, for the first time on record a judge argued that the concept of nature sustaining Article 534 has no legal grounding. The presiding judge explained to the court that the 'law did not define the specific meaning of nature or had adopted an accepted criterion confirming to what extent the reason is contradicting nature and its laws' (International Commission of Jurists 2012). The judge then proceeded to challenge the idea that nature is fixed and unchanging, existing somehow external to social forces: 'The violation of nature is linked with the thinking and mood of a society and its traditions and its capacity to accept the new norms of nature that are not yet usual.' Deploying flowery language coloured almost with poetic imagery, the judge mused at length on the concept of nature:

> Man [sic] is part of nature and one its elements and one its cells and no one can say that any of his acts or behaviour is contradicting nature even if the act is criminal or offending simply because these are the rules of nature. If the sky is raining during summer time or if we have a hot weather during winter or if a tree is giving unusual fruits – all these can be according to and with harmony to nature and are part of its rules themselves. (International Commission of Jurists 2012)

In a further case, in 2014, the presiding judge also challenged the idea of 'nature' to protect the rights of a transwoman prosecuted under 534. The transwoman was arrested after the police received reports that the defendant was taking part 'in acts of sodomy and group sex'. In her statement, she pointed out that although her personal status registry classified her as male, she was born intersex and had undergone gender reassignment surgery in 1994 after self-identifying as female. The defendant denied that she had engaged in acts of indecency, as she considered the sexual relations that she had with men throughout her life to be classified within the framework of natural relations between men and women, and the duration of those relationships had sometimes exceeded a year and a half (Human Rights Watch 2019).

In rejecting the case put forward by the prosecution, the judge drew on the precedent set by the judge in 2009. The judge agreed that Article 534 does not clearly specify 'unnatural' in a way that is fit for legal purpose. In his final ruling the judge went further by stating that the transwoman had not broken the law since she was not in a same-sex relationship; given that the 'external appearance, disposition, and psychological state of the defendant, all of which overwhelmingly indicate a female character', sexual relationships with a woman 'would be, in the view of the court, an act "more contrary" to nature than his/her engaging in sexual relations with men'. Summing up, the judge announced: 'Gender identity is not only defined by the legal papers, the evolution of the person and his/her perception of his/her gender should be taken into consideration' (Arab Foundation for Freedoms and Equality 2018). The inference was clear: a person's gender should not simply be based on their personal status registry document, but on their self-definition

(Arab Foundation for Freedoms and Equality 2018). The ruling thus opened the way for judges to protect transpeople from prosecution under Article 534.

In a third case, in 2016, the security forces arrested a Syrian national because, according to the police report, he 'had been wearing women's clothing, given his feminine leanings since childhood' and he 'had been having sex with men in Syria' (Karame 2016). In his ruling the judge argued that what constitutes our understanding of human nature is often determined by socio-legal and political factors that are constantly in flux. Definitions of nature, stated the judge, should:

> include multiple meanings, according to which lens is used to interpret it, particularly when it comes to human relationships – which are constantly changing, subject to the development of concepts, customs, and beliefs, and are not necessarily connected to religious or social principles. (Karame 2016)

For this reason, the judge continued, it was not possible to declare that homosexuality is an aberration of nature or a product of psychological illness. To support this, the judge cited a report by the World Health Organization (WHO) stating that 'sexual orientation by itself is not to be considered a disorder'. As such, the judge pointed out, sexual orientation is protected on the basis of general legal principles ratified by Lebanon, including the Universal Declaration of Human Rights, Resolution 17 of the Human Rights Council issued in 2011, and the general leanings and principles enshrined in the UN system (Karame 2016).

While judges have pointed to the dubious characteristics of nature to determine crime, in a more recent case, in 2017, the judge dismissed the case not by referring to the spurious legal utility of 'nature' but more simply by stating that homosexuality was an individual human right. The case involved nine men arrested by the ISF after complaints were made about the men to the local municipal authorities. The judge declared in his statement that 'homosexuals have a right to human and intimate relationships with whoever they want, without any interference or discrimination in terms of their sexual inclinations, as it is the case with other people' (Rights in Exile Programme 2020). To give legal weight to his decision, the judge referred to Article 183 of Lebanon's penal code, which states that 'an act undertaken in exercise of a right without abuse shall not be regarded as an offense'. In other words, personal freedoms are legally protected if they do not infringe on others' liberties.

The judge's verdict represents the most significant thus far in regards to the legal struggle to oppose Article 534 since it provided a precedent that already existed in Lebanese law that guarantees individual freedoms. The ruling gained added importance a year later when the State Prosecution of Appeals refused to reverse the decision. The three-judge bench agreed with the original verdict that consensual sex between adults of the same-sex cannot be considered 'unnatural' as long as it is not 'seen or heard by others, or performed in a public place, or involving a minor who must be protected' (Human Rights Watch 2018b). This meant that for the first time the higher courts had made a ruling in favour of LGBTQ rights. The significance of the precedent set by the Court of Appeal's ruling was illuminated in November 2018 when the Court of Appeal overruled a conviction of three young men – two Lebanese and one Syrian – charged with same-sex relations.

In sum, these court rulings add up to a situation in which it is now difficult for state prosecutors to successfully win cases brought forward on the basis of 534. This now also applies to military as well as civilian courts. In a landmark ruling in March 2019 a military court acquitted four military personnel accused of sodomy charges. In explaining his ruling to a newspaper, the presiding judge noted that 'sodomy is not punishable by law' as the country's penal code did not specify what 'kind of relationship can be considered contrary to nature'.

'Lebanese people are still being arrested'

LGBTQ activists have made headway against 534 – successes have been gained in relation to anal examinations, conversion and reparative therapy and, more notably, in challenging criminal prosecutions. Yet, it needs repeating: none of these successes translate into formal legislative public policies. These changes may better be understood as often wrought through informal agreements and processes, which mean that all gains are essentially provisional, liable for revocation and without claim to legal permanency. At best, this activism finds and exposes weaknesses in the system that closes down by increments its space for homophobic power. This logic can best be seen in the judicial decisions to reject prosecutions of 534 cases. These decisions, over the past decade, have cumulatively narrowed the legal legitimacy and applicability of 534 without, crucially, leading to any imminent prospect of decriminalization appearing in legislation.

The character of the gains forged by activists against 534 is contingent and suspect to reversal. Rather than on the run, the state and its apparatus is willing to creatively adapt its repressive methods to a changing environment. While suspects are rarely imprisoned according to 534, this does not mean that they escape punitive action. Fadi, an activist who has been trying to monitor arrests carried out under 534, noted that 'Lebanese people are still being arrested. They may not be sentenced to prison but they still get it on their legal records'.[24] Indeed, as Zain confirmed, 'instead of 534, they arrest people under public nuisance laws; they still try to police sexuality in other ways'.[25] Maya, who has also been tracking the issue, explained 'that there are very few cases where people are actually given a one-year sentence because of 534 or other charges'. Instead, she continued, 'what happens is the torture, the abuse that goes unaccounted and undocumented'. It is this which is 'the biggest fear and that causes a lot of people from the LGBT community and specifically transwomen not to leave their homes at all once they are stopped at a checkpoint and they have to show their IDs which don't match their gender expression or if they are undocumented refugees or asylum seekers'.[26] There is the additional issue, Maya continues, of pre-detention. For those who are arrested, they 'end up staying in pre-trial detention for extended periods of time, because their cases are not monitored, because they don't have the right to make a phone call so they can't tell anyone that they are detained'. This problem is particularly acute 'for refugees and asylum seekers'. In sum, 'there is no accountability or complete mechanisms that people can access that are reliable and credible'.[27]

In fact, despite judges increasingly rejecting 534 prosecutions, the number of people arrested on the basis of 'sexual deviancy' has grown exponentially in recent years. Using figures from the Trafficking Bureau, a 2017 report by Helem noted seventy-six arrests under Article 534 in 2016 compared with forty-three in 2012 (Helem 2017a). These figures, moreover, are incomplete, as they do not include many parts of Lebanon. In addition, as noted earlier, while 534 may be increasingly inoperable security forces still arrest LGBTQ individuals on a range of charges. In addition, some of the judges issuing rulings in favour of LGBTQ suspects have themselves come under scrutiny and even punishment from the state as a result of their rulings, including being transferred to different districts.

Despite its successes there are distinct limits to an activism that is based on evading or even deactivating 534. Such activism leaves in place the nature of the homophobic system that drives and legitimates harassment and persecution of LGBTQ people. Thus, in order to achieve durable change, it is vital that activists positively alter the values, beliefs, norms and opinions of power-holders in influential institutions and the broader general public towards LGBTQ people and rights. In Chapter 5, we turn to how activists aim to gain public approval and legal recognition for their rights by fostering a transformation of societal attitudes.

Chapter 5

'I EXIST': THE POLITICS OF AMBIGUOUS
VISIBILITY AND PRIDE

In 2005, Lebanese LGBTQ activists joined activists around the world in the first International Day against Homophobia (IDAHO). The theme chosen by activists in Lebanon was 'I Exist', a simple declaration, one wrote, that 'LGBT people exist in Lebanon and we are breaking the wall of silence' (Azzi 2011c). 'I Exist' represents an example of the 'politics of visibility'. The politics of visibility has been central to the global LGBTQ rights movement since the late 1960s. At its most basic level, the politics of visibility rests on the premise that sexuality itself must be visible – a matter of public, not just private, concern – in order for rights to be secured. In the words of the renowned US activist Harvey Milk: 'Come out, stand up and let that world know. … Only that way will we start to achieve our rights.'[1]

Visibility represents the 'fusion of the personal and political' in LGBTQ activism. The personal public declaration of one's marginalized sexual identity acts as a catalyst for attracting others to copy and for positively transforming the attitudes of homophobic society. In terms of activism, visibility is central to the process of inwardly building a movement. Visibility sends a signal to closeted and isolated people that they are not alone and there is a community out there willing to endow them with a sense of pride and support in their sexual orientation. Visibility, as an 'open avowal of one's sexual identity' thus symbolizes 'the shedding of the self-hatred that gay men and women internalized' (D'Emilio 1983: 103). In this way, visible LGBTQ activists act as recruiters, drawing others to them, allowing LGBTQ people to find each other in societies where their identities are invisible, thereby increasing the potential for their mobilization (Ayoub 2016). As Jeffrey Weeks (2015: 47) writes: 'By coming out … it would show other lesbians and gay men that they were not alone, that through coming out all could come together, and construct new narratives about who and what they were.' As a strategy for LGBTQ activism, especially in the United States and Western Europe, the power of public visibility fuelled the organizational capacity of the LGBTQ movement by encouraging 'the active involvement of large numbers of homosexuals and lesbians in their own emancipation effort' (D'Emilio 1983: 238).

While visibility is central to the process of movement building, it is also important in making LGBTQ identities and politics visible in the public arena, which in itself is a challenge to the notion of a uniformly heteronormative social order. Visibility, as such, encourages society to accept and tolerate the reality of sexual diversity. There is also evidence that people are more likely to be tolerant and supportive of LGBTQ rights if they have regular contact with LGBTQ people. Exposure to sexual diversity can lead to a widespread reduction of prejudicial attitudes, what one scholar terms 'affective liberalization' among the public with respect to LGBTQ people. The contact hypothesis – that interpersonal contact between groups can reduce prejudice for minority communities – has become a guiding logic for major campaigns for LGBTQ rights. More mediated forms of contact – such as books, plays, films and television – have also been identified as generating positive attitudinal transformation. Research illuminates how positive television portrayals of gays and lesbians on US TV in the 1990s generated warmer feelings among those who did not directly know a gay or lesbian person. Pointing to public survey polls, Garretson (2018) argues that the mediated exposure to a positive gay television character had durable positive effects on attitudes about gay rights. In sum, 'visibility matters'. When LGBTQ people are seen, 'they are more able to influence public attitudes and public officials and … to advance LGBT rights' (Michelson 2019: e1).

Yet, visibility needs to be understood as context-bound to time and place and not as a universalizing strategy. It goes without saying that visibility is a highly dangerous strategy in places where LGBTQ people are criminalized, and subjected to torture and various forms of state-sanctioned violence and harassment. The act of 'coming out', while liberating for many, risks the individual being ostracized from their family and social networks. In addition, the onus on visibility as an expression of an individual's sexual practice inscribed into a clearly observable and often-gendered identity is ill-fitting in contexts marked by the existence of fluidity in relation to sexual practices. Visibility thus risks effectively eroding rather than protecting sexual diversity. How, then, do Lebanese activists harness, negotiate or abjure visibility?

'Very few people come out'

Paul, a leading activist, noted that at a basic level 'very few people come out to their parents here. There are people who are out to the entire gay community but not their parents and their family'.[2] This situation is mirrored by a shortage of activists willing to be publically visible. Hakim continued on this theme: 'Our problem is also of exposure. I mean there are two or three people in this country that don't mind having their face on camera and being out and gay. I am one of them and there's two others, and that's it. Everyone else will not do anything.'[3]

To a considerable extent this invisibility can be ascribed to the ongoing legacy of 534. Yet, as we explored in Chapter 3, some relatively privileged LGBTQ individuals prefer to remain publically invisible, as they are able to exist in some comfort as gay people in the private sphere of bars and clubs. The state and security forces rarely intrude into the spaces to harass LGBTQ members. Samer, a leading Helem member, expanded on how privilege operates for gay middle-class men:

They don't understand how things work because of their privilege. If someone is a gay man and their economic situation is fine and they have their own house and they can afford to go to bars and for them gay life in Lebanon is the ability to go to gay places and to hang out at night, which is not my perspective. I want to be politically involved and not be ashamed as a gay person. I want to be more involved at the political level. Most people are not politically involved. They say, 'Why do you want to change the law 534? You are putting a limelight on us and we don't want to be highlighted because we are having fun.' Gay men, because they are rich, can pay a lot of money just on health projects, HIV, but they don't pay money for transwomen or for a shelter. They don't care, but when they are in trouble they come to us – this happens a lot.[4]

Ali, a Helem activist, ruefully concluded that perhaps some privileged LGBTQ members needed to be shocked into activism, even if this meant that they experienced some discrimination and harassment. For this reason, activists had even considered using the tactic of 'outing' to force privileged individuals to become more publically involved in the movement:

Maybe things need to be shuffled more, maybe people need to experience discrimination on a much wider scale, but you can't force that. You can't put people in danger to wake them up, because that's not what we do. We have a strict 'no outing' policy; we never share names, faces or contacts with anyone else. But that is unfortunate, because you don't want to reinforce the shame, you want to reinforce the pride, and maybe it is an issue of pride, and maybe a lot of people here are gay, they have accepted it but they are sure as hell not proud of it.[5]

Lebanese activists have been forced to be creative by developing a range of tactics to emphasize the visibility of the movement. These tactics often eschew or do not primarily involve activists becoming visible in public spaces. For instance, since the movement's outset, activists have employed the internet as a major tool to communicate and disseminate information to their audience. Helem's online magazine, called *Barra* – meaning 'out' in Arabic – provided a regular source of information about the movement, covering issues ranging from sexual health to legal advice. *Barra*'s presence provided a tangible signal of the existence of LGBTQ people in Lebanon. Since then, a number of LGBTQ groups in Lebanon maintain an active presence on the web, including their own websites and social media, especially Facebook and Twitter accounts. One notable video by Helem (2017b) released via its various social media accounts, which was called 'Homophobia is Terrorism', attracted more than one hundred thousand views.

In addition, as the first major LGBTQ movement in the MENA region, Lebanese activism attracted the attention of the media both in Lebanon and internationally. Major reports on the Lebanese movement have been published in renowned newspapers and TV channels boasting a global reach, including the *Washington Post*, BBC, and CNN, to name just a few. These reports typically provide positive and even moving portrayals of Lebanese LGBTQ people and activism. One article in the *New York Times*, called 'Coming Out in Lebanon', features the stories of individuals and activists who have 'come out'. The writers claim: 'Openly gay, lesbian and transgender people face persecution across the Arab world. The exception may be in Lebanon, which has slowly grown more tolerant thanks to the work of activists' (Boushnak and Boshnaq 2017). Lebanon's print media, which can boast to be a largely free and liberal sector, has, on the whole, been a powerful ally of the LGBTQ movement, providing favourable content and reports on LGBTQ issues. Even newspapers that are seen to be supportive of particular sectarian factions have on occasion published articles in support of LGBTQ rights.

Television perhaps represents the key battleground in the representation of sexuality. Although Lebanon has a national broadcaster – Tele Liban – the postwar era witnessed the sector fragment into a large number of channels funded by the main sectarian parties. Lebanese televised media, in particular, is identified as 'fanning the fires of sectarianism and political differences' (Salloukh et al. 2015: 136). In this light, television presents a potentially hostile medium for LGBTQ people, which indeed it has often been.

Television coverage of LGBTQ issues has notably changed from when the activist movement emerged in 2004. In 2005, a well-known TV station broadcast a report accusing Helem of promoting perversion among the youth. As we saw in Chapter 4, the 'investigative' reports on the MTV show 'Anta Hurr' ('You Are Free') on cinemas catering to gay men was not only an example of the most insidious type of homophobia but it also led to the arrest and torture of thirty-six men. Yet, change has occurred on the screen in how LGBTQ people and issues are represented. In response to the arrests, a rival station to MTV, LBCI, broadcast an introduction to its main news programme damning the security forces for its use of torture against LGBTQ suspects. MTV also put out a statement declaring that 'MTV has been always known for supporting sexual freedoms and "marginalized" homosexuals' (Mandour 2013). The channel itself quickly changed tack as 'Anta Hurr', in reaction to the critique directed its way, even began to broadcast reports on acts of harassment and violence against LGBTQ people.

For Hakim, the immense power wielded by the media in Lebanon to shape public opinion and political discourse means that it is perhaps the key arena of social movement activism: 'Getting positive coverage is important. I am a firm believer that in this country if you are with a cause, as soon as you get the media on your side, it's a matter of time.'[6]

Driven by this belief, the energy of activists is often exercised by gaining TV coverage, and this is an area that they can claim some positive progress. In 2018, for instance, MTV dedicated extensive airtime to exposing LGBTQ abuses in Lebanon. The concept and development of the episode featured the input of activists. Fadi, an activist involved in producing the show, explained:

> We had a huge programme on MTV. We worked on it with MTV to prepare the whole episode on the issues that LGBT people are facing based on the report we published which deals with detention and torture, and we had cases in which

people were sharing their experiences, we had expert lawyers, talking from different perspectives. The impact was very important. We did this. I was there on everything. On every meeting they were having, I was making sure that all of the messages are LGBT friendly.[7]

The battle is far from won, however. Portrayals of LGBTQ people on TV can still lean towards the patronizing or camp comedic. An activist noted:

It's either people are being covered on the TV when there are grievous human rights transgressions or they are guests on talk shows, where they are asked to tell about their sex habits. This again contributes to visibility, but I doubt if it contributes much to making things better. It's not like no one has ever given a microphone to a gay person in Lebanon and said: 'What do you have to offer?'[8]

It is also important to stress that media visibility for LGBTQ generates hierarchies of representation. While representations of gay men and lesbians have largely improved, the appearance of trans* people in the media involves routinely being 'misgendered, mocked and humiliated'. In some cases, interviews with trans* people are accompanied by religious figures and health 'experts, who are invited as surprise guests to shame trans individuals and confirm the normative assumption that they have a disease that must be cured' (see Human Rights Watch 2019).

'The closet can't contain us anymore'

The politics of visibility becomes perhaps even more tricky when activists enter into public spaces to challenge state power, to demand rights and celebrate sexual difference. It is here where activists increase their risk of exposure to the security forces. Unlike Stonewall activism, which was predicated on activists taking to public spaces to fight for rights, resist state oppression and articulate pride in sexual diversity, Lebanese activists rarely engage in street politics. Part of this results from a distinct want in activist numbers. Street demonstrations carry the risk of being counterproductive if they attract only a small number of protestors – the 'regular faces' – thus drawing the criticism that the movement is weak and merits little attention.

Activists have on occasion used public protest as an instrument to highlight incidents of state harassment. One notable example involved a series of demonstrations in response to an ISF raid on a sauna in Beirut in 2013 during which a number of men were arrested and subsequently detained and tortured under 534 (see Chapter 4). Ali, who helped organize the protests, noted how the demonstrations ultimately suffered from a lack of momentum: 'To be honest with you the protest had been dwindling in size. The first protest was really big, the second protest was smaller and the third smaller, and we were sure the next one would be even smaller.'[9] Part of the problem, argued Hakim, is a generational gap: 'It's young people who do this, that's where the passion and commitment is, that's where activism truly resides.' Yet, 'you have this gigantic gap where there's no people in their 20s and 30s', as this cohort have careers outside of activism. Hakim ruefully noted that 'very few people can do this fulltime, can do this as a career'.[10]

The low returns received for investing in street protests mean that activists often prefer to direct their energy into different forms of activism, particularly those that – as we illuminated in Chapter 4 – involve working behind the scenes. An activist explained how the sauna protests tended to use up valuable time and resources better spent doing activities that while they may not garner much visibility appear to yield better returns:

> The protest took a lot of time and resources to plan and the protest itself became the endgame and not the really hard long-term work that went into following up this case and making sure that people that did wrong were held accountable. So people suffered, but at least there was some sort of policy change or an apology, something in order to make it worthwhile. So we sat down and decided that we are not going to do a protest, we are going to dedicate all of our work, all of the resources into making sure that we are going to maximize the impact on this sort of thing as opposed to calling in everybody.[11]

The pursuit of visibility has most conspicuously been sought in recent years through the development of 'Beirut Pride'. Beirut Pride, of course, takes its inspiration from a long lineage of Pride events, which first emerged as part of Stonewall activism in the early 1970s to eventually become a celebration that takes place in hundreds of cities across the world. While Pride began as rather discrete communal commemorations of LGBTQ resistance against police oppression, events nowadays in places like New York City, Rio de Janeiro and Sydney are known for their carnivalesque celebrations that regularly attract millions of attendees and state support. Mirroring this exponential growth is the intense commercialization of Pride. The insertion of Pride into the economic and political mainstream in many places has led to fierce debates among activists internationally about whether such visibility represents an important vehicle for advancing LGBTQ rights or its taming through commercial co-option. For proponents, Pride celebrates sexual difference in the public sphere, helping to make 'visible the LGBTI community and to transform the public perception of LGBTI communities leading to a concomitant change in laws regarding civil partnership, marriage, blood donation, and adoption' (McGarry 2016).

Compared to the public visibility gained by a number of Pride celebrations worldwide, the development of Beirut Pride is a more modest affair. Beirut Pride does not feature a public parade, an event that typically serves as the culminating showpiece of Pride celebrations. Instead, Beirut Pride is restricted to an eight-day series of indoor events, ranging from discussions on sexual health, a Grand Drag Queen Ball, gender-fluidity fashion shows, 'coming out' storytelling, poetry and dance performances, art exhibitions and film festivals. Beirut Pride is further noteworthy in terms of an absence of explicit political activism guiding its mission. On its website, Beirut Pride (2020) makes clear that 'it does not endorse or encourage clashes with any social or religious actors, and is entirely run by Lebanese volunteers with no political affiliations'. This apolitical perspective reflects the fact that many of the main organizers for Pride have not come through

LGBTQ activist networks. In a media interview, one of the organizers explained that Beirut Pride is 'not looking to promote legal rights', such as the repeal of Article 534. The aim of Pride, instead, is to 'banalize' LGBTQ people, to make them seem ordinary and less of a threat to society (Beirut Pride 2020).

The premise that Pride can somehow remain above the fray of politics quickly became unsustainable. First, Pride has been critiqued by some LGBTQ activists, who argued that Pride was 'intentionally depoliticized' and it only catered to 'economically privileged gay men and their consumption habits'. For one writer, Beirut Pride emphasizes the image of an 'ideal gay subject', who 'is worthy of visibility and hence inclusion as a model of diversity within capitalist culture' (Bitar 2017: 33). Pride, in this analysis, simply advances the interests of middle-class cisgender gays at the expense of the 'unrespectable' poor, gender non-conforming trans and gay communities. Second, despite the wish of Pride's organizers to avoid conflict with religious and political actors, this desire was not reciprocated. As noted in Chapter 2, one major event for Pride 2017 was cancelled after threats by a religious organization with ties to Al-Nusra and ISIS. Then, on the eve of 2018 Pride, members of Beirut's vice squads, General Security and the intelligence bureau arrested Pride's lead organizer for allegedly 'encouraging debauchery and offending public decency', leading to his detention in Hobeish police station, infamous for its use of torture against LGBTQ individuals (Amnesty 2018). The activist was released only after committing to cease Pride's activities, a fait accompli since the general prosecutor of Beirut had already issued a ruling on this.

In response to the crackdown on Pride, LGBTQ activists and sympathizers hit back with demonstrations of LGBTQ visibility. These verged from spectacular public performances to subtler manifestations. In one display a group of activists hired two boats to sail around Pigeons' Rock, an iconic landmark of Beirut, and waved Rainbow flags for onlookers. In a show of solidarity, fifty bars in Mar Mikhael, a hip district in Beirut, flew the Rainbow flag for one night. Graffiti then appeared across Beirut stating, 'The Closet Can't Contain Us Anymore.'

The difficulties in sustaining protest and public celebrations are thus clearly apparent to activists. An LGBTQ activist pointed out to us that protests, if not organized in the context of a significant catalyst, such as a heavy-handed police response or a crackdown against LGBTQ individuals, may not have the intended effect.[12] An LGBTQ parade of visibility and pride that has not carefully considered the context it is situated in, and the consequences of its action for more marginalized queer individuals, might neither attract a broader audience nor serve the purpose of securing LGBTQ rights.

'Ambiguously visible'

'We work underground. We cannot carve a space of public visibility if the people we work with are in the dark.'[13]

The politics of visibility is not an agreed-upon strategy. Visibility is problematic for a number of interrelated reasons. As noted already, the politics of visibility can attract violent backlash from state and non-state actors. Constructing visibility further entails the construction of forms of sexual subjectification and identity that do not neatly map onto the ways in which sexuality is understood in particular contexts. This is not merely an epistemological issue; it relates more powerfully to how visibility operates to extend privilege to particular groups while simultaneously violently excluding others. Thus, while visibility may generate a backlash from the state, the effects of this dynamic are felt unevenly across groups depending on power relations.

For these reasons, some activists choose to eschew or at least negotiate visibility as a tactic. Krystal, an independent activist, explained how the network she belonged to preferred to be underground and largely invisible. What was more important for the movement was to find space for its members to engage in the building of collective identity and an awareness of the problems that confront women in Lebanon:

> In our feminist collective we are not open for the public, the only way to access the collective is to become a member. There are meetings and you need to attend events, we have a policy handbook which shows where we stand. We are now fifty women and we politicize ourselves. Every week we have two or three sessions in which we meet and talk about different topics just to be more aware.[14]

Meem, the lesbian movement discussed in Chapter 3, also posed invisibility as a core part of their activism. In a speech to the International Lesbian, Gay, Bisexual and Trans and Intersex Organization (ILGA) at a meeting in Sao Paolo, an activist from Meem issued a challenge to the 'shared international understanding of "visibility" and "coming out" as signs of progress in LGBT movements across the world'. In other words, visibility – 'a standard validation of one's identity' – is a largely Western form of identity politics that does not necessarily resonate with the conditions that confront LGBTQ people in Lebanon. Thus, 'visibility … has to be played with, refined, and attuned through strategies that respond to our very own contexts'. In response, Meem developed what they described as being 'ambiguously visible', a position that 'rejects the binary between the closet and coming out'. In practical terms 'ambiguously visible' meant that activists creatively and spontaneously combine different approaches to being seen and concealed (Meem 2010b). While their meetings were largely underground and functioned as safe space for women, they were able to announce their existence and politics through *Bekhsoos*, a self-published weekly online Arab magazine and *Bareed Mista3jil*, a collection of anonymous stories from members 'whose sexualities have been mocked, dismissed, denied, oppressed, distorted, and forced into hiding' (Meem 2009).

Inspired by Meem's repertoire of contention, various queer initiatives have proliferated, adopting an ambiguous politics of visibility as their preferred mode of activism. In their strategic engagement, activists involved in such initiatives shy away from overt political lobbying, legal approaches to activism or the search for legal visibility. Rather, they engage with a variety of tactical strategies such as art, theatre, culture and knowledge production to press their claims. At the heart of this engagement lies the desire to create frames that resonate with wider audiences and that tap into shared narratives and meanings. In so doing, they aim to impact everyday practices and discourses usually articulated outside conventional political spaces such as the legislature. This engagement also seeks to interrogate mainstream scripts of activism revolving around identity politics and the binary between the closet and coming out. Activists curating these projects are well aware that seeking legal recognition by the Lebanese state implies negotiation with the very forces they seek to eradicate and that make them even more vulnerable (Sayegh 2019). They also recognize that the very act of repealing Article 534 is embedded within a broader infrastructure of power that underlies rhetoric, imagery, narratives and cultural framings.

So how do initiatives that do not focus on earning the state's legal acceptance seek to secure LGBTQ rights and expose discriminatory practices? Let us consider Haven for Artists (HFA), a Beiruti organization formed in 2011 that defines itself as an 'all-inclusive women-led arts organization' (HFA 2020a). Focusing on supporting LGBTQ and all women, the organization draws on art as a tactic of 'non-violent confrontation' to challenge oppressive structures and injustice (HFA 2020b). Through film screenings, workshops, literary salons, art exhibitions and in-residency programs (HFA 2019a, 2019b, 2019c, 2019d), HFA connects women and LGBTQ artists and activists. By curating their research and artistic projects, it seeks to disseminate knowledge on the multiple forms of discrimination that they face. Creative art hubs evolve into cultural and discursive spheres where activists 'spread collective awareness about people's vulnerability', narrativize and unpack through readings, paintings, or theatrical performances the hidden and visible implications of laws and power practices affecting their struggle.[15]

In two large-scale exhibitions – respectively entitled 'Radical Choices and Consequences' (2017) and 'Vices and Validation' (2019) – more than twenty artists exposed the restrictions and social pressures that women and the LGBTQ community grapple with. Targeting the very socio-economic inequalities that the queer community suffers from, residencies in which artists critique oppressive structures and laws aim to create shelter spaces and employment opportunities with emphasis on trans* persons.

At the core of HFA's artistic activism lies the objective to localize the plight of the LGBTIQ community in its 'indigenous' context, away from transplanted narratives drawn from non-local contexts. A play on 'queer courage' aims to 'deconstruct' the conceptions of the closet and interpret what courage implies for queer individuals in Lebanon and the broader Middle East. In the play's script, coming out is not only about gaining the approval of friends and family; rather the act is mired in a complex struggle: fighting the darker forces of social and structural persecution that both formal authorities and informal codes have imposed on the community for decades to strengthen their rule. In this view, the lives of queer individuals are not necessarily structured around 'coming out' as a desired goal. Instead, a spectrum of everyday challenges outside the dual realm of *outness* versus *closetness* shapes their lived realities (HFA 2019b).[16]

Contextualizing queer narratives, exposing discrimination and 'achieving equality' for LGBTQ people and women through art does not however preclude HFA from weaving broader coalitions with organizations that are more visible such as Helem and the Arab Foundation for Freedoms and Equality. HFA has co-organized public discussions on contentious issues at the heart of the LGBTQ activism, namely repression and activism in political spaces. Marrying art with activism allows it to bridge the divide between visibility and the more discreet and quotidian conceptions of politics.

These issues can be illuminated further by looking at *Kohl*. Created in 2014, the *Kohl Journal*, an online queer feminist journal dedicated to body and gender research, builds on a discursive current of activism that aspires to disrupt established power practices. In response to the so-called exotification of the Middle East's queer community by Western audiences and the multiplication of LGBTQ-friendly projects that do service provision (paying often lip service to donor agencies' agendas), the journal aims to create a platform which engages with 'the infrastructure of knowledge' and the positionalities of power.[17] Its editors recognize that building new discourses and unpacking existing power structures through writing rather than merely striving for recognition and visibility are key to reclaiming LGBTQ spaces and voices. Ghiwa Sayegh, the founding editor of the online journal, notes:

> In Lebanon, discursive work is not seen as a site of activism ... we see discursive work as ground-breaking. We would like to distinguish ourselves from the humanitarian, single-issue approach to service provision and advocacy. We call for a different political project rooted in the historical, the discursive and the intersectional.[18]

'Advocacy is about the here and the now, but what does it do to our imaginaries and sexualities?' she adds poignantly. Ghiwa reminds us that negotiating legal reforms in the context of Lebanon's sectarian system suffers from various pitfalls. In one of her articles written during Lebanon's 2019 October uprising, she writes that negotiating reforms with the state may evolve into a channel for strengthening the system and keeping it 'intact'. Reforming a law in return for extracting concessions turns vulnerable communities into 'bargaining chips'. Rather, the answer is to resist negotiation 'with the forces we seek to eradicate' (Sayegh 2019). In this spirit, the journal stresses the limitations of activist approaches that focus on advocating for legal reforms without nesting them into wider and quotidian power struggles and recognizing their differentiated impacts on the ground:

> Article 534 is not necessarily making middle-class LGBTQ people miserable. It is rather the destitute people, refugees and the lower class who suffer from Article 534. We need to look beyond the article in that regard. Changing it is important but there are so many legal norms that affect non-normative sexualities ranging from censorship to codes on public decency. Resisting and dismantling hegemonic patriarchal norms, economic norms, the bank system's norms ... the people in power, heteronormative sexual identities. ... This is a wider political project.[19]

In practical terms, the journal and its supporters call for a broader intersectional queer feminist project which rises beyond identity politics, the politics of visibility and the binary of *the closet versus coming out* (Bitar 2017). This project has both an applied and a discursive dimension. It is important to weave solidarities with communities on the ground and to work with them across localities, geographies and borders to envisage alternative ways of organizing around economy and politics. At the same time, building new discourses and producing local knowledge on queer political imaginaries help to unsettle the very formal and informal norms as well as rhetorical legacies that feed into discriminatory laws. As Lebanon's 2019 October uprising started, instead of solely taking part in protests, the *Kohl* editorial team decided to pitch in a special issue on feminist revolutionaries to position Lebanon's anti-sectarian uprising in a broader discursive and historical legacy of activism (*Kohl: A Journal of Body and Gender Research* 2019).

Positioning itself as an underground approach targeting the everyday right to sexual and emotional well-being, the A Project is yet another initiative which negotiates LGBTQ rights beyond conventional forms and places of politics. The project, whose acronym stands for *Agency, Autonomy and Alternatives*, offers a sexuality hotline where all individuals irrespective of their sexual orientation can seek information about sexual and reproductive health including HIV, unplanned pregnancies and abortion, topics considered as a taboo in Lebanon's medical practices. The objective of the A Project is to provide both a discursive and counselling platform where 'women and gender non-conforming people' can reclaim sexuality and mental health services rather than having them utilized against them in a patriarchal setting (The A Project 2020b). Interested in how power disparities cut across queerness, gender, race and class, the project has curated a blog centred on the politics of sexuality and mental health. Since 2014 it offers 'sex and society reading retreats' where participants critically interrogate sexual politics in Lebanon (The A Project 2019).

At the heart of the A Project's work lies the desire to offer safe spaces for LGBTQ people. In that regard, the initiative shies away from what Van Laer and Van Aelst (2010) frame as high-threshold action repertoires such as engagement in protests, sit-ins and occupation of public spaces. Rooting its activism in a deconstructionist approach, it calls for decoupling sexuality from what it frames as 'medical patriarchy'. Its blog and reading retreats interrogate both through theoretical and praxis-based approaches the intricate interdependencies between sexuality, politics, patriarchy and sectarianism. Though its activism remains nested in semi-secret spaces, its aims are still confrontational. The A Project advocates for reproductive justice for all gender non-confirming individuals in Lebanon. Its retreats and discussion groups seek to equip participating individuals with discursive arguments geared at eroding the impact of patriarchal and sectarian politics on sexuality.

Dammeh, a collective focused on women and queer individuals, adopts the approach of community empowerment as a core strategy to strengthen grassroots activism (Dammeh Coop n.d.). Through fundraisers, community gatherings over food or cultural activities such as the production of a yearly calendar narrating feminist and LGBTQ activism, the coop aims to create public spheres bringing people together. While working behind the scenes, Dammeh negotiates its presence in select episodes of contention. At times, its members may mobilize and take to the street to demand rights for marginalized communities (Dammeh Coop n.d.).

The policy consequences that these subaltern and alternative forms of engagement yield on the ground remain disputed in the literature. In fact, if an organization is active in peripheral spaces, how can it alter public and policy attitudes and, most importantly, institutionalize LGBTQ rights? It emerges from our research however that cultural, artistic and discursive performances staged by such queer and feminist initiatives have several functions. Certainly, they raise awareness about LGBTQ rights and the forms of precarity that they face. But they also mobilize action. As Nancy Whittier (2001) has demonstrated, movements have historically drawn on cultural activities such as artistic and theatrical activities to elicit a spectrum of emotions such as grief, fear or anger to rally for change. Lebanese LGBTQ activists have long understood that to rally more endorsers, and solicit more support, they have to search for new cultural, material and human resources and craft innovative activities that are not solely focused on dismantling laws. Indeed, the establishment of initiatives that seek a politics of (relative) visibility such as Meem were partly motivated by a need for alternative engagements with discourse, power and practice (Moussawi 2015).

Events such as grassroots fundraising events, storytelling nights, theatrical performances not only allow LGBTQ activists to share information and ideas, but also to recruit more supporters. Such activities constitute key resources for extending their networks and building coalitions. In such events, activists could draw in bystanders. They could also connect with like-minded organizations such as feminist, environmental, anti-racist or migrant associations that would mobilize with them in the next protest, consolidating their intersectional base and the potential spillover effects that intersectional struggles yield for each other. Most importantly, such grassroots initiatives understand queer mobilization as a broader project operating outside conventional spheres of politics and rooted in everyday politics. In this viewpoint, resisting Lebanon's sectarian politics means primarily rethinking relationships with the political system in which the LGBTQ community is situated.

Yet, categorizing the work of LGBTQ organizations through the lens of gradations of visibility and invisibility fails to capture that almost all LGBTQ organizations in Lebanon have developed a hybrid mode of activism. Even LGBTQ organizations which have traditionally focused on legal advocacy have diversified their menu of activism. Most of these organizations justify this choice by referring to Lebanon's local realities in which resorting to strong tactical repertoires such as political lobbying against the penal code and performances of visibility may backlash against the community.

Helem, which lobbies for the decriminalization of homosexuality and the advancement of personal freedoms in Lebanon, has in the last years included in its repertoire of contention an array of softer discursive and cultural strategies.

Hosting storytelling nights where transgender people discuss their personal stories (Helem 2018), organizing open discussions on LGBTQ intimate lives (Helem 2020a) or opening a community centre which hosts book and film clubs (Yan 2016; Helem 2020b, 2020c, 2019a) have become part of its modular performances. MOSAIC (Mosaic MENA 2020a,b),[20] an organization based in Beirut which focuses on advocacy and service provision to LGBTQ and vulnerable communities with focus on transgender people, has increasingly embraced a rich cultural repertoire of action. In collaboration with international initiatives, it partakes in a global digital film festival, screening movies portraying the legal hurdles that Lebanon's LGBTQ individuals grapple with. Part of its menu of action is hosting drama and art therapy sessions where transgender women learn acting techniques while enacting scenes from their lived realities (Mosaic MENA 2020b). According to the organization, art activism must embrace the kind of visibility that can empower the community rather than stifle its engagement. In 2019, MOSAIC organized a play in which LGBTQ refugees shared their narratives. The play negotiated visibility in a selective way. Shying away from the limelight of the media, MOSAIC chose to invite a broader yet sympathetic audience that made the actors comfortable enough to seek visibility.[21] Keen on local knowledge production and on a contextualized understanding of the Lebanese LGBTQ community, MOSAIC has moreover partaken in various research projects. Most of these projects aim at elucidating the history of LGBTQ activism in Lebanon and understanding local modes of expression and mobilization.

The organization expresses a choice for a softer style of activism combining service provision, public awareness campaigns, cultural performances and research in Lebanon's geopolitical realities. An excessive politics of visibility which hinges on political lobbying and decrying politicians' rule may be of disservice to LGBTQ individuals who often prefer invisibility. In the light of the episodes of crackdown that Lebanon's security forces have staged against LGBTQ individuals, affecting public attitudes and partnering with institutions arise as effective strategies to achieving safe spaces for LGBTQ individuals.

> We are not interested only in dismantling the penal code. Rather incremental activism … who knows? The National Commission for Lebanese Women, the order of nurses, the order of Physicians or the Ministry of Health might hear us out.[22]

Though MOSAIC has not adopted any project that directly aims at dismantling the 534 law, it has adopted softer strategies to negotiate legal reforms. Currently involved in Lebanon's Universal Periodic Review (UPR), it has attracted attention to the recurrent violation of LGBTQ privacy rights.

In this vein, further organizations – such as the MARSA Sexual Health Centre – which inaugurated in 2014 the first trans* project (MARSA Sexual Health Centre 2018) or LebMASH which seeks to advance reproductive and sexual health for the LGBTQ community (Lebanese Medical Association for Sexual Health (LebMASH) 2017) – have negotiated a hybrid form of activism. Recognizing that service provision is essential in the absence of a state that has defaulted for years on providing access to public goods including healthcare, such organizations embrace subtle forms of legal advocacy while emphasizing the need for safe and protected spaces.

'Ana Shaz'? – 'I am a pervert'?

In a 2013 TV news interview, Marwan Charbel – the then minister of interior – was asked to comment about the arrests and torture of a number of suspected LGBTQ individuals. Charbel proudly announced to the cameras that the Lebanese were opposed to 'liwat', an Arabic expression translated as 'sodomites' but more commonly used to denote the slur 'faggots'. In its coverage of LGBTQ people, the Lebanese media has historically tended to favour the term 'shaz', which means 'pervert/deviant'. In a draft document by the state to specify and expand the legal coverage of Article 534 the word 'sihaq' was used for lesbianism, a term that refers to the act of 'rubbing'.

These descriptors for sexuality have various provenances, ranging from religious texts ('liwat') to descriptors developed by medieval Islamic philosophers ('sihaq'). In essence, these terms are, notes Shareen El Feki (2014: 221), often related to action rather than orientation – having intercourse with the same or opposite sex being a question of activity than identity. Whatever the origin, all of the terms are highly derogatory descriptors of LGBTQ people, which reinforce the widespread view that LGBTQ people are unnatural and deviant categories, thus constituting a threat to the moral order of society. These linguistic and discursive devices derive real-world consequences as forms of symbolic violence legitimating the harassment and persecution of LGBTQ individuals, especially as they are employed by a range of authorities, including political leaders, the media, the judiciary, medical and religious institutions. As a Helem activist explained, the usage of 'shaz' generates a particular 'mindset of people using this word',[23] which stymies their potential to accept the legitimacy of LGBTQ rights.

Given the tremendous power of language to engender oppression, Lebanese LGBTQ activists seize the means of production by participating in forms of linguistic neologism designed to generate positive descriptors to frame sexual identity. This linguistic activism, notably, predates the emergence of the LGBTQ movement in Lebanon. As detailed by Gabriel Semerene (2019), the Gay Lesbian Arabic Society (GLAS), an organization based in New York City, wrote a letter in 1996 to a London-based Arabic newspaper requesting that they cease using 'shaz' to describe LGBTQ people. Problematically, there are no existing terms in Arabic to describe sexual identity, such as 'homosexual' or 'lesbian'. For this reason, GLAS coined the expression 'mithliyya jinsiyya' as an attempt to translate the word 'homosexuality' into Arabic.

Further linguistic innovation was performed by another North American Arab group, Mujadarra Grrls, which produced a detailed bilingual (English to Arabic) glossary of terms to provide 'more positive expressions' in Arabic for various types of sexual identity. Beyond 'mithliyya' for 'gay', the glossary introduced 'mozdawij' for 'bisexual' and 'moghayir' for 'transgender'. Further terms have been developed, including 'thuna'iyand thuna'iyya', from the word 'double', for male and female bisexuals; 'mutahawwill' and 'mutahawwill', from the word 'to change', for transsexual and transgender people.

These linguistic developments clearly resonated with Lebanese LGBTQ activists. By the time Helem formed in 2004, 'mithliyya' was becoming a commonly used term by activists, who had broadened it out to describe 'gay'. Helem's online magazine, *Barra*, which means 'Out' in Arabic, also used and expanded the glossary of terms advanced by Mujadarra Grrls in its first issue. While these terms provided a new lexicon for LGBTQ activists and individuals to describe their identity and politics, for them to derive the power to stimulate social change, they needed to be disseminated and embedded into all spheres of public life. In effect, this meant encouraging the media, health professionals and educational institutions to begin the practice of using the preferred terms in their communications. With this objective in mind, a leading LGBTQ NGO, The Arab Foundation for Freedoms and Equality, published a manual catering to journalists, writers and audiovisual media professionals who tackle issues of gender and sexuality in their material.

Activists can certainly claim to have effected linguistic change. The term 'mithliyya' is increasingly becoming commonly used by the Lebanese media, judiciary and academics. Yet, despite the increasing prevalent usage of new terms, this does not mean that they cannot be refashioned once more to service homophobic politics. For example, in his televised rant against LGBTQ people (noted above), Marwan Charbel used the phrase 'zawaj al-mithliyyin', which translates as 'gay marriage'. The new lexicon produced by activists is also problematic in a different way. They are almost exclusively terms that have been directly translated from English into Arabic. Indeed, there are no linguistic equivalents of these English words in local dialects or classical Arabic. In so being, there is a risk that LGBTQ activists are merely importing Western terms for sexuality that do not necessarily map onto the experiences of people in the MENA region. As Semerene (2019) explains, many of the Arabic translations of English words for sexuality derive from concepts that originated in nineteenth-century European psychiatry and sexology, queer studies and from LGBTQ activism in the United States. The translation of these terms originating in the Global North potentially sustain the allegation adopted by opponents of LGBTQ rights in Lebanon that homosexuality identity is largely a product of Western sexual imperialism.

Partly in response to some of these issues, LGBTQ activists have occasionally sought to reappropriate some of the pejorative Arabic expressions for sexuality. In deciding on the theme for their 2010 IDAHOT celebrations, Helem chose 'Ana Shaz', which translates into 'I am a deviant'. As noted above, 'shaz' is perhaps the most commonly applied slur against LGBTQ people. To an extent, such co-option of derogatory terms is clearly evocative of the tactics employed by activists in the United States during the 1990s to reclaim the word 'queer' from its existing location as an offensive epithet to instead describe a progressive form of sexual identity and activism. The political meaning of 'queer' came to denote a form of activism dedicated to the disruption of the normalcy embedded in male/

female and heterosexual/homosexual binaries. Queer activism thus rejected the perceived assimilationist tendency of the existing gay rights movement; rather than mobilizing for acceptance within the system, it is an activism that represents a radical, confrontational challenge to the status quo (Meem 2010b).

Like the reclamation of 'queer', the 'Ana Shaz' campaign aimed to make the idea of sexual 'deviance' a rallying call for radical politics. A statement by Helem called 'Am I Queer? Ana Shaz?' announced that the 'Ana Shaz' theme was 'chosen to support all those who are considered queer/deviant by the governmental aspects of society' (Helem 2010). Queer, in this sense, can be seen as articulating an intersectional form of politics, an inclusive and interlinked identity marker for all individuals and groups oppressed by the sectarian system. Queers, the document stated, 'choose to be different from this social system and the racism and exploitation it represents, simply because we are "different" in a society ruled by sectarianism, sexism, classism, racism, and discrimination'(Helem 2010). 'Ana Shaz?' called for political alliances across society, since 'discrimination against LGBTIQ persons is similar to that against women, foreign workers, persons with low wages, people with special needs, sex workers, and even heterosexuals who choose to have a sex-life outside the framework of marriage or religious confession'. In its list of demands, the 'Ana Shaz' campaign called for a political activism that made connections between these various issues, including abolishing 534, ending discrimination against LGBTQ individuals in schools, promoting environmentalism and calling for rights for migrant workers. Yet, despite the power that could potentially be harnessed by reappropriating 'shaz', many activists felt that the term was far too deeply entrenched as a slur in public consciousness.

Recently, various LGBTQ initiatives have adopted linguistic activism as part of a softer-action repertoire that could catalyse a variety of incremental changes. The intent is not to shock political and public spheres into paying attention to the plight of LGBTQ people, but to position LGBTQ semantics as tools for accessing protection, information and services. A case in point is Shabakat el Meem ('queer web'), an LGBTQ-friendly project hosted at the Arab Women's Institute at the Lebanese American University. The project aims to develop a widely accessible glossary containing more than four hundred terms in Arabic relevant to the community, and to provide an online forum where LGBTQ individuals can submit their questions anonymously to sexual health and mental health experts. The glossary is not solely focused on correcting the terminological constructs used to designate LGBTQ people. Rather it has some practical dimensions. First, it seeks to redress regional and power inequities at the heart of Lebanon's LGBTQ community. Most services targeting LGBTQ individuals are usually found in Beirut, the capital, unlike the country's remote towns where LGBTQ individuals, especially queer women and transpersons, have hardly had access to information or counselling. Also, traditionally, the first organizations working on LGBTQ rights in Lebanon have focused on gay rights. In the last decade or so, in the wake of Meem's inception, activists have become increasingly aware that queer women and trans* individuals have lacked adequate linguistic tools that personalize their access to information and healthcare services. Taking language as a point of departure, the queer web that Shabaket el Meem is in the process of developing aims at creating an online space both for conversation and representation.[24] It positions language as an important vehicle for the expression of the LGBTQ populations' heterogeneity.

An additional project offered by LebMASH, an association that seeks to advance sexual and reproductive health in Lebanon with focus on the LGBTQ community, has drawn on linguistic activism as an essential strategy for accessing health equity. Mahmoud, a LebMASH activist, explained in detail:

> All information that is important to the LGBTQ community is generally available in English. We translated international protection clauses on transsexual health in Arabic. … Also, if one does not have a fixed gender identity, you cannot refer to them as he or she. In Arabic, there is so far no corresponding pronoun. We aim to release soon a list of pronouns in Arabic. This is extremely important, especially when doctors write memos and prescriptions. The person does not have to explain their identity every time.[25]

As noted earlier, there is the risk that translating terms from English to Arabic may gloss over local contexts and understandings of sexuality. Yet, the desire to appropriate language as an arena for accessing local services has become an inescapable need, especially given that there is a dearth of semantics in the MENA region representative of sexual complexities.

Drawing on language as a key vector for reclaiming LGBTQ voices has become extremely important to organizations seeking locally grounded methods of activism. As mentioned earlier, many underground projects have raised the question of decolonizing knowledge and reclaiming LGBTQ political subjectivities. An important obstacle consists however in the scarcity of literature on sexual politics and queer imaginaries in Arabic unlike the dense academic materials that can be found in English. Often in reading retreats and open discussions, LGBTQ organizations find themselves grappling mostly with theoretically inspired readings in English. When hosting its theory-driven reading retreats, the A Project became increasingly conscious that there is limited material in Arabic to discuss sexual politics. Creative techniques such as translating readings in English, conducting discussions in Arabic, English or in an Arabic/English mix have served to make the material more accessible (The A Project 2019) and to delink its content from Western academic spheres, often associated with colonial legacies.

Beyond the binary of visibility/invisibility: Subaltern imaginaries

> Queer and trans people find the space to mark their presence through poetic chants, bold graffiti, public discussions, and by taking their struggle to the streets day after day. (Younes and Bailly 2020)

In February 2020, a consultative meeting on Lebanon's Parallel Report for Beijing +25 took place in Beirut.[26] Various civil society organizations as well as some feminist and LGBTQ actors had come that day to deliberate on the key messages that the report put forward. In some of the side discussions, some actors started debating whether policy actors have been attuned enough to the multifaceted forms of activism that Lebanon's feminist and LGBTQ organizations practice. Those forms of activism do not necessarily revolve around sit-ins, lobbying and advocacy. Rather, as underscored earlier, they embrace alternative engagements with rights and politics, theatre, poetry, storytelling, art and discourse building. They also do not necessarily conform to the mainstream scripts of 'doing activism' by staging campaigns or writing petitions – the typical politics of visibility and pride. Mehdi, an activist who had participated in the consultative meeting, reflected, 'People from abroad tell us to change laws, but this is not necessarily the way to go about' and following this formula can be tricky.

This chapter has reviewed the menu of activist strategies that LGBTQ organizations navigate. It has shown how LGBTQ organizations have navigated a continuum of hybrid repertoires ranging from a politics of visibility to a zone of ambiguous visibility. At the same time, we have shown that capturing their strategies through the binary of visibility and invisibility makes us lose sight of the broader picture. Desirous to root their activism in local realities, LGBTQ activists have crafted creative strategies to interrogate deep-seated inequalities undergirding class, race, gender and language. At the outset, Helem's core approach has mostly relied on a politics of advocacy and visibility. Seeking to change laws that criminalize homosexuality has been one of its key goals. Nonetheless, as noted earlier, Helem has diversified its menu of action, recognizing that engaging in activities such as storytelling or literary readings are highly effective to building new discourses, interrogating patriarchal practices, connecting communities and educating the public. Also, as shown in this chapter, emerging feminist and queer movements have pointed out to the shortcomings of legal approaches, deemed as insufficient to build new discourses and reconfigure power asymmetries that map themselves onto lived realities. For other LGBTQ organizations such as MOSAIC, achieving visibility incrementally is seen in complementarity rather than in isolation to strategies aiming at cultural resonance or at deconstructing power and patriarchy.

The choice to adopt a mix of action repertoires ranging from 'high threshold' to softer methods has complex reasons. According to some grassroots feminist and queer organizations, following conventional scripts of activism, namely lobbying and advocacy, may reduce them to mere service providers or may run counter to a locally grounded style of activism (Laruni, Maydaa and Myrttinen 2018). Such approaches lead at times to the NGOization of their work, and to making them followers of external funding agencies' agendas. Alternative scripts of activism have become particularly important for LGBTQ initiatives seeking a locally grounded presence in the face of international policymaking. In the wake of mass displacement from Syria since 2011, Lebanon has become a key site for international agencies that have sought to provide aid to host refugee communities. In that regard, questions around the visibility of gender and LGBTQ rights have taken centre stage in the programmatic agendas of external funding agencies. The implementation of the Sustainable Development Goals (SDGs) or the Women, Peace and Security Agenda and their localization in Lebanon have led to heated debates as to how Lebanon's grassroots actors could shape and influence international policy. A predominant concern is how gender and LGBTQ grassroots actors could steer this agenda without being reduced to service providers or policy followers. A core concern here is whether their diversified forms of engagement, which do not necessarily align with lobbying around the penal code, shape policy on the ground and count on a world scale.

Indeed, as noted in this chapter, Lebanon's complex sectarian system which stifles institutional and legal change requires that activists become innovators rather than emulators of what worked in other contexts. In recent years, some LGBTQ organizations have developed a softer and subaltern repertoire of contention to expose the failings of Lebanon's sectarian system and to attract broader audiences through alternative strategies. An affirmative politics of visibility in which they overtly call for legal recognition or for the annulment of Article 534 is not necessarily everyone's preferred strategy. To many LGBTQ organizations, art, storytelling and theatre constitute powerful avenues through which they can access 'subaltern imaginaries' (Sharp 2011), interrogate power relations and expose how their lived realities are enmeshed in broader inequities that are often times articulated discursively and informally. Various LGBTQ initiatives approach linguistic activism not only through the lens of an affirmative politics of visibility but also to equip LGBTQ communities with daily linguistic tools that guarantee their local access to health, knowledge and services. Decolonizing knowledge and positioning queer individuals as knowledge producers rather than foci of study are increasingly on some of the activists' mind.

The founder of HFA, Dayna Ash, argues that looking at LGBTQ organizations through the lens of their strategic repertoires rather than through the binary of visibility versus invisibility may allow for a better engagement with how they seek to secure LGBTQ rights. To that end, she distinguishes various strategic approaches that have characterized LGBTQ work in the last decade.

In addition to legal forms of activism that Helem has engaged with since its inception, she adds that LGBTQ-related organizations have diversified their modes of strategizing. Some, such as LebMASH, engage with issues related to psychological warfare, trauma and mental health. Others such as the Arabic Foundation for Freedoms and Equality have sought to position themselves on the research scene. Collecting evidence-based and empirical information on LGBTQ perceptions and lived realities is key to policy change. Others such as MOSAIC engage with the full spectrum of vulnerable communities in Lebanon, seeking to address the everyday forms of precarity that touch refugees, trans* and disenfranchised people alike. A fourth type of organization, she continues, relates to underground art and cultural initiatives which seek to debunk narratives and connect people in peripheral spaces that are not necessarily visible to the policymaker and the practitioner. In such spaces, as underscored, people may unpack the content of a law and expose its failings through a theatrical play, a dramaturgical performance or a painting. It is in such spaces, explains Dayna, that people can perform the consequences of laws on their lives and illustrate their oppressive effect as well as their potential for protection.

So, how do we ascribe value to hybrid forms of activism in Lebanon's LGBTQ scene? And would a discourse centred on the binary of *outness* versus *closetedness* and visibility versus invisibility capture their repertoires of activism? An understanding of Lebanon's LGBTQ activist scene remains incomplete if we do not tap into the visible, ambiguously visible and concealed spaces to see how LGBTQ diverse groups negotiate the peripheries and the margins, trying at times to position the margin as the centre. This hybrid sort of politics signifies a deeper engagement with what Joanne Sharp (2011) frames as 'subaltern geopolitics'. In Lebanon, as underscored, the infrastructure of the sectarian state stretches into every corner of public and private lives. One way to dispute the way power is exercised over the lives and intimate spaces of LGBTQ people is to engage in 'subaltern imaginaries that offer creative alternatives to the dominant (critical) geopolitical scripts' (2011: 271). In that regard, a subaltern queer activism is not to be interpreted as a counterpoint to the sectarian state's dominant geopolitical power. Rather it makes direct reference to that power, seeking to renegotiate it, disperse it and diffuse its oppressive grip.[27]

Actions such as combining legal change with art, carving a space for storytelling, redesigning linguistic tools and building new discourses inscribe themselves within the realm of this 'subaltern geopolitics' where LGBTQ individuals seek to reposition the exercise of power over territory and space. Reclaiming the underground and the peripheral margins allows for capturing how a single law, such as 534, may impact people differently, generating various shades and forms of inequality and vulnerability that cut across class, age, gender, social networks and employment status.

The case of Lebanon's LGBTQ activism(s) has broader insights to convey. As some activists and researchers have already pointed out, it disputes the hegemonic definition of queer organizing often grasped through the prism of advocacy, coming out and visibility (Darwich and Maikey 2011). This prism may gloss over manifold nuances and narratives rooted in the local, the banal and the everyday. More particularly, it is to be understood in the various ways through which the geopolitics of the Lebanese sectarian state permeates the daily life that is performed in public squares, the working place, the pubs or the bedroom.

As various scholars have already demonstrated, Lebanon's LGBTQ activists are aware that laws are not the only hindrances. Unequal access to discursive power, economic capital and spaces, even if they are gay-friendly, has significantly shaped their plight. In this context, 'multiple exclusions' nested within hierarchies of power forge their everyday experiences and interactions (Moussawi 2018). In addition to legal restrictions, multiple oppressive sites of authority, at times tacit and informal (Moussawi 2018; Allouche 2017), hinder access to resources. A Western affluent LGBTQ migrant or a middle-class Lebanese gay is welcome in a gay-friendly bar in a gentrified Beiruti district unlike a disenfranchised Arab LGBTQ refugee or migrant (see also Moussawi 2018).

To some underground LGBTQ organizations, legal activism hides also various traps. Seeking the acquiescence of Lebanon's sectarian state makes them complicit with its practices and leads to a de facto acknowledgement of its authority.

Table 5.1 Typology of LGBTQ Activist Groups

Type of activism	Key characteristics
Advocacy politics	• Lobbying official institutions, ministries and health institutions • Calling for repealing of Article 534 and decriminalizing homosexuality • Seeking legal visibility • Organizing marches and sit-ins • Providing evidence-based research to reform policy
Community empowerment	• Providing services and emergency assistance • Creating safe spaces
Everyday politics	• Contesting sectarianism through everyday practices such as drawing graffiti, organizing storytelling nights and reading groups, altering semantics and building new discourses to recast homophobia and patriarchy • Wrestling daily with a variety of problems ranging from censorship laws, bureaucracies to power outages and crumbling infrastructures
Underground horizontal activism	• Drawing on 'Artivism' to raise awareness on the state's discriminatory practices • Crafting coalitions with grassroots actors namely feminist, anti-racist, migrant and refugee groups • Reflecting on movement building as un-institutionalized resistance • Cautioning against NGOization and dependency on external funding agencies
Confrontational activism	• Staging protests • Blocking roads • Shaming politicians online and offline • Organizing sit-ins in front of financial institutions and politicians' houses

Reclaiming visibility through the eyes of the sectarian state is another way to strengthen it and nurture its infrastructure whereas the goal is to disrupt its grip on LGBTQ people's everyday lives. As Meem argues, considering the ways Lebanon's sectarian system stifles LGBTQ rights, it is hard to imagine how queer activists can reclaim their rights by working with the system.

Table 5.1 provides a typology of dominant forms of LGBTQ activism in Lebanon and cites some of their defining characteristics. These types of activism are not mutually exclusive. Rather they intersect, converge with and borrow from each other. An LGBTQ-based organization or initiative may choose to incorporate hybrid forms of activism in its menu of action (see Table 5.1).

Exploring the various and hybrid strategies through which LGBTQ organizations rally for their rights, whether through discourse building, rethinking political thought, community empowerment or public awareness, brings us a step closer to understanding the multifaceted contexts that shape their struggle. While some draw on a rights-based discourse, others are more concerned with the geopolitics of sectarianism or the way sectarian rule grafts itself onto territory, space, resources and discourse. Here, a closer understanding of how individuals reclaim their agency through their political subjectivities, their bodies and their discursive capacity to 'trash the sectarian system' (Kraidy 2016) is particularly important. Not only does it bring us closer to the way they perform politics in lived and imagined spaces, but it also helps us to shy away from a conception of LGBTQ groups as victims rather than policy and norm shapers – a view often highlighted in practitioner and policy reports.

Chapter 6

'LGBT IS AT THE BOTTOM OF OUR LIST': INTERNATIONAL ACTORS AND RIGHTS

'We have our eyes on you'

In response to the detention and arrest of the organizer of Beirut Pride by General Security in 2018 Lebanese activists drove to a number of embassies in the city to hand out rainbow flags for them to fly as a declaration of solidarity with Lebanon's LGBTQ population. On 18 May 2018, which also marked the International Day against Homophobia, Biphobia and Transphobia (IDAHOT), some thirteen embassies across Beirut hoisted the rainbow flag from their missions. In a joint statement posted on social media, the UK, Australian and Danish embassies declared, 'We raise the rainbow flag at our embassies to support the full enjoyment of human rights for all' (UK Lebanon 2019). For an activist who had distributed the flags, the flying of the rainbow flag was a 'big statement' by the embassies to the Lebanese authorities. 'It was a statement to say that "we have eyes on you".'[1]

The public backing given by embassies and other international groups to Lebanese LGBTQ activism appears unsurprising. The promotion of LGBTQ rights has increasingly become a component of international development programmes and human rights policy. So-called 'norm entrepreneur' states and supranational actors incorporate LGBTQ rights into their institutional mission and underwrite core policies supporting rights transmission in places where LGBTQ populations experience oppression and violence. LGBTQ movements and activists in developing countries are identified by agencies for funding so that they can oppose homophobia and provide support services for a vulnerable LGBTQ population. In consequence, while LGBTQ issues were once marginalized in development programmes, the recent attention to and funding for LGBTQ activism within international development programming represents what has been called a 'queering' of human rights (Jolly 2000).

There are a number of potential benefits for local social movements working collaboratively with international human rights actors. Appealing to the support of powerful international agencies gives an opportunity for movements to upscale their activism to the global arena where they can encourage international actors to use their offices to leverage human rights change at the local domestic level and to lend legitimacy to their claims. International agencies can also distribute vital funds and material support required by activists to build and sustain campaigns and services for vulnerable LGBTQ populations. Established international activist groups share long-accumulated advice gained from operating at a transnational scale and dispense training for local social movements as they emerge and develop, thus establishing transnational activist networks.

Yet, these encounters between global and local actors, human rights ideas and practices may not always generate predetermined, predictable and positive dynamics. As a number of writers and activists have noted, the idea of sexuality, let alone LGBTQ rights, is not universal and the idea of global norms in relation to these processes obscures their Western roots (Massad 2007; Rahman 2014). Such concerns are not academic; the local consequences of Global North actors pressuring states to adopt rights may be an increase in state harassment of LGBTQ people rather than triggering reform. Thus, resistant states and groups conveniently conflate opposition to LGBTQ rights with resistance to Western imperialism (Nuñez-Mietz 2019). In addition, encouraging local movements to adopt the language and architecture of LGBTQ rights risks reducing activism to one nodal point – thus eliding the intersections between multiple forms of political struggle, which include class, gender and ethnicity.

These meetings – or collisions – between the global and local therefore can be both a site for empowerment and for domination for local activists and populations. For this reason, rarely is it the case that human rights norms simply descend downwards unchanged from international to local actors. In her research on women's movements in India, Merry (2006) notes that activists may either 'replicate', 'hybridise' or 'subvert' international human rights norms.

In this chapter we examine the relationship between international actors and the Lebanese LGBTQ movement. From practically the moment it formed, the Lebanese LGBTQ movement attracted the attention and support of international actors seeking to promote and effect a 'norm cascade' of human rights across the MENA. The Lebanese movement quickly situated itself within transnational networks of LGBTQ activism. Yet, at the same time, Lebanese activists debate amongst themselves the extent to which their activism should be crafted to the specific conditions of the local environment that they operate within or even if they need to remain largely independent of international actors. How, then, do international actors involve themselves in LGBTQ rights in Lebanon, and how do local activists respond to these interventions?

LGBTQ rights diplomacy

Speaking of global and international actors in LGBTQ rights risks homogenizing what is a large and diverse collection of institutions, groups and agencies located at different levels and which exercise varying amounts of power and influence. Among these we can include supranational actors, such as the UN and EU; the aid and development agencies and diplomatic missions of some states; transnational LGBTQ activist organizations (e.g. International Lesbian, Gay, Bisexual, Trans and Intersex Association); and international non-governmental organizations dedicated more generally to documenting, protecting and advocating human rights (e.g. Amnesty International and Human Rights Watch). These various actors deploy a range of support for LGBTQ groups to try and enforce rights change, including funding and aid, training and advice, and even using diplomatic and economic pressure against resistant states.

What unites all of these actors is that to different degrees of commitment and influence they promote LGBTQ rights as a policy that forms part of their international mission. It is worthwhile briefly illuminating how these various international actors and institutions have publicly made LGBTQ rights components of their work.

Foremost among these is the UN, which has created a number of measures and policies designed to expedite the worldwide decriminalization of homosexuality and other measures to tackle violence and discrimination against LGBTQ people. These declarations of support for LGBTQ rights were given added emphasis in 2015 with the unprecedented joint statement – 'Leaving no one behind' – calling on states to act urgently to end violence and discrimination against lesbian, gay, bisexual, transgender (LGBT) adults, adolescents and children (Office of the High Commission for Human Rights 2015). Alongside the UN, the EU represents a transnational organization that has LGBTQ rights at the heart of its policy on human rights diffusion. EU Action is further designed 'to promote and protect the enjoyment of all human rights by lesbian, gay, bisexual, transgender and intersex (LGBTI) persons' (EU Commission 2015). More broadly, in line with its diplomacy role outside its member states, the European Instrument for Democracy and Human Rights (EIDHR) is used as a tool to support 'several projects worldwide for the defence of LGBTI rights'. These projects have a wide remit, including 'improving LGBTI organizations' visibility and acceptance, and enhancing their dialogue with authorities to change laws' and 'combating homophobia and prejudices against LGBTI persons'.

A number of states have increasingly engaged with what could be called LGBTQ human rights diplomacy: international policies and programs with the long-term goal of promoting the social, political and economic equal rights of LGBTQ persons. The United States is particularly notable for embedding LGBTQ rights into its foreign policy. In 2011, the then Obama presidency encouraged 'the potent enticement of foreign aid, to promote gay rights around the world' (Encarnación 2016). The Global Equality Fund, an initiative started in 2011 by Hillary Clinton, has spent $12 million on efforts supporting LGBTQ rights and LGBTQ activism at some fifty US embassies. To spearhead this activity, in early 2015 the Obama administration created the US envoy for the promotion of LGBTI rights abroad.[2]

Many European states also specify LGBTQ rights as part of their diplomacy work. Some of these states publicly proclaim to use their economic and cultural influence in their former colonies, especially since anti-homosexuality laws were imposed during periods of imperial control. Thus, France supports the objective of universal decriminalization of homosexuality, especially in countries where the French colonial authorities created laws decriminalizing homosexuality, of which Lebanon is included (France Diplomatie 2019). Under the tenure of then Prime Minister José Luís Rodríguez Zapatero, Spain made LGBTQ rights a foreign policy priority in Latin America. Between 2004 and 2008, Zapatero's administration spent more than $2 million promoting rights in Latin America, including backing a successful campaign to legalize same-sex marriage in Argentina (Díez 2015). The UK is a founding member of the new Equal Rights Coalition, launched at the Global LGBTI Human Rights Conference in Montevideo in July 2016 and the Equal Rights Coalition (ERC), the first intergovernmental network to promote and protect LGBTQ rights. UK Prime Minister David Cameron claimed to deploy his country's leverage in former colonies where LGBTQ populations are criminalized, including declarations warning states – particularly Uganda and Nigeria – that the UK would withdraw aid from these states if they continued homophobic policies (APPG 2016). Such LGBTQ rights diplomacy is not the preserve of the Global North. Brazil, in particular, has assumed a 'leading position as a LGBT norm promoter at global and regional levels' (Nogueira 2017: 545).

International actors are increasingly promoting LGBTQ rights across the world. Yet, the question is the extent to which and in what ways the involvement of these actors helps secure LGBTQ rights in states where LGBTQ people are criminalized and persecuted? In relation to LGBTQ rights, a growing research illuminates how the successful impact of transnational norms and external resources can only be achieved through their adaptation at the local context in which they are received (Ayoub 2016; De la Dehesa 2010; Friedman 2012; Nogueira 2017; Waites 2017). At a broad level, the rise of same-sex-union laws are predicated on the actions of transnational networks that bring together human rights and LGBTQ activists and organizations, national and regional policymakers, and legal experts (Ayoub 2016).

Numerous single case studies reinforce these observations. The repeal of Uganda's so-called 'kill all gays' Anti-Homosexuality Act is identified as the outcome of the 'close working relationship between international actors and national civil society' (APPG 2016). Friedman's (2012: 29) analysis of the successful campaign for equal marriage rights in Argentina demonstrates that 'Spain's support was essential to the Argentine law's shape and passage'. Spanish norm entrepreneurs – including the Spanish government and LGBTQ activists – bolstered Argentinian LGBTQ activists through both the procurement of material resources and in providing help to build strategies (Díez 2015: 127). At the same time, the 'receiving' context is important – the receptivity of Argentinean organizations to transnational organizing and norm promotion. De la Dehesa (2010) thus examines how Mexican and Brazilian LGBTQ movements appropriate and readapt transnational human rights discourses to make them salient to their own environments. These case studies cumulatively indicate that the development of transnational diffusion is not just a top-down flow of information, but involves much creative reinvention and pragmatist agency on the part of receiving actors. Local LGBTQ activists represent 'norm brokers', whose role it is to take international human rights norms and translate them into modes of expression which fit the domestic context. International actors, themselves, often recognize the need to take 'into account the local realities in which human rights defenders need to advance their struggle' (Council of the EU 2013).

While research captures the dynamics that engender fruitful collaboration between local and international activists, it is also important to be mindful of the equally problematic forms of engagement. Some research claims that international actors trade human rights for geopolitical and security concerns. The EU, in particular, has drawn criticism for its inconsistent policy on LGBTQ rights. While the EU's accession criteria are designed to condition states into accepting LGBTQ rights, the EU allowed Macedonia to drop anti-LGBTQ discrimination legislation out of the list of requirements for visa liberalization. In an analysis of postwar Kosovo, Rexhepi (2016: 49) argues that '[t]he EU does not really seem to be concerned about the rights of the LGBT communities'. More important for the EU is to police its symbolic borders to construct and maintain an image of Europe as multicultural, tolerant and secular. Similar claims are made that the US follows double standards on LGBTQ rights, sanctioning Uganda and Gambia for its homophobic policies while simultaneously ignoring the record of human rights abuses carried out in a number of MENA states, arguably due to its strategic interests in that region related to oil and counterterrorism (Peale 2015).

An additional anxiety concerning international actors is that their intervention extends Western framings of sexual categories to non-Western contexts at the risk of ignoring local understandings and cultural meanings about sexualities. This is a process that Brown et al. (2010) describe in relation to sexualities in the Global South as colonial regimes of knowledge constituting neocolonial practices. Underlying such desires are neocolonial notions of liberating MENA people from repressive political and social structures, including homophobia. In this regard, Mohmin Rahman (2014) has coined the phrase 'homocolonialist' to describe how Western states frame societies that are resistant to LGBTQ rights as inferior to superior Western values. Such concerns are not merely academic; the local consequences of Global North actors pressuring states to adopt rights may be an increase in state harassment of LGBTQ populations rather than triggering reform. Thus, resistant states and groups conveniently conflate opposition to LGBTQ rights with resistance to Western imperialism.

It thus appears as if there is something resembling an international push to support and propagate LGBTQ rights around the world. To what extent, then, do international actors, whether supranational institutions or states, as part of their stated policy positions engage in efforts to advance LGBTQ rights in Lebanon? And are these interventions helpful or of negative impact in fostering rights change?

'Protecting minority rights is in our DNA'

The offices and community centre of the LGBTQ NGO were located in a small and cramped basement room of a residential housing bloc, which appeared to have little in the way of facilities. Yet just over a year later, the NGO had moved into an entire apartment on the second floor of the bloc. The centre was spacious, modern and freshly decorated. One room was reserved for a doctor to visit on a weekly basis to conduct HIV tests and another was used for a counsellor to tend to the users. The main room of the apartment was the community space, used for various events, such as poetry nights, workshops to deal with homophobic bullying, and sessions where lawyers explained the rights that LGBTQ people have when dealing with the security forces and state apparatus. In the reception stood a small table on which stood a toy kangaroo holding an Australian flag and small plaque recognizing the significant financial donation made by the Australian embassy to allow the NGO to move into and develop its new space. The services of the NGO were additionally resourced by the Swiss embassy, the director explained.

Money is the most obviously tangible form that international actors support LGBTQ groups. It is distributed to help LGBTQ groups perform their work on a daily basis, build long-term campaigns, engage in advocacy work and allocate vital services for their vulnerable constituency. Samer, a director of one Beirut-based LGBTQ NGO, explained that funding allows them to provide a wide variety of services to different communities, 'like clinical management for rape cases and social intervention and psychological intervention. Every year we are doing more than hundred sessions training for NGOs and INGOs, UN and SOGI organizations, alongside casework for LGBT people'.[3] Funding also allows some activists to become professional NGO workers willing to dedicate their energy on LGBTQ issues.

All LGBTQ NGOs in Lebanon rely upon international funds for them to survive, since it is clear that the Lebanese state has no largesse to lavish on the sector. Some international actors directly finance specific groups and projects. On the whole, as one European embassy figure who works on LGBTQ rights explained, in 2019, 'no one is really giving money', a reference to the various embassies.[4] Instead, the tendency is to encourage Lebanese LGBTQ groups to competitively apply to various state agencies around the world for funding. Most of the LGBTQ NGOs aim to work on discrete projects that do not overlap for the purposes of funding. Thus, while some groups work on legal advocacy and activism, others work on health, social work and psychological support. Samer explained how most of the main LGBTQ groups meet on a monthly basis to discuss funding applications: 'We always collaborate together to avoid duplication. We are working on a coalition of NGOs'.[5]

A European embassy worker practically sighed, noting that the fractured NGO landscape in Lebanon made it difficult for her embassy to come up with more comprehensive support. While it is not the case that embassies seek to apply some form of divide-and-rule split and weaken the NGOs, the fact that some embassies are willing to fund some projects and not others creates the conditions for rivalry between NGO groups. This process of splintering into service-based organizations also risks incorporating NGOs into a 'social movement market', where bonds of solidarity are replaced by competition for the next external grant (Thayer 2010).

International actors can utilize economic power in a different way than directly funding LGBTQ groups. A number of states from the Global North provide economic aid to support basic infrastructure projects that build state capacity in the Global South. In some cases, international actors fund initiatives that they see as contributing to fostering stability and security in places characterized by volatility and conflict. For example, the UK government has ploughed in the region of £20 million into the Lebanese Army Forces (LAF) to assist their fight with Syrian Islamic radicals on the Lebanese border. Other states and international institutions, such as the EU, provide aid to the Lebanese police, prison system and judiciary, respectively (Meaker 2017). This funding, which is designed to strengthen these institutions, overlaps with LGBTQ issues in the sense that it can be used to incentivize these institutions to improve their human rights performance. This is particularly salient in regards to how the security forces and the prison services represent citadels of abuse for LGBTQ populations.

One notable way in which funders can use their leverage in respect of LGBTQ rights is by threatening to withdraw aid when a state and its public institutions are seen to be homophobic and oppressive when it comes to LGBTQ populations. This is certainly the case when we consider the ongoing legacy of the security forces and elements of the judiciary in harassing and persecuting the LGBTQ population.

In Lebanon there is little evidence that international actors use aid and funding in a punitive fashion to coerce state institutions to be less homophobic. A leading figure in a Western European embassy involved in LGBTQ issues explained that his government had 'given a lot of funding to the LAF, we have given a lot of funding to prisons'. Yet

> we know that when we're funding certain organizations, or certain things like a prison and we know that abuses are going on there, we have got a direct lever to very easily say, 'That's not OK.' I have never seen us use that funding as a lever in that way, not directly like that.[6]

There is an argument that economic leverage provides little evidence of efficacy when it comes to engendering human rights reform and instead is more likely to make resistant states even more recalcitrant on the issue, even to the extent of instigating a backlash against the local LGBTQ population (Jones 2015). Yet, a senior political advisor to a Lebanese political party leader who has worked with activists on drafting a policy to end Article 544 counters this argument:

> The ambassadors have leverage on the government, and the government wants funds for their governmental projects, social affairs and other ministries, so they [the embassies] can put pressure on the government and tell them that they cannot conduct gender discrimination. So they have the leverage and we need to play at that level.[7]

A human rights worker responsible for LGBTQ rights also stressed the importance of international actors using funding in ways to encourage Lebanese state institutions to respect the rights of LGBTQ people:

> We are saying that the funding that is being directed to Lebanon is not used to violate human rights under international law. That's not to say that we advocate

for governments or embassies or UN agencies to withhold funding from Lebanon but to hold the Lebanese government accountable, and specifically the security forces for the violations that they are committing with this funding. A lot of the funding and a lot of the way that the institutions function is because of external funding, so it's the only leverage that we have because we see that there isn't a concern or an attention to these issues internally. Opening up a dialogue with the government in the presence of donors and funders might go a long way. The ISF, for example, are primarily funded by the EU, so the EU should have leverage over them. However, the priority may be that refugees in Lebanon don't go to the EU, so it is much more political than it is really on a human rights values and morals point of view.[8]

In fact, there is some indication that economic leverage represents a powerful weapon in domesticating Lebanese leaders. A good example of how international actors can generate positive outcomes was illustrated in 2019 after the storied Lebanese band Mashrou Leila was forced to cancel a concert as part of the Byblos festival, a major international event. The decision to cancel the event occurred after threats and homophobic statements by religious figures – mostly Christian – against the band that was effectively condoned by the major political parties through their deafening silence on the issue (see Thomas 2019). A senior worker at an aid agency in a Western European embassy recounted:

> I think what worked the most for the Mashrou Leila thing is when ambassadors and the international media, the senior members of the diplomatic community were talking about it publicly, how bad this was for Lebanon's reputation and you could see politicians squirming a bit about what it was doing to Lebanon's reputation and its climate for investment and for tourism and I think that economic case resonates a lot more especially in the current economic climate rather than the human rights perspective.[9]

Fadi, an activist, backed up this argument, noting that

> the Lebanese state is always afraid of the international media and international states. For example, when they cancelled our event for International Homophobia Day in May [2017] we held a press conference and the BBC, CNN, Reuters contacted us. It created a very big pressure on the government. The government is always worried about its image.[10]

Paying 'lip service'?

Legitimacy is where international actors demonstrate support for LGBTQ groups. It reveals that these NGOs are legitimate movements with rightful aspirations and demands. A senior EU diplomat in Lebanon with a portfolio in human rights explained that 'protecting minority rights is in our DNA. LGBT rights are part and parcel of these rights'. Towards this, the diplomat continued, 'we politically support LGBT groups – we raise the rainbow flag for IDAHOT, we send a delegation to LGBT events and seminars. We give moral support to the LGBT community. They know that they have the credibility of the EU'.[11] The fact that a powerful institute like the EU is a visible supporter of the LGBTQ population in Lebanon lends legitimacy to the existence of LGBTQ groups. Fadi emphasized the importance of international support, such as the EU:

> I was at the EU consultation in Brussels, me as part of an LGBT organization, a human rights organization serving LGBT people, we are in such a meeting, we are putting the LGBT agenda forward in this meeting. We were in Brussels, it is always important to remind that LGBT people and LGBT rights are part of the humanitarian and human rights agenda, we don't believe that we should live in a ghetto, we are part of the human rights movement ... because of me the Lebanese minister of social affairs said loudly for all of the Lebanese delegation, which was about fifty people, that he is supporting LGBT rights in Lebanon. He said it in Brussels, and it might just be a political statement to please the Europeans to try and get money, but at the same time it is important he can be asked about it later on: 'What have you done?'[12]

An aid worker from a Western European embassy provided extensive detail about how international actors can legitimate LGBTQ rights activists:

> A certain legitimacy is conveyed when politicians and religious groups know that these activist groups are engaging with embassies, and when they know there is an ongoing dialogue, and when they know that there are these networks, when we have conferences and joint seminars together, then they know that are a lot of meetings are going on, that offers NGOs a lot of cover and legitimacy. Having really good connections with a range of embassies gives them a lot of cover because it gives them something to fall back on, it gives them a safe space to go to, because they know that they have support, and if something does go wrong they have the confidence to go out and act, so it gives them legitimacy, and for politicians to know that actually this is a well-integrated network; it's not just a fringe group who don't know anything or anyone, this is a well-integrated activist community that is well connected, that helps.[13]

Indeed, as detailed at the start of the chapter, a number of embassies flew the Rainbow flag in 2018 as a declaration of support for LGBTQ people detained by the security forces. Such symbolic work demonstrated that the embassies were monitoring transgressions by the Lebanese authorities. The activist responsible for handing out the rainbow flags to the embassies said, 'I hope it's not only the flag what they do – what I know from the embassies that I talk to is that they discussed this with the authorities as part of the human rights commitment that LGBT rights are respected.' Embassies can thus provide tangible legitimacy and support when the Lebanese LGBTQ population is under attack from state forces.

An activist remembered that when the Lebanese censors banned movies from the Beirut Film Festival in 2016 because they had LGBTQ themes, the movies were 'screened inside the French Cultural Centre, the French Embassy, because it's not Lebanon it's French territory'.[14] In 2018, when Beirut Pride was shut down, a North American embassy held some events in its embassy, knowing that this is a space that the Lebanese authorities would not interfere in. Zain, a former leading Helem activist, admitted that 'the intervention of foreign funding will create this type of space that the state will not intervene in'.[15]

At the same time, the premise of legitimacy may encourage actors to mainly offer symbolic gestures of support, such as hoisting the rainbow flag from their missions on IDAHOT day and/or sending messages from their official social media sites. A senior diplomat in a European embassy rather resignedly noted that while 'LGBTQ rights is a priority of our foreign policy, we have no budget to fund projects in this field, so our support is limited to moral support, for example by attending events organized by the LGBTQ community or raising the rainbow flag at our embassy on the International Day against Homophobia and Transphobia'.[16] More pointedly, a representative from another embassy described much of the support offered by international actors as essentially paying 'lip service' to LGBTQ rights. In connection with his own country's efforts in Lebanon, he said:

> We're going to raise the rainbow flag, issue a press statement and send a tweet, and I'm sorry but literally you cannot do much less than that. That's very good for satisfying ourselves, satisfying your host government, satisfying your staff, but it does disappoint the LGBTQ community. It offers a bit of an association, it offers a bit of solidarity with the local community that is supporting it and a bit of visibility, but beyond that it's not much.[17]

Such tokenistic approaches to LGBTQ rights lead some international actors to support high-profile events and initiatives that reflect well on their reputation. Sometimes the gestures made by diplomatic missions risk being categorized as rather banal acts of virtue signalling, forms of self-promotion designed to categorize these actors as bastions of progressive and liberal principles. For example, one Global North embassy held an event celebrating its nation's 150th birthday, and as part of this they included representatives of Lebanon's LGBTQ groups to demonstrate how tolerance for LGBTQ groups is a core part of its state's identity.[18]

At worst, while such acts may appear as if support is being given, it can instead have destabilizing effects on the LGBTQ movement and population. Consider for example that a number of Western embassies in Lebanon have cultivated a relationship with the organizer of Beirut Pride, a figure who works outside of the established activist networks. Despite having a rather idiosyncratic way of operating, with little reference to the advice and strategies of more seasoned activists, the organizer of Pride has become the poster boy of these embassies. He is feted by the international media and therefore provides an easy symbol for international actors to publicize themselves through association with this figure.

The embassies, furthermore, have invited the organizer to speak for and provide analysis of the needs of the movement at high-profile events on human rights and democracy in Europe.

This co-option of particular individuals that some international actors perceive as giving added visibility to their human rights diplomacy risks rapidly undermining the long-term gains and objectives of the local activist movement. In the context of Beirut Pride, which now garners major global media attention, the event has the potential to be provocative, especially as it has proposed a major public parade that goes past an ISF station in Beirut. A development worker from a European embassy noted that the event 'has a lot of risk of backlash'.[19] This strategy essentially disregards the forms of activism developed by the LGBTQ movement over a long period, which is based upon being non-incendiary and avoiding any potential for people to be put in harm's way. As such, the co-option of Pride's organizer ignores the accumulated wisdom and expertise of established activists who have been working in the area since the movement was formed and do not have the same access to international policymakers and actors.

In a similar way, some of the embassies have supported initiatives that align more with Western forms of activism, which do not necessarily resonate with the conditions faced by the Lebanese movement. An example is the support given by the embassies to some Lebanese LGBTQ representatives to draft laws to overturn Article 534. This desire to bring about decriminalization in a number of countries around the world has become, in particular, a core goal of the US foreign LGBTQ policy (Encarnación 2016). While this support is perhaps well meaning, it is an initiative that few Lebanese activists are involved in or would be willing to participate in at this time. As explained in earlier chapters, demanding decriminalization in the parliamentary system is seen as the endpoint of a long period of mobilization aimed at ensuring that the optimal political and social conditions are in place for this policy to find a responsive social and political audience. Demanding decriminalization at this current juncture in time threatens to expedite a strong backlash from state and wider society. There is in addition a question to what extent any or a significant body of embassies can use their leverage to place pressure on key Lebanese political figures to permit decriminalization without backlash from various arms of the security forces that tend to run as autonomous fiefdoms.

'LGBT is at the very bottom of our list'

On the whole, the actions of international actors do not lead to LGBTQ rights in Lebanon. The tendency of international actors, especially the diplomatic missions, is to invest in symbolic gestures or to associate themselves with high-profile initiatives that do not clearly lead to positive outcomes. Why is this the case? Why do so many international actors proclaim that LGBTQ rights is central to their foreign policy and obligation to diffusing human rights yet do little in relation to concrete deeds that back up words of support?

Perhaps the simplest yet most powerful answer is that LGBTQ rights in Lebanon rank as a low priority for most international actors. A senior aid worker admitted:

> In the real world we are supposed to mainstream inclusion into all of our programmes but in reality when we are doing humanitarian delivery here LGBT is at the very bottom of our list. When it comes to inclusion, we have gender first, obviously, and then violence, children and disability, who are all groups we would be asked to prioritize ahead of LGBT. These are just higher in the agenda for inclusion.[20]

Rarely are LGBTQ rights dealt with by international actors as an issue that derives specific and tailor-made polices. A leading EU diplomat in Lebanon explained that LGBTQ rights for his organization comes within the broad remit of human rights: 'What we are doing basically concerns human rights. We touch on LGBTQ issues, which are cross-cutting with other human rights issues, such as gender and refugees. Human Rights is based upon justice and culture.'[21] Dina, a human rights worker and activist, confirmed this observation, noting that funding is rarely funnelled 'towards a specific issue like transpeople's health needs or access to shelter, this does not exist, or employment opportunities, and not stereotypical things like hairdressing and makeup.'[22]

While the idea that LGBTQ rights cross-cuts with other human rights issues promises to allow international actors the scope to deal with sexuality in relation to how it intersects with a range of identities and forms of inequality, in practical terms it means that these organizations tend to dilute LGBTQ rights within this wider pool of human rights. A diplomat, from a Western European state, explained that LGBTQ rights are not directly targeted by their embassy, but are touched upon in relation to their work on human rights, particularly in democratization and peacebuilding.[23] Indeed, after receiving blank responses upon contacting a number of embassies requesting to speak to the individual responsible for LGBTQ rights, we soon learnt that this issue is subsumed within wider portfolios.

LGBTQ rights is only one of a number of human rights issues that international actors are involved in. Yet, as one leading aid worker ruefully noted, 'We are not necessarily willing to put our capital in those discussions about LGBT.' For many diplomatic missions, as one diplomat from a small Western European country admitted, it is paramount to maintain 'good distance with the political parties', which entails doing little to provoke them on issues that are sensitive to them, such as LGBTQ rights.[24] For the diplomatic missions of most Global North states and institutions their number one priority in Lebanon is maintaining peace, security and stability. Ensuring that Lebanon is protected from the spillover effects of the Syrian civil war and minimizing the spread of the refugee crisis to the West is the fundamental foreign policy ambition of Western states vis-à-vis Lebanon (see Fakhoury 2020). A human rights worker noted that the main concern of some international actors was refugees, and this had the knock-on effect of working against LGBTQ issues:

A senior aid worker, who works on LGBTQ issues, noted that the priorities of his government's mission in Lebanon, is 'focused around refugees and refugee returns, and now increasingly it's focusing on political stability, so LGBTQ issues are not on the agenda'.[25] In this sense, international actors reproduce the narratives of Lebanon's sectarian elites who claim that gender equality and rights for LGBTQ populations would threaten to unravel the delicate civil peace that Lebanon enjoys.

There are other reasons why international actors are wary of getting involved in the imbroglio of LGBTQ rights in Lebanon. Chief among these is the concern that tactless intervention by international actors into this delicate issue would ultimately aggravate rather than ameliorate the process. Thus, international actors are cognizant of the dangers of being seen to promote sexual imperialism by imposing Western understandings of sexual identity into the region. A senior diplomat of a European embassy responsible for human rights explained that the work of his embassy, in relation to LGBTQ rights, needed to be 'particularly sensitive to Lebanon's specific cultural norms and practices'.[26] Another aid worker, who was an LGBTQ activist in his home country, explained how he sought to engage with LGBTQ issues in Lebanon in a way that did not reproduce a colonial relationship:

I wanted to know how we as a collective embassy could support some of the NGOs and these activists, and if there is a way that we could lend our voice that wasn't colonial, that wasn't trying to lead, or trying to steal the voice of a space that those NGOs needed but we are behind what they are doing and being supportive as much as possible without occupying that space or taking away from those organizations.[27]

At best these positions express an understanding that local activists rather than international actors should lead the campaign for rights. This approach also demonstrates awareness among international actors, especially from the Global North, that they have the capacity to deeply exacerbate the situation for local activists through well-meaning but, ultimately, naïve gestures. Indeed, as a director of one Lebanese NGO noted, one of the most common accusations that the movement faces in Lebanon, and not just from politicians and religious figures, is that 'we are importing homosexuality in Lebanon, it is an alien concept and construct to Lebanon'.[28]

In this sense, international actors need to tread lightly when intervening in LGBTQ rights issues as any false step is likely to see local activists being framed as not only in the pocket of Western states but of being handmaidens of sexual imperialism. Such allegations can endanger activists and the wider LGBTQ population by amplifying the likelihood of backlash. In some cases, activists ask international actors to hold back from becoming too publicly vocal on LGBTQ issues. A leading development worker from a European embassy noted:

It's the fear that we are damaging the community, because LGBTQ issues here will then be associated with the West in a way that the local community doesn't want. Ambassadors still want to do stuff, but the lesson learnt is be careful what you do.[29]

In this sense, it is important for international actors to take a steer from activists, even if this means they are required to say or do little. An aid worker explained that some local activists told him to

> support the community but speak with politicians privately. Use your press in the West to raise the issue, but don't say anything publicly because anything we say publicly gets construed as a Western thing and the local movements that are against LGBT rights will pick up on that straight away and say it's a Western thing funded by the West, the West is supporting you to promote this agenda, it's not a Lebanese value.[30]

Similarly, another representative from the embassies made a case for holding his tongue when it came to speaking out on LGBTQ issues in Lebanon:

> Believe me there are a bunch of ambassadors who are willing to put their neck out there and take a hit because they believe in it. But the argument against it by the [LGBTQ] community is actually that this is going to hurt us if you do it. Sometimes I cringe because stuff happened and we should be saying stuff because it's the right thing to do, but I know in my heart that it wouldn't help if we said something. It would make me feel better and it would make people back home feel better that we are saying and doing stuff but actually here it would be counterproductive in the short term. Maybe in the long term it would actually help.[31]

Thus, rather than assume the role of exporters of Western sexual imperialism into the Middle East, international actors instead prefer to stay out of the fray. In fact, the cultural relativist notion that homosexuality is at best a thorny issue in Lebanon and, at worst, essentially alien to the Middle East provides a get-out card for international actors to do little or nothing in terms of LGBTQ rights. Dina, an internationally famous writer and local activist, sighed: 'I am convinced they [the international community] should use their leverage. Too much political correctness can be deadly'.[32]

However, this issue is played out differently in terms of the colonial history of particular states. Countries like France and UK, whose lasting legacy included the imposition of many anti-LGBTQ laws in their colonies, have an image problem when preaching the virtues of sexual tolerance. Similarly, the United States, which has a deeply problematic past and present in relation to LGBTQ rights in its own backyard, is seen as hypocritical when it comes to extolling anti-homophobia abroad. Indeed, it is fair to say that the United States lacks a lot of credibility in the eyes of much of the Arab world when it comes to talking about human rights in general. States that do not have much of a history as colonizers are perhaps able to work on LGBTQ rights in Lebanon without attracting the usual allegations that they are sexual imperialists, using sexuality as a tool to browbeat and weaken Lebanese society. Notably, in Lebanon, the Scandinavian embassies have been able to visibly associate themselves with LGBTQ groups and issues in a way that appears to be neither obtrusive and self-serving nor is seen as a former empire seeking to exercise its influence. Yet, the question in relation to these diplomatic missions is the extent to which they have any leverage when it comes to pressuring the main Lebanese agencies in regards to protections and rights for the LGBTQ population.

In addition, international actors do not intercede too far on LGBTQ rights since there is a misconception that the situation in Lebanon for LGBTQ people is rapidly improving or is at least better than that confronted by LGBTQ populations across the MENA region. This impression is reinforced by media coverage of Lebanon as a gay paradise in the Middle East – a place of tolerance and sexual licence – and by reports of steady gains by the LGBTQ movement. A development worker in a European embassy explained:

> When you look at our county brief on Lebanon, it is an internal document, when it talks about LGBT issues, we see it as this beacon in the Middle East and how it's getting better, and how it's rosy, and that they are going to take steps for repealing [Article 534]. We don't recognize all of the shit stuff that is happening. There is still a misconception in my home capital and again I suspect elsewhere that Lebanon is in a good place.[33]

This situation is compounded, the development worker continued, by a lack of documentary evidence that would allow his government to raise many specific incidents of abuse meted out by state forces against the Lebanese LGBTQ population:

> With Internal Security, General Security, we have flagged incidents of torture, detainment in custody to them, not necessarily directly to General Security but through politicians. So when I went to an LGBT group's community meeting, I heard a whole bunch of stories and anecdotes of incidents that had happened, whether it was LAF, General Security, ISF, where there had been various cases of detainment, arrests, torture and harassment, blackmail but it is not documented in a way that allows us to raise it a lot of the time and that's one of the issues. We need to be able to corroborate with evidence whatever we charge, so it's difficult. It does happen, but we could do more, we could do a lot more. If it was higher on the agenda, we would, but we're here for refugees.[34]

Part of the reason why international actors may not have data necessary for them to intercede is that – as noted in Chapter 4 – suspects are often arrested and detained under a number of articles, not just 534, and in many cases they do not know what the exact charge is. In one example a transwoman was detained in Roumieh – a notorious men's prison located east of Beirut – under a sodomy charge and held for more than five months underground. She was only released because a representative from the International Committee of the Red Cross happened to be visiting the prison and found her working as a service, thereby reporting the case to the authorities.[35]

'We don't simply cut and paste projects from the West'

In this chapter we have examined some of the ways in which international actors both intervene and withdraw from the issue of LGBTQ rights in Lebanon. While we argue that the work of international actors can stymie positive rights change, it is important to take into account how Lebanese LGBTQ activists view the role of international actors.

We can explore some of these issues by looking at the extent to which the Lebanese movement sees itself as connected within global LGBTQ activism. From its beginnings, Helem associated itself with transnational movement politics. Since 2005 Lebanese activists have joined LGBTQ people around the world to mark the annual IDAHOT. Activists participate in yearly celebrations for International Women's Day. As noted in Chapter 4, since 2017 Beirut has become part of the global Pride celebrations. The International Gay and Lesbian Human Rights Commission (IGLHRC) presented the prestigious Felipa de Souza Award to Helem for their human rights work. Lebanese activists participate in the meetings of the International Lesbian and Gay Organization (Helem 2008).

Through these numerous networks and linkages, the Lebanese movement is clearly involved in what could be called the Global LGBTQ movement. The 'globalizing ... gay community' is seen as a 'political identity struggling for equality' (Nardi 1998: 571), 'where members of particular groups have more in common across national and continental boundaries' (Altman 2002: 86–7) than with those from within their own countries. The movement has supposedly 'helped create an international gay/lesbian identity ... by no means confined to the western world' (Altman 2001: 86–7), and they generate activism by a process of transnational diffusion.

For Lebanese activist groups, the Global LGBTQ movement provides obvious benefits. As noted earlier, being seen to be associated with international institutions gives the movement a sense of legitimacy – it is recognized and included within established transnational networks. This legitimacy is particularly important in terms of promoting the profile of Lebanese activism on the global stage and for requesting funding from various international agencies. The global character of the Lebanese movement additionally strengthens the idea that it is non-sectarian as a consequence of its supranational and cosmopolitan identity.

Yet, we should refrain from repeating the simplistic fallacy that Lebanese activism represents a distant outpost of the global movement. Lebanese activists do not see themselves as facsimile pieces in a template of activism first moulded in the Global North or as the next step in the process of rights radiating outwards from the North to the South. Joey, a leading Helem activist, argued that 'this concept of gay nationalism for us is misleading. We are not trying to import models and then implement them here; we are trying to create our own struggles'.[36] Samer, who was director of an NGO, similarly explained that 'we don't simply cut and paste projects from the West here. We don't want to be part of this big global ghetto'.[37]

Lebanese activists distinguish themselves from the global movement to varying degrees. For some radical activists, their sense of distinction from the global movement and international actors is articulated as one of complete rejection. Krystal, an independent activist situated on 'the radical left', voiced at length her opposition to the internationalization of LGBTQ rights in Lebanon:

> In Lebanon ironically the more that we get funding the more we realize fuck your Western funding. On international things, such as international gay pride, some LGBT groups spoke to all of the embassies and put the rainbow flag on many buildings. I am here on the radical left and for me these are the governments that occupy, that are funding weapons. Is it good that the Finland embassy raised the rainbow flag? How did it help? Some LGBT activists go to the US, the UN, conferences in Washington, and they cooperate with senators and politicians. We are on the radical left, we are anti-imperialist and anti-colonial; I don't go to the US to get fed ideas on how it should be, I know how it should be, I have agency, I am an LGBT activist in Lebanon, I have exactly what I need. Why do I need to go to Washington?[38]

Zain, a former Helem activist, explained how he left the movement because of NGOization: 'I did not want to become stuck in a donor-driven relationship. You can see that a lot of their work [LGTBQ groups] are aligned with visions of Global North human rights funders.'

For Samer, a director of an NGO, rather than simply reject wholesale funding from international actors, the trick is to be selective when accepting support:

> The first time we took funding from MEPI [Middle East Partnership Initiative] I resigned. It was one of the American Ministries, like US Aid, we don't take money from these organizations. They make you sign a lot of papers; they request a lot of information. You need to sign a paper that you will not be involved with terrorism in your country, which I don't believe we have terrorism in my country. I don't want to be part of the American system.[39]

Funding from US agencies is often subject to conditionalities that may impose various constraints on LGBTQ organizations. For example, it may restrict their scope of work in some remote areas such as southern Lebanon where Hezbollah is the key political player. In the last years, the US administration has sought to isolate and impose various sanctions on the Shiite political party. A key player in Lebanon's government and legislature, the party has however refused to demilitarize despite repeated calls that it constitutes a dual power infringing on Lebanon's sovereignty. It frames its military arsenal as necessary resistance in the face of Israel's external threat. Within this contentious context, Assaad, who has worked with various international donors, cautions against the consequences of conditional funding:

> The idea that Western countries are bastions of freedom is not true. Imposition of values has counter-effects. Receiving funding from sources that sanction

working with Hezbollah does not allow us to reach out to households living in Hezbollah-controlled areas. It thus limits access to people in need of aid and creates a dichotomy between the good and the bad. The economic dependency and disempowerment of LGBTQ communities living in remote areas of the country will only sustain patronage networks. People will resort to parties to get services and jobs.[40]

Assaad narrates to us how in the wake of various negotiations, his project team decided to cooperate with a donor that has not imposed conditions, favouring 'localization' strategies instead.

In this way, activists that work for LGBTQ NGOs mostly strive to engage with international actors in forms that allow them to craft campaigns and services that resonate with local requirements. Hakim explained: 'We are not closing the doors to international collaboration. We need funders who realise the specific situation in this region.' Yet, this has not necessarily been the case. Samer admitted that international funders had not always been attuned to local needs:

> We were trapped in different projects, we were doing it because of the funders who were not very culturally sensitive. If we want to provide training on a micro health project, they are not interested, and they want to do training on international law, they say that they have money for this. And this is not our needs. Funding is always a trend for two or three years and then they change.[41]

One notable problem in terms of a lack of cultural sensitivity from international actors is the assumption that Lebanese activism should follow the trend set by the Global North. Hakim, a Helem activist, pointed out that 'the LGBT agenda in the rest of the world is very different. You are fighting for gay marriage, for adopting, we are years away from this.'[42] Another activist reinforced this observation in his dealings with international funders: 'They say we have gay marriage so you should have gay marriage. We do not even have civil marriage, so why are you talking about gay marriage?'[43]

For activists, international actors best support the work of local movements when they give them space to mould their services and initiatives to the specific conditions that confront them. Samer provided an example: 'When we created our organization we created our own SOGI toolkit. We have a vision based on our findings on the local society that we work within.'[44] Joey provided a further example of how 'we are trying to create our own struggles. That's why we don't celebrate one day of IDAHOT, we celebrate one week of IDAHOT because of the attention that people give to that day in order to highlight our causes.'[45]

The way forward?

A number of international actors now have policies promoting LGBTQ rights in places where LGBTQ populations confront violence and persecution. An important body of research has explored the effects of LGBTQ rights diplomacy by so-called 'norm entrepreneurs' and found a positive relationship occurs when international and local actors collaborate. Despite such successes, it is also the case that rhetorical commitment to LGBTQ rights by international actors does not necessarily translate into progress towards rights and their actions may even regress progress.

Lebanon provides a real test for the commitment of international actors to foster LGBTQ rights. International actors frame human rights as norms that reinforce state-building and democratization. Yet, in a postwar state located in a region viewed as marked by conflict and instability, international actors are primarily focused on maintaining security in Lebanon, which means that the promotion of human rights may be compromised. One reason for this is that in some contexts, such as Lebanon, sexuality and gender is in itself bound up with ideas about citizenship and how it intersects with morality and state security.

It is undeniably difficult for international actors to advance LGBTQ rights in Lebanon where there is strong resistance to same-sex relations and non-normative gender. LGBTQ rights are framed as forms of Western sexual colonialism and for this reason local activists are wary of being too closely associated with international actors and being labelled 'native informants … complicit with imperialism' (Massad 2007: 172). In this sense, international actors confront a seemingly intractable dilemma in dealing with LGBTQ rights. Intervention may lead to a backlash against local actors while inaction makes it appear as if international actors are uncommitted to human rights. However, in Lebanon, international actors either pursue forms of intervention in relation to LGBTQ rights in Lebanon that do little to secure transformation or instead position rights as a low-order priority.

It is important here to understand how, in critical junctures such as mass protests or periods of polarization, Lebanon's political elite weaponizes LGBTQ cooperation with Western actors to brand activists as traitors, instigators of change or agents of embassies. This is why LGBTQ activists, who have staged pivotal contentious performances in Lebanon's October 2019 uprising, have sought to distance themselves as much as possible from external donors and European as well as American embassies as the protests were taking place.[46] The aim is to convince local audiences that their plight is indigenous and not externally induced.

What, then, modest proposals can we suggest in relation to how international actors deal with LGBTQ rights in contexts such as Lebanon? The first suggestion concerns fragmented actors. While it is unrealistic to expect that all of the international actors involved in LGBTQ rights will create uniform policies, there is a lack of consensus and communication binding international actors. This means that international actors often pursue individual policies that risk clashing with or contradicting the initiatives of other actors in the field. This situation has the consequence of not only diluting the influence of international actors but also of providing mixed messages for activists. In fact, the absence of unanimity of approach means that the activist movement is increasingly fragmented into a large number of NGOs competing for funding from different international actors. Thus, an obvious step forward for international actors is to consider greater unity of purpose when promoting LGBTQ rights in specific places.

Second, it makes sense for international actors to treat LGBTQ rights in terms of how sexuality intersects with other issues, especially gender, refugees and disability. Yet, by creating broad-based human rights policies that are designed to accommodate a number of groups and issues this often has the unfortunate tendency of relegating LGBTQ rights down the order in relation to other issues, as we have seen in this chapter. Moreover, the specificity of how conflict and political instability impacts sexuality and LGBTQ populations needs to be recognized. To do this, international actors need to design tailor-made policies to support LGBTQ rights.

Third, in order to create and deliver better policies for activists, we need to develop scholarly thinking by going beyond reductive dichotomies, which either promote normative universalizing notions of LGBTQ rights – thus obscuring their Western roots – or see rights as a neocolonial project designed to further Western geopolitical projects. As Waites (2017) convincingly argues, greater attention is required to craft rights discourses and practices which resonate with specific contexts. This project connects with the geographies of sexual citizenship, which indicates how sexual identity and practice operates in a range of contexts and societies, particularly given its varied meanings.

Chapter 7

'WE HAVE ALWAYS BEEN THERE': TACTICAL ALLIANCES AND PROTEST SPACES

It is the first day of February. Days are getting longer but when the sun goes down, chilly temperatures are felt by the few people left on the streets to protest. Lebanon's October uprising of 2019, framed as the thawra or 'Revolution', has given way to a darker undercurrent. At night, the city's Riad al-Solh and Martyrs' Squares – the main public spaces of the city centre – which have been buzzing with protests, gatherings and teach-ins for three consecutive months, are now desolate places where the colder wind blows through the empty protest tents.

The anatomy of Lebanon's thawra has changed since the heady days of autumn 2019, and so have the mood, tactics and aspirations of its actors. Back in November, when the uprising was in full bloom, Helem called for protests to fight homophobia. With protest policing becoming more aggressive and Lebanon's economic meltdown weighing heavily on peoples' minds, the organization has changed its tactics. Activists now convene storytelling nights to reflect on the political and economic impact of the 'revolution' (Helem 2020d).

Some LGBTQ activists who were chanting slogans calling for dethroning all political leaders (*Kellon ya'ani kellon* meaning 'All of them means all of them') (Majed and Salman 2019) convene in Beirut's coffee shops and bars to discuss capital controls imposed by the banks, and the restructuring of Lebanon's debt. Some vaguely brood on immigration after sharing stories of how Lebanon's financial crash has led to the slashing of their salaries or even countless thousands losing their jobs, making their status even more precarious. At the same time, they insist that the thawra, which sought to dismantle the politics of sectarianism, decry the 'public looting of fund' and revoke homophobia, has evolved into a 'lifestyle' that has infiltrated private and public spaces (Najib 2020).[1] The thawra may have temporarily subsided in visible protest spaces, yet it continues in peripheral sites, and through new forms of collective action such as the formation of new professional associations as alternatives to the defunct trade unions and labour syndicates.

The involvement of queer activists in Lebanon's 2019 protests has been unprecedented. Graffiti denouncing homophobia and celebrating LGBTQ rights have adorned Beirut's city walls like never before. Inside the Egg, a partially abandoned brutalist cinema at the heart of downtown Beirut that stands as a de

Figure 7.1 The Egg
Source: Photo credit – Roy Chaoul.

Figure 7.2 LGBTQ graffiti inside the Egg: 'Queer for the revolution'
Source: Photo credit – Roy Chaoul.

facto monument to the destruction wrought during the civil war, pro-LGBTQ graffiti inscribed within a wider tapestry of bullet holes and anti-government slogans have attracted the attention of international reporters and photographers (see Figures 7.1 and 7.2).

To understand how the thawra intersected with LGBTQ politics of contention we must however look beyond the day-to-day events and retrace a multilayered field of informal alliances that goes back to years of coalition-building and activist networks. As many LGBTQ activists told us, this upsurge in activism is neither accidental nor sudden. In fact, it is no upsurge as it builds upon the years of activism that has been highlighted in this book. Farah notes that the effort began long before the thawra, and the thawra only helped to magnify it and bring it into the open (Harb 2019). As social movement scholar Asef Bayat puts it, it is important here to descend into the subterranean aspects of activism.[2]

When asked to narrate their involvement in the recent protests, LGBTQ activists relate to us the importance of retracing more than a decade of 'hard work'. At the height of the protests, the solidarity that has been forged with intersectional feminists, intellectuals and students may have never felt that strong. Yet at the core of these protests lie precursory cross-cutting alliances.[3]

In the last decade, LGBTQ activists' involvement in protest spaces has waxed and waned, yet their repertoire of contention has made strides. The coalitions they have built go beyond queer spaces. They permeate civil society and grassroots platforms and to some extent political coalitions. As Maya Mikdashi underlines, LGBTQ communities were 'hyper-integrated' in the 2019 protests, but this requires accounting for the multilayered entanglements, alignments and ties that bind them with others.[4] Following Ruud Koopmans, contention is 'a multi-actor process' that cannot be captured by focusing on 'one actor and reducing the others to the role of context variables'. Rather, 'interactions between actors become the fundamental units of analysis' (Koopmans 2004).

So, what intersectoral coalitions have LGBTQ activists built, and how have these coalitions shaped their contentious performances in Lebanon's 2019 uprising? In this chapter, we account for the broader coalitions that LGBTQ activists have crafted in recent years, and that have shaped their contentious performances. We then address their presence in Lebanon's 2019 protests and explore some of the narratives and strategies of contention that they have deployed. In so doing, we show that their protest performances are nested within a multilinear trajectory of coalition-building. Looking at the broader interactional context or at the way LGBTQ activists relate to sectarian politics and policies, we finally describe the dilemmas and constraints that they face in building alliances and crafting contentious performances.

'We have always been there'

In Riwaq, a casual restaurant in Mar Mikhael known for organizing storytelling performances, Rida, who describes herself as a queer activist and an artist, explains while sipping a cup of tea: 'How do you ascribe meaning to our presence in protests? Visually? Numerically? We have always been there.'[5] She then adds with a broad smile:

All LGBTQ organizations are interlinked. We have all overlapped at some point. We know each other. We all know what the other organization is doing. We have created in the last years an overarching system, a myriad of reference networks. We know that the Arab Foundation for Equality and Freedoms does research and that Helem does service provision and lobbies to change laws. Yet we also work together and seek to influence each other. We are also positioned within a wider grassroots constellation of NGOs and feminist collectives such as Kafa, Abaad and Dammeh.[6]

As we explored in earlier chapters, LGBTQ activists have developed various ties with civil society, grassroots and political spheres, as well as key actors in some of Lebanon's postwar iconic protests, including the 2005 Cedar Revolution. Still, as Rida argues, adopting a linear chronology to understand LGBTQ politics of contention, or attempting to quantify their presence in Lebanon's protest scenes, makes us miss out on the broader picture. Queer activist spaces are nested within a broader assemblage of coalitions, narratives and temporalities.

Take for example the 'Arab Spring'. In 2011, a broad protest wave engulfed the Arab world. Anti-regime protests spread from Tunisia to Yemen. In some of these protests, LGBTQ communities played an important role in denouncing authoritarian practices and social injustice. At the time, Lebanon appeared impervious to the wave of Arab uprisings, making it appear as if Lebanon's complex sectarian infrastructure inhibits mass mobilization around non-sectarian issues, hampering LGBTQ activists from formulating a politics of claims-making. Yet the picture is more complex, requiring an insight into the various types of collective action that have shaped LGBTQ activism. If we reconstitute the event-history of activism in Lebanon in the past decade, we notice that a series of major events has created a spectrum of opportunities for LGBTQ activists to build coalitions and strategize. In February 2011, while Hosni Mubarak was about to renounce power in Egypt, protests calling for abolishing political sectarianism broke out in Beirut. At the time, Helem activists joined the crowds, decrying patriarchy, homophobia and the entire sectarian political class. In subsequent months and years, key events that would jointly galvanize feminist as well as LGBTQ activism started cascading to the extent of making significant changes. In August 2011, thanks to the mobilization of feminist platforms, the honour crimes article was revoked in the criminal code. In January of the following year, civil society and feminist platforms organized protests against rape in Lebanon. Later that year, activists Kholoud Sucarrieh and Nidal Darwish signed the first contract of civil marriage in Lebanon, breaking a deeply seated taboo and defying the authority of religious officials. In this context, as researcher Henry Myrttinen notes, Lebanon witnessed a rapprochement between women's rights platforms and LGBTQ organizations, and many of these organizations adopted an intersectional feminist perspective to advance both women's and queer rights.[7]

A further key development that deepened LGBTQ grassroots alliances was the consolidation of Lebanon's migrant and anti-racist activist scenes.[8] The creation of the grassroots collective the Anti-Racism movement (ARM) in 2010, the building of the First Migrant Community Centre in 2011 and the establishment of the Congress of Domestic workers Union in 2015 created a broader scene of grassroots activism within which LGBTQ activists have sought to position themselves.

LGBTQ organizations and activists started working on intersectional projects connecting the struggles of LGBTQ, migrant and refugee communities. With widespread displacement from Syria, grassroots NGOs such as MOSAIC have sought to extricate the association of LGBTQ activism from exclusivist notions of (Lebanese) citizenship. Instead, they have called for positioning LGBTQ rights as an issue that transcends Lebanese citizens and cuts across Iraqi, Syrian, Palestinian refugees, lesbian, gay and transpersons. According to Myrttinen, the proliferation of community projects catering to both refugee and host communities' needs made new alliances possible. The presence of LGBTQ refugees, he explains, has affected self-perceptions and understandings of the LGBTQ community in Lebanon.

> Grassroots organizations started working with refugees and migrants from Syria but also from Iraq and Egypt, and projects brought together host and refugee populations in ways that were not previously possible. Lebanese Transwomen started meeting with Syrian and Palestinian Transwomen. An upper middle-class gay in Lebanon initiated a conversation with an uneducated Syrian from a rural background. It became evident that sectarianism is not the only variable. Rather the politics of sectarianism feeds upon many issues such as xenophobia, misogyny against effeminate men, class antagonisms etc. Multiple levels of discrimination, such as Lebanese identity versus the external other, intersect and confer additional layers of complexity to the everyday struggles of the LGBTQ community.[9]

Broader alliances with academics and universities have also allowed LGBTQ activists to amplify their frames and to reach out to wider alliances. These alliances have enabled them to position their claims-making politics within a wider human rights and feminist academic discourse. In recent years, some academics have joined forces with LGBTQ student clubs on campus to denounce homophobia, framing it as a human rights issue (Farah 2012). With the creation of LGBTQ-friendly student clubs such as the Secular Club, the Feminist Club and the Gender Sexuality Club at the American University in Beirut (AUB), the intersectional Feminist Club and the more recently established Gender and Sexualities Club at the Lebanese American University (LAU), queer activists started organizing talks and awareness-raising debates on campus. In some instances, they lobbied hard to cancel 'deeply homophobic events' (Gender and Sexuality Club – AUB 2017).

Leila, a pro-LGBTQ activist we met in a coffee shop in the lively Beiruti district of Badaro, underlines that strategies such as carving a space on campus or working on a research project with activist scholars have helped LGBTQ activists to integrate their narratives within the more recent wave of feminism which embraced the queer cause.[10] Nadine, an LGBTQ activist and student, explains that deploying vocabulary from queer theory and borrowing from debates on sexual citizenship has helped to 'mainstream' LGBTQ-related discussions in some university circles. In some of the classes that she has taken, she recounts, students have engaged in debates deconstructing the narrative that homosexuality is a Western or transplanted construct. They have also discussed literary and historical texts to evidence the embeddedness of queerness in the history of the Arab peoples.[11] Manal, the founder of an LGBTQ student club, relates to us how LGBTQ and LGBTQ-friendly student clubs have called for integrating in the curriculum sections that account for LGBTQ health awareness, protection and rights.[12]

Though confined to some university spheres, activist scholarship has sought to generate pedagogies and knowledge on queer history and rights. Academic institutes and initiatives such as the Arab Institute for Women (AiW) at LAU and the AUB Women Faculty Alliance, created after the 2019 protests, have integrated queer activism at the heart of their projects and activities. Previously, some professors were reluctant to supervise dissertations on LGBTQ political subjectivities in mainstream disciplines such as political science and international relations, relegating this subject to an area of exceptionalism. Today, however, as our informal conversations with academics reveal, producing knowledge on LGBTQ claims-making politics is portrayed as important to understanding the dynamics of political sectarianism.[13]

Against this background, and as mentioned in Chapter 5, Lebanon witnessed the proliferation of grassroots queer initiatives that draw on a spectrum of strategies ranging from art, literature, poetry, storytelling and sexual health awareness to spread their narratives. In 2011, Haven, the women-led arts organization that seeks to raise awareness on women's and LGBTQ rights through art, theatre and storytelling was established. In 2014, LGBTQ and LGBTQ-friendly activists launched the A Project, a semi-secret civil society organization which seeks to consolidate 'the agency, alternatives, and autonomy of sexuality, sexual health, and gender in Lebanon' (Shamma 2017). By creating a sexuality hotline, inviting women and transpersons to access information on reproductive and mental health, and staging frequent community involvement workshops, the A Project has carved a safe space for LGBTQ activists to meet regularly. That year, the launching of the journal *Kohl* has allowed for the development of a queer and feminist activist platform in which the nexus between 'discourse-making', online activism, deconstruction of gender stereotypes and social justice is strongly articulated. As Rida, the activist we met in *Riwaq* tells us, all these initiatives, far from operating as self-contained projects, have woven links with civil society initiatives, artistic spheres and other LGBTQ organizations. Some of them shy away from engaging in legal activism or direct action. But their artistic and literary techniques of contention are as 'confrontational' as protests, clarifies Rida with a large smile.

Have such coalitions however remained purely grassroots alliances? Have they seeped into Lebanon's political spheres or affected political agendas and electoral platforms? And to what extent have these intersectional ties created a receptive environment for LGBTQ activists to 'assert their presence' (Helem 2020d) and 'take up space'[14] in Lebanon's 2019 protests?

'Trashy politics': The 2015 Hirak *and LGBTQ voices*[15]

Commenting on the emergence of new LGBTQ grassroots organizations in recent years, Samir, a graduate student writing his dissertation on queer identities and sectarian politics, wonders whether new analytical tools are needed to explain LGBTQ organizing in protest spaces. He asks whether the recently formed LGBTQ organizations, such as MOSAIC or the A Project, are part of a wider movement which connects at the heart of its claims-making the dismantling of sectarianism with cross-sectoral reforms around health services, waste management, LGBTQ rights, refugee rights and gender-based violence.[16] Samir argues that this broader movement may lump various grievances. But it goes beyond what Raymond Hinnebusch (2016) frames as 'everyday sectarianism' or banal sectarian identities.[17] Rather, it primarily condemns the institutionalization of Lebanon's politics of sectarianism which has in recent years weakened social justice, strengthened political clientelism and neglected issues related to the delivery of welfare and health services. As explored in Chapter 2, Lebanon's politics of sectarianism has created deep societal discontent in the postwar order. A chasm between what James Muir frames as Lebanon's 'sectarian barons' (LSE Middle East Centre 2020) and the general populace has been widening by the day. A Lebanese Centre for Policy Studies (LCPS) report shows that Lebanon's legislature which has extended its rule twice in 2013 and 2014 has passed 'only a fraction' of laws addressing peoples' priorities (Atallah 2018). Before the outbreak of the 2019 protests, Pew Research Centre surveys demonstrate that Lebanon's citizenry is deeply unhappy with the country's economic and political situation (Mordecai 2019).

In this context, LGBTQ activists have become increasingly aware that altering laws affecting their intimate and everyday lives is imbricated within a complex process: the reproduction of political sectarianism through clientelist networks and exploitative elite cartels. It is in this vein that dynamics undergirding LGBTQ activism cannot be isolated from Lebanon's wider political processes. As Charles Tilly and Sydney Tarrow (2006) explain, contentious politics unfolds within complex processes and structures. Delineating the field of contention means looking at manifold actors, identities, episodes, performances and mechanisms of contention, and how they all interact together (Tilly and Tarrow 2006; Koopmans 2004). Certainly, reading the contentious politics of Lebanon's LGBTQ community requires such an analytical lens.

Illustrative of complex intersections between LGBTQ struggles, citizen grievances and sectarian policies came together in the 2015 wave of protests, known as the *Hirak* (movement). In the summer, amid a blistering heat wave, protests broke out in Beirut over an unprecedented waste management crisis which resulted in uncollected trash accumulating in head-high piles in the street and in the open burning of waste. The origins of the garbage crisis are linked to political squabbling between the respective sectarian elites over deals for garbage collection. The closure of a landfill that summer left piles of garbage lying for months on highways; in this period people feared the outbreak of disease, and the world's media downgraded Lebanon from a touristic attraction to a site of environmental decay.

Soon, the garbage protests evolved into a broader movement, commonly dubbed as #Youstink (*Tol'it rihetkoun*). Equating the garbage smell with politicians' stinking odour of corruption, protesters adopted slogans decrying governmental incompetence and corrupt elite practices (Fakhoury 2015). In their slogans and chants, they connected various grievances ranging from the lack of public services such as electricity, water distribution, sanitation to Lebanon's stagnating economy, staggering debt and inefficient governance. In those protests, there was consensus that all these ills are to be ascribed to Lebanon's corrupt elite and to their 'garbage' politics of sectarianism. The #Youstink campaign explicitly called on politicians to resign for having neglected citizen well-being. Back then, key LGBTQ activists joined the crowds and aligned their frames with broader public discontent. Soon, however, the protest movement splintered between activists (the original #Youstink campaign), who argued that focusing on the waste management crisis would be more strategic than bringing various grievances together, and those who sought to expand contention to various areas such as the #WeWantAccountability group, a group of activists who aimed to turn the garbage protests into 'a more fundamental' uprising against the sectarian system (Stel and El-Husseini 2015; Rønn 2020).

Though the protest movement had fizzled out by October 2015, it shaped in intricate ways Lebanon's activist scene more broadly, and LGBTQ activism more specifically. The *Hirak* made it clear that accessing citizen services such as sustainable waste management is deeply interconnected with the sectarian political regime (Mouawad 2015). In its aftermath, the movement led to the establishment of new political alliances such as *Kallouna Watani* ('We are all the Nation') and *Beirut Madinati* ('Beirut Is My City'). Those alliances made up of civil society activists, intellectuals, professionals and university professors were determined to challenge the traditional sectarian political class in the next municipal and parliamentary elections. The movement also inspired the creation of new grassroots initiatives such as *Citoyens Citoyennes* launched in March 2016. Such initiatives were keen on drawing in people interested in a variety of issues ranging from social and environmental justice, citizen welfare to women's and queer rights.

During the Youstink Protests, LGBTQ activists did not find it particularly strategic to graft their specific grievances onto the protests, yet the movement constituted a favourable discursive opportunity for many LGBTQ activists and organizations. It also facilitated alliance building with environmental activists, feminist platforms and civic spheres contesting ruling incumbents' power. Intersectional protest frames that extended beyond the garbage crisis provided queer activists with the opportunity to address issues such as homophobia, patriarchy and hegemony. Behind the scenes, feminist and queer meetings targeted issues at the heart of lesbian activism in Lebanon, namely the patriarchal culture of sectarianism which has historically given prominence to men as speakers, instigators and leaders in protest spaces. Krystel, a feminist activist who participated in the Youstink protests, relates to us the complex alliances that the movement heralded for LGBTQ activism:

> The Youstink movement was not particularly conducive to articulating a pro-LGBTQ agenda. But there are many intersectional coalitions that emerged during or in the aftermath of the movement and that indirectly inspired LGBTQ

activism. I am referring here to citizen initiatives such as *Al shaab youreed* (the people want), *akhbar el se'a* (the news of the hour), *tol'it rihetkoun* (Youstink) and informal feminist initiatives such as *saker ejrayk* (close your legs). Feminist and queer activists criticized how male activists gained visibility in protest spaces and activist meetings through hegemonic gestures such as 'spreading their legs' and interrupting others.[18]

Within this context, owing to its focus on intersectional issues (Geha 2018) and its call for eradicating the sectarian system, the 2015 *Hirak* has arguably created a terrain for LGBTQ activists to emerge as more visible actors in protests and public campaigns. In 2016 LGBTQ activists, holding a banner that said 'The Only Disease Is Homophobia', organized a protest denouncing the criminalization of homosexuality outside a police station in Beirut. Modular and ritualized feminist performances such as the annually celebrated International Women's Day and the Feminist Bloc March in 2017 saw a remarkable increase of supporters rallying for LGBTQ rights.[19]

Describing the feminist march in 2017, Krystel recalls:

> That day we saw LGBTQ groups come to the fore, raise flags calling for the freedom to live, the freedom to love without prejudice, the right to jobs, the right to have a family without being convicted and the right to hold accountable people who shame you for your sexuality. That day, our demands were intersectional. That day, we saw incredible coalitions emerge between secular, feminist and LGBTQ groups.[20]

At this juncture, post-2015 movements that sought to challenge Lebanon's ruling elite or the traditional 'Zu'ama' adopted LGBTQ rights as a key frame in their public campaigns. In 2016, Beirut Madinati, which endorsed LGBTQ rights in its public campaign, competed with Lebanon's traditional sectarian leaders in the Beirut municipal elections. Although it did not win the election, scholars and journalists celebrated its 'impressive share' in the electoral votes as a turning point that is set to shape the upcoming legislative elections (Chaaban et al. 2016). Indeed, by May 2018, after a suspension of legislative elections for nine years, more than six hundred independent candidates took part in the parliamentary polls, calling for an end of Lebanon's 'century-old sectarian framework' (Geha 2018). For the first time, more than hundred candidates advocated for LGBTQ rights and called for decriminalizing homosexuality. Twenty-four candidates articulated plans to achieve legal reforms with regards to promoting gay rights. *Kallouna Watani*, the sixty-six-member coalition of civil society members, made the decriminalization of homosexuality part of its electoral campaign. As Gilbert Doumit, one of the *Kallouna Watani* candidates, stressed: 'We are definitely pro eradicating law 534 that discriminates against homosexuality. We are pro-equality on all levels' (Qiblawi 2018). To the surprise of many, the traditional Christian-based Kataeb party, as stated in Chapter 4, spoke publicly on LGBTQ rights in Lebanon, calling for revoking Article 534. Back then, the executive director of the Arab Foundation of Equality and Rights, Georges Azzi, argued with some jubilation that 'before now, there was no politician that was able to publicly endorse the removal of Article 534' (Qiblawi 2018).

The result of the polls however (re)confirmed the resilience of Lebanon's sectarian-based parties. Only one independent candidate made it to the 2018 parliament. At the same time, doubt hovered as to whether political platforms such as *Kallouna Watani* and *Beirut Madinati* could appeal to poorer classes as well as leftist activists including Lebanon's very diverse queer community (Rønn 2020).[21] Notwithstanding this, the pre-electoral period can be credited for introducing the debate on LGBTQ votes and rights as a defining characteristic of electoral politics in Lebanon and, arguably, as some commentators enthusiastically stated back then, in the Arab world.

As noted in Chapter 4, LGBTQ activists doubt the usefulness of engaging with the legislative process in a sectarian system that inhibits change. Also, LGBTQ and feminist activists have cautiously pondered the motives that prompted electoral candidates to advocate for LGBTQ rights in 2018. To some, the Kataeb's endorsement of LGBTQ rights was only an attempt to attract new young voters and to rebrand a party that has lost its attractiveness. At the same time, there is consensus that the post-garbage crisis period has invigorated LGBTQ activism. It diversified the choice of allies and expanded its spectrum of tactical coalitions. Precipitating circumstances (such as a garbage crisis or an economic meltdown) provide 'sparks' that expose the weaknesses of the regime, leading activists to 'invent new combinations of identities, tactics, and demands' (Koopmans 2004).

'Queers for Marx?': The 2019 thawra

It is against such a background of complex intersectional spaces that we can understand the involvement of the LGBTQ community in Lebanon's unprecedented 2019 protests dubbed as the thawra or the 'revolution'. As Lebanese academics such as Bassel Salloukh, Carmen Geha and Sari Hanafi have underlined, the 2019 wave of intense mobilization generated new dimensions.[22] It is credited for articulating strong connections between social injustice, the corrupt economy of sectarianism and 'the sextarian system' which reproduces itself through regulating and bureaucratizing gender.[23] It has also cut across social classes, bringing together vendors, merchants, housewives, students, disgruntled lawyers, private businesses and teachers, among many. This has created a discursive opportunity for LGBTQ groups to insert their narratives and echo the grievances of the general populace that felt betrayed by the ruling elite. Munir, an LGBTQ activist we met several times, tells us:

> This 2019 October uprising suits us much more than any other protest. ... As soon as we realized that the revolution is calling for social justice, secularism and for ending the sectarian system, we endorsed it. Those are our ideals.[24]

So, what is so new about this thawra that 'has opened up new spaces and opportunities for alternative solidarities and modes of collective organization' (Majed and Salman 2019) and has it served as a catalyst for new LGBTQ organizational fields?

On 17 October, a proposed WhatsApp tax led to the eruption of protests that spread across cities and rural towns in Lebanon. The following day, motorcycle convoys closed the roads, inaugurating a series of roadblocks that would evolve into a ritual daily performance. Mass protests that encompassed large and diverse sections of the society called on all politicians to resign, decrying corruption and the looting of public funds. On 29 October, Lebanon's Saad Hariri government resigned but it was too late to contain the public outcry. For weeks, protesters were singing daily in Beirut's Riad al-Solh and Martyrs' Square, Jal al-Dib and Zouk Mosbeh, Tripoli's Al-Nour Square and central areas of Sidon and Nabatieh, chants calling for the resignation of all sectarian elite (see Figure 7.3).

The early demands that they communicated on protest banners, Facebook posts and petitions consisted in staging early elections, phasing out sectarianism and appointing a new technocratic government that would set an urgent rescue plan to resolve the deepening economic crisis which led to the devaluation of the Lebanese Pound.

Avoiding the risk of runs on them, Lebanese banks shut down for two weeks and imposed heavy capital controls that curbed cash withdrawals and prevented depositors from accessing their accounts. Amid a context of outrage, protesters went on to organize demonstrations and sit-ins in front of financial and political institutions. Chants and slogans sprayed on the walls of high-end shops and banks in Beirut condemned rampant corruption and economic mismanagement.

Figure 7.3 The 'revolutionary fist' in Martyrs' Square, Beirut, 2019
Source: Photo Credit – Roy Chaoul.

Figure 7.4 Graffiti inside the Egg, denouncing the public looting of funds and the dollarization of Lebanon's economy
Source: Photo credit – Roy Chaoul.

A protest campaign targeted Lebanon's National Bank for protecting the economic interests of the so-called sectarian political elite. Tirelessly, protesters chanted slogans prompting the bank's governor, Riad Salameh, framed as the guardian of the political economic elite, to leave (*Falwasqot Hami el Hitan* – down with the protector of the whales).

The 2019 thawra was essentially an uprising against banks, looted public funds, political greed and corruption (see Figure 7.4).

At the same time protests quickly evolved into a site for interconnected struggles. In the absence of organized trade unions and syndicates, feminist organizations and collectives took the lead in organizing some of the uprising's iconic marches and campaigns (Majed and Salman 2019; Malmvig and Fakhoury 2020). Throughout November and December, feminist groups staged recurrent women's marches in Beirut, Tripoli and Saida raising banners targeting the homophobic and patriarchal nature of Lebanon's political system. In their chants and slogans, they called at the protests' frontlines for equal nationality and citizenship rights for women, the promotion of queer rights, and protection against sexual harassment and violence (UN Women 2019). In towns outside of Beirut that have not known protests for years, such as Nabatieh, Hermel and Baalbeck, women called for ending discriminatory rulings detrimental to women's custody rights in the religious court systems (see Figure 7.5).

In this landscape, the protest movement has been credited for capturing the ubiquitous reach of political sectarianism. Through a diverse array of framings, graffiti and slogans, protesters went on to show how this politics governs their economic livelihoods, bank accounts, quotidian lives and intimate relations.

Figure 7.5 Drawing – 'The revolution is female'
Source: Photo Credit – Tamirace Fakhoury.

On TV, a group of young people captured best the far-reaching grip of political sectarianism and protesters' need for an intersectional approach: 'In my dorm the toilets do not work in Akkar (one of the poorest regions in Lebanon) and this is why we want to change the regime' (Mouawad 2019).

In this context, as Munir tells us, it felt natural for LGBTQ activists to join the crowds. At the same time, he argues, it is important to account for how other movement actors propelled the interests of LGBTQ activists, and how LGBTQ activism is embedded within a web of solidarities. He goes on to explain how feminist organizing has cleared the way for LGBTQ visibility.

Since women were already at the frontlines of the protests, rallying under the feminist umbrella gave some of the LGBTQ activists a sense of protection and security. Feminist challengers targeted the patriarchal and homophobic sectarian system, but they also articulated the interests of the LGBTQ community in some of the marches they have organized in Beirut. For Munir, the protests provided literal space for him and others to shout out and spray slogans.

Scholar Maya Mikdashi clarifies this point. To understand why LGBTQ rights came to the forefront, one needs to abandon a monolithic lens focused solely on LGBTQ activism. Rather, she invites us to look at relational and interactive mechanisms. LGBTQ activism played out as a dynamic enmeshed within wider feminist queer groups and a broader intersectional feminist movement.

> The feminist initiatives brought something amazing to the protests. Queer rights, anti-racist organizing, refugee organizing, coalition work. It all started to 'come out'. One of the most visible set of actors were feminist activists. Many

of these activists embraced LGBTQ activism. And they were at the frontlines of the protests.[25]

Echoing this narrative, the editor-in-chief of *Kohl*, Ghiwa Sayegh, relates how the thawra forged a site for a 'political project' in which queer feminists chanted slogans and organized events targeting intersections between sexuality, migration, economies and oppression.

> We pushed for a discourse that's intersectional: Let's talk about sexuality as much as we talk about migration. We curated intersectional chants that brought together non-normative sexualities, refugees, and domestic workers' rights. We also organized public discussions about the economy and the banks.[26]

As underscored, intersectional and organic mobilizing was not sudden. In recent years, feminist activist platforms have routinized queer involvement in their contentious performances. In marches and sit-ins, LGBTQ and feminist activists have intertwined gendered expressions of their vulnerability with broader manifestations of social precarity targeting what Sabiha Allouche frames as 'the repetitive failures of the [Lebanese] state' (Allouche 2015). In such a terrain, reclaiming legal rights and sexualities has become deeply intertwined with revoking the politics of sectarianism that grafts itself onto legal norms, gendered bodies and sexualities.

Though multi-actor coalitions have certainly galvanized LGBTQ involvement in the 2019 protests, their implications for the emergence of an LGBTQ movement are unclear. Does this mean, as some have written, that the LGBTQ community was 'at the core of the uprising' (Harb 2019)? Or does it rather indicate, as some scholars have cautiously pinpointed, that LGBTQ agency in driving protests was propelled by other actors?[27]

Munir elucidates this question by relating to us how LGBTQ organizing took on varied forms, oscillating between strategies of visibility and invisibility:

> Our identities as protest actors are complex. As LGBTQ activists we rallied under the wider feminist umbrella. At other times, we stepped out of our role as LGBTQ activists to perform the revolutionaries, not the feminists, not the queer revolutionaries.[28]

Describing to us how his protest days unfolded, he says:

> Over the course of the revolution, we held monthly meetings that feminist and queer groups led. We held discussions about whether to go fully visible or not. A consensus finally emerged that it was not in the advantage of the LGBTQ community to go fully visible. Instead of adding additional layers of complexity to the uprising, we agreed that the October uprising with its broader frames and demands is beneficial to the LGBTQ community. So, we started strategizing as to how best we can mobilize and collate our grievances on to the claims of

the revolutions. We wanted to pre-empt politicians' arguments that the LGBTQ community was seeking to hijack the uprisings. We started organizing with feminist cooperatives such as the *Dammeh collective*. Feminist cooperatives were calling for meetings to discuss how to frame the slogans, the chants, how to strategize over roadblocks and how to provide protection to the LGBTQ community. Protection emerged as an essential topic to the LGBTQ community. Since we felt vulnerable, we wanted to ensure that we are protected. So initially, we joined the protests in buddies. We removed dating apps that can pose a threat to our security. We joined initiatives that were seeking to create safe spaces for the queer and for vulnerable communities. At some point, some pro-LGBTQ tents were removed from downtown, yet our meetings moved to other sites.

Indeed, for LGBTQ activists, achieving public visibility as protest participants and organizers soon evolved into a subject of contention. Some LGBTQ organizations told us that they avoided public visibility in the 2019 protests such as setting up tents in the fear of making LGBTQ groups more vulnerable. By November, accusations had multiplied that Western actors have been funding the thawra tents. This has made LGBTQ organizations reluctant to provide services in protest spaces. Still, their representatives joined as independent activists.

Helem opted for a more visible role in the protests though it chose not to make decriminalizing homosexuality central to its involvement. At the outset of the protests, it set up a tent in Martyrs' Square. The tent acted as a venue for providing services, assistance and legal protection to members from the LGBTQ community and vulnerable groups. Political parties' supporters commonly framed in the media as 'militia thugs' destroyed the tent a week later. Helem's rainbow-coloured banner *Kilna Yaani Kilna* ('All of Us Means All of Us') was torn to the ground. Notwithstanding this, Helem continued to bolster LGBTQ activism. On 22 November, Lebanon's Independence Day, Helem called for a march that equates the country's independence with emancipation from the patriarchal, racist and homophobic regime.

Today we go down to the streets to celebrate our independence.
Our independence from patriarchy and racism.
Our independence from all that coerces our voices and bodies.
Our independence from the regime. (Helem 2019a)

As days passed by, Helem's involvement became subtler. Towards the end of December, protest policing got more invasive and security forces started arresting protesters, regardless of whether or not they were LGBTQ activists. By mid-January 2020, state repression escalated. The riot police and security forces started forcefully dispersing both confrontational and more peaceful protests. Angered by capital controls and limitations on dollar withdrawals, protesters started attacking banks and high-end shops in Beirut with rocks and metal poles. During the day, they attempted to bar access to state institutions such as the parliament. In one of the protests that took place on 15 January, security forces responded by attacking protesters with disproportionate force, including tear gas and water cannons, causing more than five hundred injuries in two days. Since then, Helem shied away from launching open calls for LGBTQ mobilization.

LGBTQ activism throughout the protests took on varied dimensions making it impossible to reduce contention within a binary debate of visibility versus invisibility. Indeed, as various activists told us, at the heart of LGBTQ activism in the 2019 uprising lies a continuum of shades varying between direct and more concealed exposure. LGBTQ activists were emboldened enough to leave lasting 'physical marks' on the city walls reminding people that the uprising had a strong focus on their rights. At the same time, the machinery of LGBTQ contention such as offices and protest tents remained 'semi-secret'.[29] It is within this spectrum of (in)visible spaces that queer activists have negotiated their protest presence. It emerges from our interviews that three broad tactical repertoires have characterized their forms of organizing: claiming intersectionality, debunking homophobic counter-narratives and 'beautifying' the LGBTQ community through linguistic activism. Each of these repertoires unfolds in a complex terrain of divisions and contradictions.

Crafting intersectional solidarities

As noted earlier, central to the 2019 protests are the intersectional rhetorical frames that exposed the many vices of Lebanon's political regime. A wander by night in Beirut after the protests had started quickly becoming a luring invitation to read the city as a patchwork of slogans. On most of the protest tents activists had juxtaposed manifold slogans written in various colours such as blue, red and yellow: 'No to Political Parties and to Sectarianism', 'No to Homophobia', 'This Is a Feminist Revolution' and 'Domestic Migrants' Rights'. In such spaces, LGBTQ activists claimed intersectionality as a frame that could consolidate rather than weaken their plight. Within days of the start of the protests, pro-LGBTQ slogans reflecting the intersectionality of demands were sprayed onto the protest tents and the city walls. Here and there, meandering through the narrow and larger streets of Beirut, we could see a proliferation of pro-LGBTQ slogans enmeshed in an intersectional framing: 'Queers for Marx', 'LGBTQ Rights', 'Love Wins', 'Feminism', 'Lesbians against Homophobia,' 'A Revolution for Workers' Rights … Homosexuals … for Lebanese Transgenders' and 'Black Poor Black Gay Trans' (Bustanji 2019; Qiblawi, Wedeman and Balkiz 2019). The list goes on. At the heart of Beirut, in the downtown area, graffiti appeared: 'LGBTQ Rights', 'Abolish Article 534', 'Intersex Rights', 'I Am Tired of Being in the Closet' are intertwined within broader frames celebrating the 17 October uprising and denouncing political corruption (Younes and Bailly 2020). In *Megaphone*, a media source created during the thawra, activist Nidal Ayoub explains how these pro-LGBTQ slogans are nested within a wider intersectional project:

> Every day, my group and I write new slogans. We always try to reflect on the things that matter to us, including trying to respond to hate speech against racism, domestic workers, and homosexuality. (Obeid 2019)

Assaad, a researcher managing A Project on LGBTQ labelling words, explains to us that inserting LGBTQ rights within a broader intersectional frame helped to achieve a dual objective. It enabled queer activists to immerse their narratives within the wider wave of popular contention. But it also provided a protective space. Collating LGBTQ grievances to home-grown claims, he argues, was a tactical strategy to persuade broader audiences of 'the LGBTQ local struggle'.

> By joining the crowds and identifying with the protests' multiple framings, LGBTQ activists wanted to convey the message that Lebanon's queer community existed outside external forces. It has its local history and is deeply interconnected with local struggles.[30]

In this thawra, he adds, LGBTQ activists wanted at all costs to avoid any suspected affiliation with Western NGOs. At the same time, he clarifies that intersectionality is a protective shield:

> Complex identities and queerness are interwoven in Lebanon's protest spaces. Many LGBTQ activists were reluctant to designate the thawra as an explicitly queer revolution. This would bring activists into trouble. They already suffer from so many vulnerabilities. They have problems finding jobs. They have most to lose if they radicalized and appropriated protest techniques. Intersectionality arises here as a protective space.[31]

Hadi Damian, the organizer of Beirut Pride, explained that inserting 'gay rights' in the broader demands of the 2019 thawra provided an umbrella for several goals. This time, LGBTQ activists have not specifically called for revoking Article 534 but they wanted to claim their right to have intimate sexual lives and to combat wider anti-LGBTQ sentiments (Harb 2019).

'Don't be afraid to respond and fight back'

As more LGBTQ graffiti proliferated, the more hostility and backlash they ignited. Indeed, as Assaad, the curator of the LGBTQ semantics project, underlines, the thawra was no easy playing field. LGBTQ visibility in the protests as well as pro-LGBTQ graffiti started soon enough to spur animosities. Some local journalists rushed to denigrate the current thawra as a 'sodomy revolution' (*thawrat al louwat*) and claimed that the goal of some protesters was to phase out sectarianism so that they could pass laws supporting homosexuality. Local TV producer Charbel Khalil warned Lebanon:

> If this revolution is successful, and they implement non-sectarian laws, they'll pass laws related to their homosexuality. We know what they think. Your homosexualities and your demons will not pass. (Nadeem 2019)

Reacting to such attacks, Helem launched an online campaign with the motto that 'homosexuality is not an offence'. On 28 October, it released a Facebook post that stressed the LGBTQ community's 'right to take to the streets'. The post explicitly called on pro-LGBTQ advocates to stand against harassment and homophobia (Helem 2019b).

> To all our followers and believers, if you hear hateful, homophobic, or transphobic things against the LGBT community during the protests, don't be afraid to respond and fight back. We're a part of the protest and we have the right to take to the streets too. Homosexuality is not an offense.

In the light of the post, LGBTQ activists and pro-LGBTQ advocates felt emboldened to shout out and spray slogans such as 'homosexuality is not an insult' and 'gays for the revolution'. The slogan 'LGBTQ rights' sprayed on the wall of the Maronite Saint George Church at the heart of Beirut led to an uproar. In a TV talk show, decrying the so-called 'sodomy revolution' and the presence of LGBTQ slogans in religious places, one journalist called on the LGBTQ community to erect temples for themselves somewhere far away 'in the sea' (Rebellious Lebanon 2019; Bustanji 2019). By February 2020, even though the protests had contracted, the slogan on the church continued to ignite heated debates. In one of the coffee shops that hosted revolutionary talks, one activist tells us that the slogan drawn on the façade of a religious institution divided various protesters. It is true that religious institutions are key resisters of same-sex relations. Yet, should the revolutionaries protest against religion at this stage?[32]

Reshaping popular protest slogans

In this context in which LGBTQ frames were increasingly contested, organizing in the thawra started taking more complex forms. For LGBTQ activists, it meant finding creative ways to assert their presence in a not so well-marked and orderly arena. It soon became clear however that debunking narratives that tarnished their involvement was not the only challenge. Organizing in an intersectional space where protagonists brought in diverse framings is a minefield. A key dilemma consisted in what stance LGBTQ individuals are to adopt vis-à-vis popular slogans and chants that were disdainful of their plight. Throughout the uprising, protesters started using anti-gay slurs such as 'louti' (sodomizer or faggot) or sexual profanities to defame some politicians.

In response, protesters started singing chants such as 'faggot is not an insult' to counter the prevalent 'normalized oppression of queer and trans people' (Younes and Bailly 2020). Some LGBTQ activists took on the task of rewriting protest slogans and chants that contained anti-LGBTQ and gender-biased rhetoric. As Munir tells us:

> We changed and rewrote many slogans. We changed their rhythm. We sought to alter chants that targeted in pejorative manner sexual parts of the body such as the vagina. Our aim was to beautify the community: my vagina is no place for insults.[33]

In the women's marches, queer and feminist groups started challenging masculine and patriarchal generics as well as disrupting mainstream slogans. Assaad however ponders such strategies more critically. He argues that changing rhetorical frames is not only an attempt at 'beautifying the community' or reclaiming power. Rather, it is a critical moment of 'of self-assessment'.[34] Seeing that protesters draw on such slurs as a tool of political contention is certainly a moment of reckoning.

In a podcast, feminist and queer activist and writer Nadine Mouawad (2019) talks about the 'long list of compromises' that activists had to undergo during the thawra. Language is one of them. Semantics emerged as powerful revolutionary platforms. At the same time, they brought about quandaries. By distancing themselves from predominant protest chants, feminist and queer activists could open cracks within the protest's trajectory and alienate themselves. In such times, she says, 'people check each other out', eager to determine who is on their side and who is not.

It is in that vein that LGBTQ linguistic activism in the protests evolved into a double-edged sword. It brought many underlying questions at the heart of the struggle of queer Lebanese to the fore: At what stage of the protest cycle can LGBTQ activists bring in their specific claims and frames? How do they validate their importance amid multiple framing contests? And at what stage do they carve their own discursive path and assert discursively that the revolution is also about them? (see Figure 7.6).

Figure 7.6 LGBTQ graffiti during the 2019 protests
Source: Photo credit – John Nagle.

Indeed, though the LGBTQ community, as Helem argues, has 'asserted its presence throughout the revolution' (Helem 2020d), the protests epitomized at the same time its vulnerability, and reflected its long-winded struggle and organizational dilemmas. As previous chapters have shown, this struggle is shaped by complex intersections between structures of power and agency. Following scholars such as Ghassan Moussawi (2015), Sa'ed Atshan (2020) and Sabiha Allouche (2015), the contentious performances and imaginaries of feminist and queer activists in politically charged contexts such as Lebanon or Palestine cannot be analysed in isolation from local geopolitical struggles and configurations of oppression. At the same time, social movement theory reminds us that the 'fate' of activists is equally 'shaped by their own actions' (McAdam, McCarthy and Zald 2008). So, in a rather constrictive setting, what agency can queer Lebanese claim on the protest scene? And how is their agency transformed by the state's ensemble of geopolitical and security practices and by other contentious imaginaries?

Dilemmas inhabiting LGBTQ protest spaces

At the start of the 2019 thawra, Munir radiated with optimism. He spoke of the LGBTQ presence in the protests as a game changer. He related to us how he discovered a sense of agency he thought he never had, and how he spent his days connecting with activists, attending workshops and strategizing for the next protest. Three months later, as soon as he entered the coffee shop where we had an appointment, we noticed that the tone of his voice had changed, and that his facial expressions evoked sadness. He went on to describe to us how violent clashes between security forces and protesters left him and his friends feeling particularly vulnerable.

> Being a rebel, being a revolutionary, being LGBTQ ... these are all framings that compound our vulnerability. Protests started stoking up fears of persecution. Individuals who practice their gender expression more visibly started hesitating whether to join the protests. ... At the same time, tents facilitating our mobilization had closed. The Helem and feminist tents were burned down. Some organizations advised us not to join protests that could turn violent.[35]

By mid-January, as previously stated, the anatomy of Lebanon's thawra changed. Lebanon's riot police and security forces sought to forcefully disperse both confrontational and more peaceful protests. . The Lawyers' Committee for the Defense of Protesters and human rights organizations hurried to denounce the arrest of activists and the 'excessive violence' used to disperse protesters (Human Rights Watch 2020). In the eyes of an LGBTQ individual, comments Munir, such moments conjure up deep-seated memories of fear that the Lebanese state's security practices summons in one's psyche.

Securitization

The Lebanese state may not be a 'deep state' as other Arab autocracies. Yet, in the last decade, democracy and press freedoms barometers such as the Freedom House Index and the Reporters without Borders (RSF) have noted a backlash in political, civil and media liberties in Lebanon (Freedom House 2020; Reporters Sans Frontières 2020). In the shadow of Syria's civil war, Lebanese governments have prioritized security and geopolitical concerns, relegating citizen demands to 'low politics' (Fakhoury 2019). Since 2011, various governments drew on insecurity spillovers from Syria such as Islamist militants' incursions across Lebanon's northern borders as pretexts to postpone elections and quell protests. In the name of political stability and public order, security forces have recurrently arrested protesters and activists who criticized the ruling elite. During the Youstink protests, the riot police arrested more than forty-six organizers of the movement in one day (Geha 2018). The sectarian political elite branded protesters as dissident 'traitors' co-opted by international agents and paid by embassies (Geha 2020).

Within this climate, the LGBTQ predicament has become nested within a wider register of securitization through which the Lebanese state has cracked down on journalists, activists, refugees and domestic migrants, and branded the uprising as externally fomented and destabilizing to national peace. In 2018, as noted earlier, authorities suspended Beirut Pride and detained its organizer under the pretext of fostering amoral behaviour. That year, security forces also disbanded Nedwa, a major LGBTQ regional conference, barring some participants who attended from visiting Lebanon for the next fifteen years.

In the 2019 thawra, some political parties and leaders alleged that the protest tents were externally funded, making LGBTQ organizations wary to enter the fray. As soon as protest policing became more aggressive and homophobic insults uttered by the establishment started targeting gay individuals (Medina and Chehayeb 2020; CrimethInc. 2019; UN Women 2019), LGBTQ activists began to ponder the risks of visibility. Some opted for strategizing in peripheral places, behind closed doors or through convening intellectual activities such as storytelling nights. In the wake of severe confrontation between the riot police and protesters, the twitter feed of some of the leading LGBTQ activists shifted from expressing slogans of change to showcasing incidents of violence and repression.[36]

LGBTQ rights at the bottom of the policy ladder

Now it is not the time. Now we are not ready.[37]

Security practices such as clamping down on protests and restricting spaces for activism are not the only factors that have affected LGBTQ dynamics of mobilization in the 2019 protests. Other subtle yet insidious state strategies weigh in. In the context of the post-2011 Arab upheavals and their regional ramifications, the political elite have recurrently portrayed Lebanon as a state under massive security and geopolitical strains. Through 'enunciating' such 'utterances' (Balzacq

2005), they have downgraded issues at the heart of the gender and the LGBTQ struggle to the bottom of the policy ladder. In the light of Lebanon's precarious security, policymakers have framed personal-status law reforms that could have an impact on weakening the 'sextarian system' such as the passing of the Civil Marriage Law or women passing their citizenship to their children as untimely.

These discourses have not remained as purely rhetorical utterances. In practice, they have led to tensions in policy prioritization, and have contributed to relegating calls for legal reforms relevant to the LGBTQ community to the margins. The recurrent 'speech act' that the timing for discussing gender and LGBTQ issues has not yet come has had far-reaching consequences, haunting even protest spaces.

Eliding LGBTQ issues at the highest policy level creates strategic dilemmas for actors planning to defy the establishment, and for LGBTQ activists seeking to deploy contentious framings in protests. According to Krystel, this affects the extent to which new political platforms such as *Kallouna Watani* or *Beirut Madinati* can push for LGBTQ rights in the open, and the extent to which they can prioritize thorny issues such as gay marriage or violence against transsexuals.

In the wake of the Youstink protests, independent candidates strategizing for the legislative polls were confronted with several strategic dilemmas. Key concerns were how to position themselves towards governing elite cartels on the one hand, and how to appeal to broader audiences on the other. One issue of contention revolved around whether it would be more strategic to strike alliances with traditional political parties on electoral lists to access power and then 'change things'. Another issue was whether endorsing issues perceived as 'radical' could alienate traditional voters. Such electoral dilemmas are not unique to Lebanon. As elections draw nearer, candidates face trade-offs as to how to optimize their vote share and position themselves towards their divided constituencies. Such dilemmas however become more pronounced in deeply divided societies in which protagonists face the trade-off of preserving existing ethnosectarian configurations or rocking the boat.

The LGBTQ issue conjured various quandaries for independent platforms aspiring for electoral victory. First, amid the multiple failings of the Lebanese state, it prompted them to reflect on the extent to which they ought to highlight the urgency of LGBTQ-related issues. One candidate of the *Kallouna Watani* list explains the difficulties of prioritizing LGBTQ issues. Though many candidates have endorsed the decriminalization of homosexuality, she argues, the issue is rarely prominent in public spheres (Qiblawi 2018).

> I don't think it's that important of a national issue to the majority. The main issue that we are all suffering from is the lack of clean water in our homes, the lack of a functioning electrical system, the lack of economic equity.

As noted, another dilemma lies in the extent to which prioritizing the LGBTQ issue could impact the electoral victory of independent candidates. Though *Kallouna Watani* and *Beirut Madinadi* adopted pro-LGBTQ rights in their electoral campaigns, some of our interviewees concurred that they have neither laid a fully-fledged road map for achieving such rights, nor have they included LGBTQ candidates in their electoral lists. By talking about LGBTQ individuals rather than including them, such platforms, even if they are anti-sectarian, fail to represent all struggles and classes of LGBTQ communities.

Such pre-electoral dilemmas create many cracks. The argument that once contenders are able to access power they would inevitably introduce the LGBTQ debate at the heart of the legislature does not resonate well with all LGBTQ activists, and particularly with those who think that half-hearted approaches do not dignify their struggle. Krystel clarifies such dilemmas and their repercussions on the LGBTQ scene of activism:

> Supposedly, independent coalitions have claimed inclusivity in representing people's demands before the 2018 elections. But who are the people they are representing? Who is shaping the agenda and who is claiming representativeness? Do independent candidates truly represent the totality of LGBTQ grievances in their campaigns? Compromising with the regime or thrusting the sectarian wall arises here as a core dilemma.[38]

Such intra-organizational struggles within Lebanon's public and civic spheres have consequences beyond the electoral sphere and straight into the protest space. They affect the extent to which LGBTQ activists can claim their own organizational field in a popular protest movement. In such a setting, LGBTQ activists find it extremely hard to introduce thorny topics perceived as 'dissident' such as gay marriage, violence against transpersons or the abolition of Law 534 in intersectional protest movements. This leaves them in a state of organizational limbo in which they ponder whether to ally with the larger crowds or set themselves apart by highlighting their own struggles.

Claiming agency in a multisited protest field

Against this background of 'security utterances' and policy dilemmas, appropriating a queer protest space is no straightforward affair. As Nadine Mouawad (2019) illustrates, deciding in a protest when to bring in certain social issues, when to opt for 'sector-related mobilization' and how to relate to other movement actors is extremely challenging. Here, Lebanon's sectarian framework, which acts as a regulatory power pervading policy, civic and public spheres, has additional dilemmas for LGBTQ activists. It not only constricts their engagement but also makes it increasingly difficult to carve their own space. Ghiwa Sayeh perceives the act of carving a protest space as a much-needed moment of 'embodiment' through which queer activists can graft their imaginaries, histories and sexualities onto the protest site.[39]

As we explored in previous chapters, the politics of sectarianism is a multisited field of power that impinges on institutions, everyday politics, sexual and intimate lives. In this context, the intimate lives and futures of the queer community are managed by sectarian policies, recurrent institutional failings and geopolitical discourses. Power outages, unemployment, capital controls and crumbling infrastructures exacerbate the community's vulnerability.

In these multisited loci of power, what place can queer activism carve in popular protests? And is queer activism at the core or at the edge of a popular wave of contention? Within this maze, LGBTQ activists encounter a twofold challenge. They are uncertain as to whether highlighting their specific claims or calling for the fall of the regime and for the improvement of state services serves their plight better. They also realize that they must tread carefully in a protest field in which collective actors have a myriad of goals defined around varying identity, economic, ideological and class cleavages.

As noted, the 2019 protests encompassed various movement actors that had different conceptions of what anti-sectarianism entails. Even though protests created a platform where cross-cutting identities converged around forms of injustice, expressions of popular outrage varied enormously across regions. Protests which embraced the LGBTQ cause were mostly predominant in urban areas. LGBTQ graffiti proliferated mostly in Beirut. Rarely did slogans make it to protest sites in rural Lebanon or peripheral cities such as Nabatieh, Tripoli, Sidon or Akkar in which popular outrage was primarily focused on dire socio-economic conditions. In certain protest sites, though gender was at the core of the revolution, sexual identities and dissidence were not. In Nabatiyeh, women criticized the Jaafari courts for undermining their inheritance rights yet did not embrace the queer cause.

'Breaking the wall': Cracks emerge

In such a polycentric field of contention, LGBTQ activists are uncertain as to how best to contextualize their narrative in such a way so as to address the implications of political sectarianism for their legal rights, the embodiment of their sexuality and for social justice in general.

Some activists we interviewed have unpacked at length the dilemma of 'going' intersectional. Munir argues that 'thinking out slogans to fit in the crowds' is in some instances motivated by the decision not to 'overwhelm the revolution with demands and grievances.'[40] At the same time, once queer activists begin to reflect on ways to 'embody' and 'validate' their presence in the protest field, cracks are bound to emerge not only between LGBTQ activists and other protesters but also within LGBTQ ranks. Queer feminists who called for intersectional and organic organizing did not necessarily subscribe to mainstream visions of political transitions endorsed by other collective actors. Ghiwa Sayegh clarifies the clash in goals and tactics:

> We did not necessarily subscribe to the vision of staging milestones to dismantle the sectarian system in the sense that the government should resign, the president should be next, then early elections should be convened etc. Because this is still a scheme within the sectarian system. Our vision is to chip at the system so that one day it all crumbles. This is our aim. Breaking the wall through

counter-narratives, creating alternative economic systems within communities, sustaining each other as communities without necessarily passing by the bank or cashing our salary from a specific employer. Those were our concerns during the protests.[41]

As protests unfolded, LGBTQ and feminist activists clashed on some protest tactics. Some LGBTQ activists endorsed disruptive techniques such as roadblocks. Nevertheless, others were concerned with the implications of such tactics for LGBTQ safety. The quotidian ways of living the 'thawra' also caused some controversies. Some members of the drag community decided to resume their performance schedules despite ongoing protests. For them, their performances incarnate the politics of the ordinary, in which 'gender bending' exposes a state turned inside out. Other activists decried the mentality of 'business as usual'. Rather, they called for staying on the streets, engaging in confrontational methods of activism such as disrupting the traffic or barring way to certain institutions. Activists who framed themselves as 'queer communists' sought to distance themselves from LGBTQ individuals who were still frequenting elitist venues framed as 'neoliberal'. Within this context, disparities compounded by class and ideological cleavages became more pronounced in the protest scene.[42] Munir describes a plethora of discursive disagreements:

Differences of opinion are multifaceted … are they mainly class-based or ideological? LGBTQ members who are economically disadvantaged have blamed others who are more affluent of being complicit with the system. At the same time, they blamed them for not having leveraged well their privileges. Other schisms have emerged too … schisms between those who advocate same-sex marriage versus those who do not want it because it is institutional. Many argue that it is not about achieving heterosexual rights. These are imperfect too.

When will the Lebanese state 'come out'?[43]

The 2019 thawra strengthened the cross-cutting ties that LGBTQ activists forged with other grassroots actors. But it also left them grappling with a plethora of questions: How to adapt their grievances to a multisided field of contention? How do they transition from the early stages of the protests to a later phase in which they bring in their agenda, and how do they ensure that they will not set themselves apart from the broader trajectory of the uprising? Is their impact measured by their numerical presence, visibility or by broader underlying coalitions that propel them forward?

Such questions are not new. They reflect long-standing struggles within the LGBTQ community in Lebanon. Lara, a feminist activist, related to us how LGBTQ groups have been divided for years over whether to bring in their own specific grievances in protests or to support the abolition of anti-sectarianism without necessarily emphasizing their specific claims. At the heart of this challenge is how to carve their own politics of claims-making and agree on a framing that resonates with broader publics. In the last decade, protests that have restricted themselves to LGBTQ rights have not resonated much with the broader Lebanese public. At the same time, mobilizing within broader anti-sectarian protests has only allowed LGBTQ activists to superficially introduce their own grievances. Intersectional protests highlight solidarities but lead to lumping and diluting demands. In such a protest configuration, LGBTQ activists can rarely opt for more disruptive tactics that reflect their queer imaginaries and dissident bodies. As one LGBTQ artist and activist intimates, highlighting sexual dissidence through daring photos or transgressive narratives in a protest could easily evolve into a trap for LGBTQ activists. This may turn into a polarizing cleavage, giving contenders an excuse to attack the revolution.[44]

As noted at the beginning of the book, we are bound here to reflect on the structural forces that shape LGBTQ collective action. What opportunities exist in a sectarian system in which legislative and policy processes are closed to LGBTQ groups? And are protests an alternative arena for contestation? To what extent can LGBTQ activists scale up contention when the political system is indifferent to their plight?

As many scholars have argued, Lebanon's political system offers ambivalent conditions for LGBTQ activists, and the deceitfully liberal landscape of Beirut is certainly a disconcerting place for their claims-making politics (Moussawi 2020). Henri Myrttinen clarifies this point:

> There is a continuous opening and closing down of spaces for activism … in the history of LGBTQ activism, the ruling elite has selectively used degrees of delegitimization to weaken the LGBTQ community as a collective force.[45]

As the book illustrates, LGBTQ voices have found several 'iconic' occasions to voice contestation. But their politics of contention is governed by the infrastructure of political sectarianism. State's security practices have heavily targeted their activist spaces in crises, upheavals and national emergencies. Also, sectarian institutions have recurrently sidelined their demands. The everyday pathways to precarity that Lebanon's sectarian framework has in store for all its citizens magnifies their vulnerability.

The 2019 protests illustrate this predicament. LGBTQ activists identified a window of opportunity in the thawra that has curated 'alternative solidarities'. They have left 'physical marks' on Beirut's walls. At the same time, once the protest wave contracted by February 2020, activists were confronted with core questions regarding the tangible gains that they have achieved. Their claims have not only paled in the face of Lebanon's harrowing financial crash, but also the machinery of political sectarianism returned, as resilient as ever.

Will Lebanon's sectarian system constitute a durable barrier to their activism, and to what extent can their intersectional ties with wider constituencies propel them forward? Social movement theorists have expressed a variety of opinions on the effects of political contexts for activism. In a closed political environment, available discursive opportunities and coalitions enable challengers to voice their demands. In such a setting, however, challengers rarely extract concessions from the political elite. Though some opportunities for mobilization are available, the political elite will most likely resist their claims and even repress them (Kriesi 2004). Conversely, scholars such as Marshall Ganz (2000), attract attention to actors' 'strategic capacity' to utilize an array of creative techniques to achieve successful mobilization and transcend adverse conditions.

The history of LGBTQ contention in Lebanon reflects a struggle between these two approaches. In Lebanon's sectarian model where the LGBTQ community finds it extremely difficult to engage with political processes, LGBTQ activists have remained 'outside challengers' that have rarely obtained legal and policy concessions. Yet as this chapter has shown, discursive opportunities and intersectional ties abound. This allows LGBTQ groups to take up their demands and connect their struggles to feminist, migrant, marginalized and economically vulnerable groups. Intersectionality however yields disadvantages. In a labyrinth of overlapping narratives, they must make choices that often become 'forks in the road': How to deploy strategically their imaginaries in Lebanon's protests? What forms of protests celebrate best their narratives? When to align their framings with the broader demands, and when to bring in their own 'political projects'? Could intersectional ties propel their struggle forward? Is it more strategic to remain at the margins of protest spaces or (re)claim the protest field? Should they subscribe to normative models of political transitions, negotiate with the ruling elite or remain outside challengers?

According to Lara, the feminist activist we interviewed back in 2016, this situation, far from representing an impasse, offers an opportunity. She clarifies this point:

> Sectarian politics presents huge challenges for LGBTQ and gender activism. One of them is the puzzling question as to whether we should coalesce with the political elite to achieve change or strategize from 'outside the system'. In fact, we can only change the system by disrupting it from afar, from outside. That means avoiding collusion with the ruling elite and calling for the end of political sectarianism in protests and other sites of activism.[46]

Ghiwa Sayegh describes this pathway of activism with particularly powerful words: 'Our vision is to chip at the system so that one day it all crumbles.'

Chapter 8

CONCLUSION: CONTESTING SECTARIANISM

The darkness drops again; but now I know
That twenty centuries of stony sleep
Were vexed to nightmare by a rocking cradle
                              --William Butler Yeats, *The Second Coming*

In August 2019, shortly before Lebanon's October uprising erupted, anonymous activists painted in big red letters graffiti that read 'Let's Go Lesbians' on one of the walls of Tripoli, a city on Lebanon's north coast. The graffiti drew much attention for various reasons. One of them is its location in Tripoli itself. Known formerly for its Mediterranean flair in the 1960s, its souks and its famous pubs on the *El-Mina* Harbour, such as *Le Bateau Ivre*, Lebanon's second largest city barely resembles its glorious heyday. Postwar representations of the city frame it as a fairly 'conservative' and underfunded city characterized by economic hardships and years of governmental neglect (Ismail, Wilson and Cohen-Fournier 2017). Some Westerners visiting Lebanon usually prefer spending time in Tripoli because it is portrayed as a 'more authentic' city where one could learn Arabic away from the multilingual conversations of the busy streets of Beirut that usually start with *Hi, kifak, ca va?*[1]

In the wake of the Syrian civil war, media and international aid agencies took interest in Tripoli as a playground for the Bab-al-Tabbaneh versus Jabal Mohsen[2] conflict as well as a host city for Syrian refugees rather than a site for LGBTQ activism. In 2013, as a result of divided loyalties over Syria's war, clashes broke out between the Bab-Al-Tabbaneh's Sunni community that sided with the Syrian opposition and the Jabal Mohsen's Alawites who are loyal to the Syrian regime (Fakhoury 2014).

Contestation between the factions escalated, and armed skirmishes broke out. What seemed to be at first a conflict drawn around sectarian lines was in reality a complex struggle over authority and order in a city which had to rely on informal providers of services and resources in the presence of a neglectful state. With large-scale displacement from Syria, the city welcomed many displaced Syrians who constitute by now a sizeable community living in extremely challenging urban settings (see Figure 8.1).

Figure 8.1 Tripoli seen from the *Citadel of Raymond de Saint-Gilles*, also known as Qala'at Tarablus
Source: Photo credit – Stu Cook.

During the first months of Lebanon's 2019 protest wave, Tripoli would become the 'bride of the revolution', challenging the myth that Lebanon's iconic protests only happen in Greater Beirut. In its famous Al Nour Square, hundreds of thousands of citizens sang for days and nights, and devised chants and slogans calling for the toppling of the political elite. With the outbreak of the Covid-19 pandemic in 2020, compounded by Lebanon's harrowing financial crash which led to an 85 per cent devaluation of the Lebanese currency by June 2020, the citizens of Tripoli condemned the closure of their shops and businesses. Many directed their wrath against banks and politicians' houses. As the newly appointed prime minister Hassan Diab urged the Lebanese to observe strict rules of confinement, Tripoli's citizens defiantly opened the souks, arguing that 'staying home' is no option when hunger is at the doors. A fortnight into the Covid-19 quarantine, another LGBTQ piece of graffiti appeared in big red letters 'Gay Is Okay' on another street in Tripoli.

Sprayed in glaring red, both pieces of graffiti, according to activists, were much more than simple writings on the wall. Their timing, location and broader symbolism were important. They were basically a call to reimagine life 'on the basis of vulnerability and loss' (Butler 2004). The first graffiti, though precursory to the uprising, was sprayed in a time when grassroots contention had started to simmer, and the second during the Covid-19 quarantine which marked the ebbing of the 2019 protests and the mounting despair of ordinary citizens.

As Lana, a student activist underscored, they invite us to rewrite the history of LGBTQ activism in Lebanon from the margins, integrating geographies and moments that we thought did not matter.[3] Given that the graffiti were produced outside the peak times of Lebanon's 2019 revolutionary episode, they disconfirmed certain accounts that the spread of the LGBTQ graffiti was to be attributed to the encouraging albeit short revolutionary interval. Rather they hinted at an underground politics of resistance that aspires to permeate seemingly remote and peripheral spaces. This politics articulates itself around acts of 'everyday activism' framed as a collection of 'non-deliberate' and 'dispersed' albeit 'contentious practices' that contribute to building momentum (Bayat 2013). Conspicuously visible to the eye in a city that is no usual site for queer activism, the two graffitied walls certainly decentre attention from Greater Beirut as the key playing field for LGBTQ activists. Most importantly, they call for narrating the politics of space through queer eyes.

In postwar Lebanon, spaces, walls and squares are far from being neutral. Rather they are loaded with meaning and imbued with codes that the Lebanese state uses to deploy its power over its territory. With the exhaustion of warring parties in 1989 and the adoption of the so-called Ta'if power-sharing agreement, the green line separating West from East Beirut no longer exists. But it has transmuted into new visible and invisible borderlines structured around central and peripheral urbanities as well as gentrified and rundown districts. As Lina Mounzer (2020) puts it, with the official ending of the war in 1990, 'the old warlords became the new government; private contracts replaced contract killers'. Within this climate, postwar space-making has come to reproduce the sectarian order and decades of internecine conflict (Bou Akar 2018). Party flags, artefacts, monuments, politicians' posters, military and paramilitary signposts are key codes that engender this order. Political elite have consolidated their grip by appropriating access to space and managing urbanities. Through certain reconstruction projects such as remodelling public squares, erecting statues and rebuilding the centre of Beirut and poor suburbs of Beirut, governing powers have shaped city-making and infused their legacy onto space. The building of gentrified downtown Beirut is associated with the legacy of Sunni leader Rafiq Al Hariri and its political party the Sunni Future Movement (see Figure 8.2).

While the rebuilding of the downtown into an area of prime real estate reproduces gentrification, a broader process of urban planning in postwar Beirut plays on fears, differences and paramilitary strategies to organize everyday life via territorial contest for land sales, zoning and planning regulations, and infrastructure projects (Bou Akar 2018). Urban planning has allowed sectarian networks to create ethnically homogeneous, self-contained and exclusive spaces in Beirut, which has the effect of maintaining communal solidarity and thus the localized power of warlords. For example, the rebuilding of Dahieh or the poorer suburbs of Beirut is associated with Hezbollah's reconstruction efforts. In this landscape, public squares have paradoxically epitomized the retreat of public

Figure 8.2 The Mohammad Al-Amin Mosque, a legacy of the Rafiq Al Hariri era, seen from the Egg in downtown Beirut
Source: Photo credit – Roy Chaoul.

and green spaces, signalling instead the advances of sectarian territory. Beirut's Martyrs' square is a case in point. While during periods of imperial control Martyrs' square functioned to discipline dissent, it has evolved since the inception of Greater Lebanon in 1943 into a site for struggle between various forces: France's colonial legacy, sectarian elite cartels, developers and ordinary citizens. In postwar Lebanon, it became heavily associated with the redrawing of downtown Beirut into a gentrified, neoliberal, albeit heavily securitized spatial domain, that ordinary citizens have hardly access to.

From this perspective, each territorial domain discloses the name of its gatekeeper and profit-making power-broker. Asphalting streets, constructing highways and planting trees in public squares are governance strategies that sectarian parties use to control their governable followers and buy their acquiescence in exchange for providing social services and basic infrastructure. In other words, sectarian politics is not only predicated on enforcing laws and policies but also on regulating who has access to a certain space, who benefits from it, who gets to hang and take down a certain poster in that managed space and what political parties shape access to a city and to its political economy. The control over discrete spaces has been achieved through the social cleaning of the undesirable, whether through the erasure of 'unclean' queerspaces (Chapter 3) or via acts of violence carried out by militias against individuals deemed to be involved in same-sex relations or to be holding non-normative gender appearances.

In this landscape, graffiti represents a visual embodiment of dissent, and acquires an extremely powerful function. It certainly merits more attention in understanding the various tactical strategies that LGBTQ activists use to resist political sectarianism. By spraying surfaces, activists seek to occupy, remake and reborder sectarian geographies. Scribbling on walls becomes then an act of reclaiming territory, usually decoded through the lens of sectarian signifiers and frontiers. LGBTQ graffiti in central spaces (such as the outer wall of a central church in Beirut) or more peripheral sites (a walled fence in Tripoli) hold major implications. They are about rereading Lebanon's cartography through alternative signifiers rather than the usual 'sectarian iconographies'.[4] Enmeshed in a richly woven quilt of anti-sectarian messages, they are about crafting new imaginaries and using sexualities as sites of resistance. Graffiti that reads 'Queers for Marx', 'Let's Go Lesbians', 'My Virtuous Sister: Lesbianism Is the Solution', 'No Homophobia No Racism' reclaim access to space through the cartography of gendered bodies, dignified lives and fair economies. They call for reimagining the Lebanese 'walled state' (quoted from Brown 2010) beyond its own sectarian walls (See Figure 8.3).

As this book has explored, the history of Lebanon's LGBTQ activism is first and foremost a project to reimagine the sectarian state and its frontiers. This history has no linear path. It alternates between periods of dormancy as well as tidal waves of contention that defy regularities, sequences and patterns. It is about the artful and tactical crafting of a campaign. It is also about movement building. Yet it is equally about dispersed acts such as sprayed graffiti, social media manifestos and storytelling nights in Beirut's coffee shops. Framing this history in accordance with

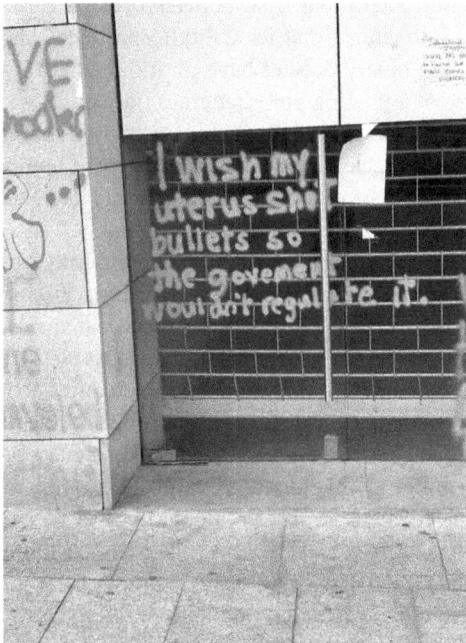

Figure 8.3 Resisting sectarian governance through graffiti
Source: Photo credit – John Nagle.

short-term or longer-term outcomes such as repealing Article 534 or dislodging sectarian leaders may gloss over its many significant moments. This certainly overlooks its deeper subaltern implications and, more specifically, how a queered politics of the ordinary continuously iterates and reiterates alternative scripts in the face of Lebanon's resilient sectarian state. As George Lawson (2019) argues in his book, *Anatomies of the Revolution*, looking at episodes of contention through the lens of success and failure may lead us to become trapped in 'contextless attributes, abstract regularities, ahistorical variables, and timeless properties' (71). This perspective may also disregard the symbolic transformations that activists may generate in terms of new beliefs, values or revolutionary identities. Assigning value to such transformations through a checklist or a set of benchmark criteria is an act that all our protagonists in the book do not embrace. Indeed, as noted in Chapter 7, the history of LGBTQ activism is both about incisive protest events such as the 2019 October uprising and the daily performative acts that build a movement and solidify its roots. It is about the contestation of official politics, shaming politicians, blocking roads, and occupying squares and financial institutions. But it is also about 'artivism', changing daily semantics and building underground coalitional strategies with various movement actors. In yet another perspective, it is about *queering* the international humanitarian order by critically interrogating donors' policy templates and advising them on how best to support locally induced change.

Heated debate has often occurred as to whether the postwar LGBTQ activist scene represents a movement that is sustainable over time, or whether it is prey to such stark internal fractures that its ability to produce change is considerably weakened. Mainstream binary debates have positioned LGBTQ activism either as a movement capable of attracting policy attention or condemned to staying at the margins. Indeed, we are tempted to attribute success to a movement in relation to the tangible successes it is able to reach and the degree of homogeneity it achieves. In recent years, however, various scholars and activists have called for a paradigm shift in understanding queer activism in the small polity. Maya Mikdashi portrays discursive disagreements among the LGBTQ community as part of a healthy deliberative conversation.[5] Ghassan Moussawi unpacks heterogeneity as an indigenous trait of Lebanon's LGBTQ activist scene, often misconstrued through expectations of homogeneity and uniformization (Moussawi 2015). Sabiha Allouche looks at the intricate dynamics of contestation between queer politics and the failings of the Lebanese state (Allouche 2015). Lara Bitar unpacks the politics of pride and visibility as a conceptual mismatch to Lebanon's multiple queer projects (Bitar 2017).

Our book contributes to this paradigm shift. It is ultimately concerned with exploring queer trajectories and political imaginings as sites of contestation and change in their own right. We dedicated these pages to narrating the many tactical strategies that LGBTQ activists draw on to contest sectarianism, be they tacit or explicit, non-deliberate or carefully crafted, discursive or non-discursive. We have shown that their visions of change are plural, and they are not to be locked in a sectarian, post-secular or liberal democracy framework. Their visions often debunk accounts of a gradualist political transition, commonly described as a series of steps ranging from governmental overthrow to the instalment of some kind of democracy. For many, unmaking the politics of sectarianism is much more than launching a transition delineated through electoral sequencing, revamping constitutions and establishing new secular official institutions. Such a political transition traps queer imaginaries in a sectarian/desectarian binary. Rather some propose breaking away from the conception of politics as secular versus sectarian governmentality. They call for a grassroots political project that presupposes the capacity to imagine new grassroots politics and economies outside capitalism and representative legislatures. This vision however coexists with other scripts that aim to contest sectarianism through reforming laws and weakening the grip of the patriarchal order on lived realities. Repealing Article 534 and reforming laws of censorship and privacy are seen as important to emancipate the queer community from the apparatus of control that the sectarian state has bureaucratized. Another camp of activists prefers a politics that serves community empowerment. In the absence of the social state, they see LGBTQ activism as a vital infrastructural power that can work with the community on the ground and provide services allowing individuals to adapt to economic hardships and exclusionary policies.

Equally important to this book has been recasting narratives about LGBTQ activism in Lebanon, typically seen either as a queer feminist versus internationalist gay project, or as a quest towards visibility versus staying underground. The narratives of LGBTQ activists we have collected show the necessity to embrace clashing and heterogeneous conceptions, and to account for the dynamic pathways and alliances of the movement. In the last decade, LGBTQ activists have closely embraced the feminist movement and collaborated with anti-racist, migrant and refugee coalitions. Queer consciousness has largely revolved around contesting the sectarian state's flattening sexualities, as much as it governs private lives and bank accounts. By exposing how politics of sectarianism intrudes into lived realities, queer subjects have been key to discrediting the myth of sectarian power-sharing, long celebrated as a magic panacea for coexistence by Lebanon's elite cartels.

As Lebanon sinks at the time of writing into a vertiginous financial crash, the so-called 'Ta'if republic' may have neared its collapse three decades after the end of the 1975–90 civil war. Ironically enough, even if their reserves and financial conduits have dried up, sectarian political parties have made a strong comeback following the 2019 protests, branding themselves as saviours and providers of wheat, electricity, fuel and jobs. In this scenario, subordinated to a politics of the margins, Lebanon's citizenry views their future options through the lens of Albert Hirschman's dilemma of exit or voice (Hirschman 1970). While some are still taking to the streets, many are contemplating emigration as an exit strategy. As Bernard Hage, a cartoonist, puts it, 'We're like prisoners who do nothing but try to plot our escape' (Azhari 2020). From the margins at the heart of quotidian lives, LGBTQ scripts of contention tell an everyday politics of resistance with resoundingly important lessons for imagining a possible tomorrow. Their action repertoire, which has to a great extent embraced collective organizing and underground tactical strategies, suggest that there are alternative ways to 'chip at the system' until it all falls apart.

Social movement scholars, students and writers may unlock new perspectives and findings by embracing Lebanon's queer activism as a subaltern yet continuous project that 'chips at' sectarian statecraft from below. This includes looking at precursory, underlying and dormant periods of activism rather than concentrating on salient revolutionary episodes and their outcomes. This also includes looking at queer imaginaries as an underground dynamic that interrogates deep-seated disparities and state failings ranging from power outages to foreign policies. Additionally, it is about understanding how queerness coalesces with transnational anti-racism, refugeeness and migranthood to contest sectarianism.

Acknowledging diverse pathways and conceptions of LGBTQ activism(s) allows us to let go of prescriptive approaches to understanding the 'Queer Orient'. Often these approaches, framed as 'outer-queer-(y)ing' privilege an analysis of the 'Queer Orient' in accordance with a set of expectations tainted by Western experiences (Allouche 2020). For instance, focusing on queer visibility may eclipse the heterogeneity of tactics and the manifold expressions of dissent. Indeed, approaching the terrain of queer activism in Lebanon with such expectations is like setting oneself up for finding a 'cluster of absences,'[6] a trap that many analysts end up falling into when looking at the Middle East.

Beyond questions on navigating the 'Queer Orient' (Allouche 2020), this book set out to approach LGBTQ activism as a new base for political analysis and practice in Lebanon. As Lisa Anderson (2006) reminds us, to understand actors leading change, it is essential to 'search where the light shines' rather than bring in prior assumptions and preoccupations that neglect the existing forces at play. Analysing Lebanese politics suffers to some extent from such biases. In the rich literature on Lebanon, there is an undeniable tendency to understand postwar processes predominantly through the lens of classical geopolitics such as Sunni-Shia cleavages, US-Iran polarities and Syrian versus anti-Syrian allegiances, relegating down the order the imaginaries that groups such as the queer community hold for reimagining citizenship and transnational alliances.

Running concurrent to this, Lebanon's policy workshops and public talks subsume anti-sectarian forces under classical actors such as trade unions, civil society organizations or secular political parties. Rarely are LGBTQ actors integrated in such analyses as challengers of sectarianism as well as policy and norm shapers. Their actions remain peripheral to impactful policy and academic conversations.

Capturing the manifold tactics of LGBTQ dissent allows for an elastic understanding of the anti-sectarian forces that have struggled to change Lebanon's political system. Queer political narratives offer a fascinating avenue to critique and enrich the dominant epistemology used to understand Lebanese politics. Often, dominant academic and policy analyses remain replete with references to official institutions, political elite, Islamist groups and armed non-state actors. Offering an LGBTQ geopolitical narrative unravels how the system's discriminatory practices cut across class, gender, sect and citizenship status. Activists' conceptions of dissidence as multisited present new opportunities for understanding how political change can mature as an everyday project *from margin to centre*.

In 2016, after a two-year hiatus, the Lebanese parliament elected former military chief and warlord Michel Aoun as new president of the Republic. That year saw the government adopt a localization approach towards the Sustainable Development Goals (SDGS) which, among many objectives, sets out to leave no one behind including populations on the basis of their sexual orientation or gender identity and expression (SOGIE). Ironically, the last few years saw increased crackdowns on LGBTQ activists willing to engage in political change. From this viewpoint, this book is also a critical inquiry into how the Lebanese state has consolidated its sectarian governance imaginary by seeking to discipline queer activism. By casting them into a state of continuous precarity and blocking their attempts to reach sexual freedom, the state reifies *sectarianism* as a founding myth for its survival.

Today, however, queer activists have made strides, and this founding myth has lost its grip. As they rebel against the defunct institutions of the postwar sectarian state, and some of its restrictive laws that are relics of colonial periods, they brood on what path to take next, and what uncharted journey they will travel. Next is harnessing the teaching potential of the 2019 October uprising, and learning how to *queer* Lebanon's revolutionary episodes, that have so far been fated to ebb as resilient elite cartels have staged a so-called indispensable comeback. Dilemmas await, however. Learning how to live with backlash and vulnerability in its various economic and social forms; emancipating themselves from donors' imperatives; carving their own protest space may seem almost like Sisyphean tasks. Still, right now more than ever, movement building requires stepping into the creative unknown that queer utopia calls for.

NOTES

Chapter 1

1 The 'kafala' system is where the legal residency of workers is tied to their contract with their employer. Kafala migrants are typically domestic workers employed in private households. Lebanon is home to an estimated 250,000 kafala workers. Kafala is identified for permitting abuses on migrants sponsored under the system, including employers forcing them to work excessive hours, denying them rest days and holidays, confiscating their passports, and restricting their freedom of movement.
2 Interview, Beirut, November 2017.
3 Interview, Beirut, 21 April 2020.
4 Interview, Beirut, October 2019.
5 For a broader critique of intersectionality in research and practice, see Nash (2008).
6 In some specific cases, most notably in Northern Ireland, LGBTQ rights have become embroiled in a culture war within power-sharing (see Hayes and Nagle 2016).
7 Interview, Beirut, July 2014.
8 Interview, Beirut, November 2017.
9 Notable examples of such behaviour include Brunei's decision to introduce the punishment of death by stoning for homosexuality and Russia's infamous 'gay propaganda law', which criminalizes any activity deemed as promoting homosexuality, including outlawing pride parades and even proscribing the rainbow flag (see Encarnación 2016; Nuñez-Mietz 2019).
10 Interview, Beirut, November 2017.
11 Interview, Beirut, September 2019.
12 Interview, Beirut, September 2019.
13 Interview, Beirut, November 2017.
14 Interview, Beirut, April 2020.

Chapter 2

1 Interview, Beirut, June 2014.
2 The French Mandate was a mandate given to France by the League of Nations in 1920 to exercise administrative control over Lebanon and Syria. The purported objective of the mandate was for France to provide stewardship over Lebanon until its peoples were ready, in some undefinable point in the future, to have independence. However, rather than work towards this aim, France used the mandate as a form of de facto colonial control.
3 Parliamentary quotas are operationalized by the state's electoral law which up until the 2018 election divided Lebanon into twenty-six electoral Qada (districts), wherein a quota of seats is reserved in each district for specific sects based on what the Ministry of Interior estimates to be the sectarian demography.

4 Interview, Beirut, November 2017.
5 The fact that the negotiations for Ta'if were held in Saudi Arabia, noted for its oppressive policies for women, signalled that Lebanon's postwar political dispensations had little to offer women.
6 Interview, Beirut, September 2019.
7 Indeed, it is important to add a brief caveat to note the relationship between colonialism and the legacy of homophobia. In 1885 the British government introduced new penal codes that punished all homosexual behaviour in its colonies. Of the more than seventy countries that criminalize homosexual acts today, over half are former British colonies. France introduced similar laws around the same time. After independence, only Jordan and Bahrain did away with such penalties.
8 Interview, Beirut, June 2015.
9 Interview, Beirut, September 2019.
10 Interview, Beirut, October 2017.
11 Al-Nusra Front is a Syrian 'jihadist' group with reported links to al-Qaeda.
12 Interview, Beirut, September 2019.
13 Interview, Beirut, June 2015.
14 Interview, Beirut, June 2015.
15 Interview, Beirut, July 2014.
16 Interview, Beirut, October 2017.
17 Issa Makhlouf (1988: 113), e.g., notes that during the civil war it was not uncommon for the bodies of murdered males to show sexual violence and desecration, including instances in which 'several male cadavers were discovered with their sex cut off and sometimes pushed into their mouths; the simulation of fellatio, generally repressed by morality, is very revealing as a rejection of moral codes'.
18 Some notable examples of 'za'im' – former warlords converted into sectarian political leaders – include Samir Geagea, Walid Joumblatt, Nabih Berri and Michel Aoun.
19 Interview, Beirut, September 2019.
20 Interview, Beirut, June 2015.

Chapter 3

1 Interview, Beirut, October 2017.
2 Interview, Beirut, October 2017.
3 Interview, Beirut, October 2017.
4 Interview, Beirut, October 2017.
5 Interview, Beirut, June 2015.
6 Interview, Beirut, June 2015.
7 This nascent activism was given increasing urgency in the context of what appeared to be a growing violent crackdown against LGBTQ individuals across the MENA region, evident in the infamous 2001 Queen Boat incident in Cairo.
8 Interview, Beirut, June 2015.
9 The lasting legacy of the Cedar Revolution was not only that it led to the removal of Syrian rule from Lebanon, but it also revealed a new frighteningly violent fracture in postwar Lebanese politics. In essence, the cleavage featured two camps – March 14 Alliance and March 8 Alliance – with the former demanding Lebanon's independence from Syrian control and the latter taking a pro-Syrian stance. At a broader level, the

two factions are distinguished through being supported and funded by Saudi Arabia and Iran, respectively. This reflects the degree to which Lebanese politics is deeply penetrated by Saudi Arabia and Iran and the extent to which Lebanon provides a key terrain for the ongoing proxy conflict in the Middle East, caught between Saudi and Iranian geopolitics (see Knio 2005). Notably, the March 14 Alliance and March 8 Alliances have increasingly come under strain and are no longer the key political cleavage in Lebanon.

10 Interview, Beirut, June 2015.
11 Interview, Beirut, November 2017.
12 Interview, Beirut, June 2015.
13 Interview, Beirut, October 2017.
14 The International Day against Homophobia.
15 Interview, Beirut, June 2015.
16 Interview, Beirut, September 2019.
17 Interview, Beirut, September 2019.
18 Interview, Beirut, September 2019.
19 Interview, Beirut, July 2014.
20 Interview, Beirut, June 2015.
21 Interview, Beirut, June 2015.
22 Interview, Beirut, June 2015.
23 Interview, Beirut, July 2014.
24 Interview, Beirut, June 2015.
25 Interview, Beirut, June 2015.
26 Interview, Beirut, June 2015.
27 Interview, Beirut, October 2019.
28 Interview, Beirut, June 2015.
29 Interview, Beirut, June 2015.
30 Interview, Beirut, June 2015.
31 Interview, Beirut, June 2015.
32 Interview, Beirut, June 2015.
33 Interview, Beirut, July 2014.
34 Interview, Beirut, November 2017.
35 Interview, Beirut, July 2014.
36 Interview, Beirut, July 2014.
37 Interview, Beirut, October 2017.
38 Interview, Beirut, July 2014.
39 Interview, Beirut, October 2017.
40 Interview, Beirut, September 2019.
41 Interview, Beirut, July 2014.
42 Interview, Beirut, October 2017.

Chapter 4

1 Interview, Beirut, September 2019.
2 These include Article 523: practicing and facilitating prostitution; Article 526: luring the public into acts of depravity; Article 527: relying on the prostitution of others;

Articles 531 and 532: infringing public morals and ethics; and Article 533: trading indecent material (see Human Rights Watch 2019).

3   Interview, Beirut, September 2019.
4   Interview, Beirut, September 2019.
5   Interview, Beirut, June 2015.
6   Interview, Beirut, September 2019.
7   This information was given to us by a Lebanese legal professional and political advisor.
8   For example, in recent years Lebanon's parliament has sought to repeal the Domestic Violence Bill (2014), which has provisions for women's rights and safety.
9   Interview, Beirut, June 2015.
10 Interview, Beirut, June 2015.
11 Interview, Beirut, September 2019.
12 Interview, Beirut, September 2019.
13 Interview, Beirut, September 2019.
14 Interview, Beirut, June 2015.
15 Interview, Beirut, June 2015.
16 Interview, Beirut, October 2017.
17 Interview, Beirut, October 2017.
18 Interview, Beirut, June 2015.
19 Interview, Beirut, July 2014.
20 Interview, Beirut, June 2015.
21 Interview, Beirut, October 2017.
22 Interview, Beirut, November 2017.
23 Interview, Beirut, November 2017.
24 Interview, Beirut, November 2017.
25 Interview, Beirut, June 2015.
26 Interview, Beirut, September 2019.
27 Interview, Beirut, September 2019.

Chapter 5

1   See Milk (2013).
2   Interview, Beirut, June 2015.
3   Interview, Beirut, July 2014.
4   Interview, Beirut, October 2017.
5   Interview, Beirut, June 2015.
6   Interview, Beirut, July 2014.
7   Interview, Beirut, September 2019.
8   Interview, Beirut, July 2014.
9   Interview, Beirut, June 2015.
10 Interview, Beirut, June 2015.
11 Interview, Beirut, June 2015.
12 Interview, Beirut, 19 June 2020.
13 Interview with activist, Beirut, 4 February 2020.
14 Interview, Beirut, October 2017.
15 Interview with activist, Beirut, 4 February 2020.

16 Adapted from HFA, Strategic Report for the Year 2020 and based on two interviews with HFA artist, 4 February 2020 and 21 March 2020, Beirut.
17 Interview with Ghiwa Sayegh, Beirut, 21 April 2020.
18 Interview with Ghiwa Sayegh, Beirut, 21 April 2020.
19 Interview with Ghiwa Sayegh, Beirut, 21 April 2020.
20 MOSAIC stands for the MENA Organization for Services Advocacy Integration and Capacity Building. While its projects may branch out to LGBIQ communities in the Middle East and North Africa, more than 90 per cent of its projects are based in Lebanon. See https://www.mosaicmena.org.
21 Interview with Charbel Maydaa, executive director of MOSAIC, 19 June 2020.
22 Interview with former MOSAIC employee, 10 February 2020.
23 Interview, Beirut, October 2017.
24 Authors' conversation with researchers at Shabaket el Meem, Beirut, 5 February 2020.
25 Interview with LebMASH activist, 21 February 2020.
26 The Beijing Declaration and Platform for Action was an action plan agreed in 1995 to promote gender equality and the empowerment of all women.
27 Adapted from Sharp (2011).

Chapter 6

1 Interview, Beirut, September 2019.
2 The post has been vacant since November 2017.
3 Interview, Beirut, October 2017.
4 Interview, Beirut, September 2019.
5 Interview, Beirut, October 2017.
6 Interview, Beirut, September 2019.
7 Interview, Beirut, September 2019.
8 Interview, Beirut, September 2019.
9 Interview, Beirut, September 2019.
10 Interview, Beirut, September 2019.
11 Interview, Beirut, September 2019.
12 Interview, Beirut, September 2019.
13 Interview, Beirut, September 2019.
14 Interview, Beirut, June 2015.
15 Interview, Beirut, June 2015.
16 Interview, Beirut, September 2019.
17 Interview, Beirut, September 2019.
18 Information provided from interview with LGBTQ activists, Beirut, September 2019.
19 Interview, Beirut, September 2019.
20 Interview, Beirut, September 2019.
21 Interview, Beirut, September 2019.
22 Interview, Beirut, September 2019.
23 Interview, Beirut, September 2019.
24 Interview, Beirut, September 2019.
25 Interview, Beirut, September 2019.
26 Interview, Beirut, September 2019.
27 Interview, Beirut, September 2019.

28 Interview, Beirut, September 2019.
29 Interview, Beirut, September 2019.
30 Interview, Beirut, September 2019.
31 Interview, Beirut, September 2019.
32 Interview, Beirut, September 2019.
33 Interview, Beirut, September 2019.
34 Interview, Beirut, September 2019.
35 Information provided by a human rights worker. Interview, Beirut, September 2019.
36 Interview, Beirut, October 2017.
37 Interview, Beirut, October 2017.
38 Interview, Beirut, October 2017.
39 Interview, Beirut, October 2017.
40 LGBTQ activist, interview with the authors, Beirut, January 2020.
41 Interview, Beirut, October 2017.
42 Interview, Beirut, October 2017.
43 Interview, Beirut, October 2017.
44 Interview, Beirut, October 2017.
45 Interview, Beirut, October 2017.
46 LGBTQ activist, interview with the authors, Beirut, January 2020.

Chapter 7

1 Conversations with numerous activists in Beirut.
2 Conversation with Asef Bayat, Geneva, February 2020.
3 Conversation with activist, Beirut, February 2020.
4 Interview with Maya Mikdashi, February 2020.
5 Interview with activist, Beirut, 2 March 2020.
6 KAFA and ABAAD are Lebanese NGOs working towards the elimination of discrimination and violence against women as well as gender-based violence through varied initiatives which include advocacy efforts, research, training and the provision of support. Dammeh Cooperative describes itself as a grassroots organization focused on helping women and people who do not conform to the binary division of gender, by working against the patriarchal system and seeking to achieve gender justice in Lebanon.
7 Interview with Henri Myrttinen, Melbourne, February 2020.
8 Interviews with activists, Beirut, 2 March 2020 and April 2020.
9 Interview with Henri Myrttinen, Melbourne, February 2020.
10 Interview, Beirut, February 2020.
11 Interview, Beirut, October 2019.
12 Interview, Beirut, April 2020.
13 Authors' interviews with professors in Beirut.
14 Interview with Maya Mikdashi, Rutgers, February 2020.
15 Saab (2015).
16 Interview with student and researcher, Beirut, March 2020.

17 Everyday or banal sectarianism describes the 'natural' or 'unpoliticized' sectarian identity that people are born into.
18 Interview, Beirut, February 2020.
19 Interview, Beirut, February 2020.
20 Interview, Beirut, February 2020.
21 Interview, Beirut, February 2020.
22 Authors' conversations with Lebanese academics.
23 Interview with Maya Mikdashi, Rutgers, February 2020.
24 Interview, Beirut, December 2019.
25 Interview with Maya Mikdashi, February 2020.
26 Interview with Ghiwa Sayigh, Beirut, April 2020.
27 Conversation with Lebanese scholar, Beirut, February 2020.
28 Interview, Beirut, December 2019.
29 Interview with Anne Kirstine Rønn Sørensen, Aarhus, 2020.
30 Interview, Beirut, February 2020.
31 Interview, Beirut, February 2020.
32 Interview, Beirut, February 2020.
33 Interview, Beirut, December 2020.
34 Interview, Beirut, February 2020.
35 Interview, Beirut, January 2020.
36 Authors' observation of activists' twitter feed at the time of writing.
37 Interview, Beirut, February 2020.
38 Interview, Beirut, February 2020.
39 Interview with Ghiwa Sayigh, Beirut, 21 April 2020.
40 Interview, Beirut, December 2020.
41 Interview with Ghiwa Sayigh, Beirut, 21 April 2020.
42 Interview, Beirut, 19 December 2019.
43 The expression of states 'coming out' is inspired from Ayoub (2016).
44 Artist and LGBTQ activist, Online Commentary, November 2020.
45 Interview with Henry Myrttinen, Melbourne, 5 February 2020.
46 Interview, Beirut, 2016.

Chapter 8

1 Interview with photographer, July 2020.
2 Bab-al-Tabbaneh and Jabal Mohsen are two neighbourhoods in Tripoli.
3 Interview, Beirut, July 2020.
4 Interview with artist and professor, June 2020.
5 Interview with Maya Mikdashi, February 2020.
6 The expression of cluster of absences is usually used to show how Orientalists have looked at the Middle East with the expectation of finding attributes and processes that have guided Western capitalism and democratization yet that are in essence absent in the Middle East. Such expectations skew realities and disregard local contexts.

REFERENCES

Abbas, H. (2012). 'Aid, Resistance and Queer Power'. *Pambazuka News*. Available at: www.pambazuka.org/governance/aid-resistance-and-queer-power (accessed 23 October 2012).

Abdo, G. (2017). *The New Sectarianism: The Arab Uprisings and the Rebirth of the Shi'a-Sunni Divide*. Oxford: Oxford University Press.

Abraham, A. (2019). 'Why Culture's "Queerbaiting" Leaves Me Cold'. *The Guardian*. Available at: www.theguardian.com/global/2019/jun/29/why-cultures-queerbaiting-leaves-me-cold-amelia-abraham (accessed 7 July 2020).

Adamczyk, A., and Liao, Y. C. (2019). 'Examining Public Opinion about LGBTQ-Related Issues in the United States and across Multiple Nations'. *Annual Review of Sociology*, 45: 401–23.

Afary, J. (2009). *Sexual Politics in Modern Iran*. Cambridge: Cambridge University Press.

Agamben, G. (1998). *Homo Sacer: Sovereign Power and Bare Life*. Stanford, CA: Stanford University Press.

Agamben, G. (2014). 'What Is a Destituent Power?' *Environment and Planning D: Society and Space*, 32 (1): 65–74.

Agarin, T., McCulloch, A., and Murtagh, C. (2018). 'Others in Deeply Divided Societies: A Research Agenda'. *Nationalism and Ethnic Politics*, 24 (3): 299–310.

Akerman, I. (2018). 'Photo Mario and Beirut's Collective Memory'. Available at: https://iainakerman.com/2018/06/17/1162/ (accessed 10 July 2020).

Al-Ali, N., and Sayegh, G. (2019). 'Feminist and Queer Perspectives in West Asia: Complicities and Tensions'. In *Queer Asia: Decolonising and Reimagining Sexuality and Gender*, ed. L. J. Daniel and J. Ung Loh. London: Zed, pp. 243–65.

Al-Harithy, H. (2010). *Lessons in Postwar Reconstruction: Case Studies from Lebanon in the Aftermath of the 2006 War*. Abingdon: Routledge.

Allouche, S. (2015). 'Are Sexual Dissidence and Gender Activism Necessarily Linked? Notes from the Field on the Body'. *Civil Society Knowledge Centre and Lebanon Support*. Available at: https://civilsociety-centre.org/pdf-generate/29314 (accessed 10 July 2020).

Allouche, S. (2017). '(Dis)-Intersecting Intersectionality in the Time of Queer Syrian Refugee-Ness in Lebanon'. *Kohl: A Journal for Body and Gender Research*, 3 (1): 59–77.

Allouche, S. (2020). 'Seven Analytical Recommendations for the (Un)queer-(Y)ing of the Middle East'. *Kohl: A Journal for Body and Gender Research*, 6 (1). Available at: https://kohljournal.press/seven-analytical-recommendations (accessed 10 July 2020).

Altman, D. (2002). *Global Sex*. Chicago, IL: University of Chicago Press.

Amnesty. (2018). 'Lebanon: Crackdown on Beirut Pride an Outrageous Attempt to Deny Human Rights of LGBTI People'. Available at: www.amnesty.org/en/latest/news/2018/05/lebanoncrackdown-on-beirut-pride-an-outrageous-attempt-to-deny-human-rights-of-lgbti-people/ (accessed 10 July 2020).

Anderson, L. (2006). 'Searching Where the Light Shines: Studying Democratization in the Middle East'. *Annual Review of Political Science*, 9: 189–214.

APPG. (2016). *The UK's Stance on International Breaches of LGBT Rights.* Westminster: APPG.

Arab Foundation for Freedoms and Equality. (2018). 'Activism and Resilience: LGBTQ Progress in the Arabic-Speaking States in the Middle East and North Africa Region'. Available at: https://outrightinternational.org/sites/default/files/MENAReport%20 2018_100918_FINAL.pdf (accessed 10 July 2020).

Atallah, S. (2018). 'Addressing Citizens' Concerns Is Not on the Parliament's Agenda'. *LCPS.* Available at: https://www.lcps-lebanon.org/featuredArticle.php?id=142 (accessed 10 July 2020).

Atshan, S. (2020). *Queer Palestine and the Empire of Critique.* Redwood, CA: Stanford University Press.

Awadalla, A. (2012). 'Lebanon: Inflammatory TV Show Leads to Arrests of Gay Men'. *Global Voice.* Available at: https://globalvoices.org/2012/08/01/lebanon-inflammatory-tv-show-leads-to-arrests-of-gay-men/comment-page-2/ (accessed 10 July 2020).

Ayoub, P. M. (2016). *When States Come Out: Europe's Sexual Minorities and the Politics of Visibility.* Cambridge: Cambridge University Press.

Azhari, T. (2020). 'Plotting Our Escape: Lebanon Braces for New Emigration Wave'. *Al Jazeera.* Available at:https://www.aljazeera.com/ajimpact/escape-lebanon-braces-emigration-wave-200701094323974.html (accessed 10 July 2020).

Azzi, G. (2011a). 'Secularism and Rights'. *G-Azzi.* Available at: https://gazzi.wordpress.com/2011/03/31/secularism-and-rights/ (accessed 10 July 2020).

Azzi, G. (2011b). 'Gay Beirut'. *G-Azzi.* Available at: https://gazzi.wordpress.com/2011/01/07/gay-beirut/ (accessed 4 July 2020).

Azzi, G. (2011c). 'The History of the LGBT Movement in Lebanon'. *G-Azzi.* Available at: https://gazzi.wordpress.com/2011/12/21/history-of-the-lgbt-movement-in-lebanon-3/ (accessed 10 July 2020).

Balzacq, T. (2005). 'The Three Faces of Securitization: Political Agency, Audience, and Context'. *European Journal of International Relations,* 11(2):171–202.

Barakat, H. (1995). *The Stone of Laughter.* London: Garnet Publishing.

Bayat, A. (2013). 'The Arab Spring and Its Surprises'. *Development and Change,* 44 (2): 587–601.

BBC. (2012). 'Outraged Lebanese Demand End to Anal Exams on Gay Men'. Available at: www.bbc.co.uk/news/world-middle-east-19166156 (accessed 4 July 2020).

Beirut Pride. (2020). 'Beirut PRIDE: An Analysis from the Inside'. Available at: https://may17.org/beirut-pride-an-analysis-from-the-inside/ (accessed 10 July 2020).

Bell, D., and Binnie, J. (2000). *The Sexual Citizen: Queer Politics and Beyond.* Cambridge: Polity.

Bell, D., and Binnie, J. (2004). 'Authenticating Queer Space: Citizenship, Urbanism and Governance'. *Urban Studies,* 41 (9): 1807–20.

Benoist, C. (2015). 'Lebanese Gay Rights Organization Helem Marks 10 Years with a Mixed Legacy'. *Al Akhbar.* Available at: https://chloebenoist.wordpress.com/2015/03/03/lebanese-gay-rights-organization-helem-marks-10-years-with-a-mixed-legacy/ (accessed 4 July 2020).

Bitar, L. (2017). 'Against Assimilationist Projects: Towards Queering Our Political Imaginations'. *Kohl: A Journal of Body and Gender Research,* 3 (1): https://kohljournal.press/against-assimilationist-projects.

Bou Akar, H. (2018). *For the War Yet to Come: Planning Beirut's Frontiers.* Stanford, CA: Stanford University Press.

Bourdieu, P. (2003). 'Symbolic Violence'. In *Beyond French Feminisms*, ed. R. Célestin, E. Dalmolin and I. De Courtivron. Basingstoke: Palgrave Macmillan, pp. 23–6.

Boushnak, L., and Boshnaq, M. (2017). 'Coming Out in Lebanon'. *New York Times*. Available at: https://www.nytimes.com/2017/12/30/world/middleeast/lebanon-coming-out.html (accessed 10 July 2020).

Brown, G., Browne, K., Elmhirst, R., and Hutta, S. (2010). 'Sexualities in/of the Global South'. *Geography Compass*, 4 (10): 1567–79.

Brown, W. (2010). *Walled States, Waning Sovereignty*. Boston, MA: MIT Press.

Bustanji, S. (2019). 'Gays for the Revolution: LGBT Rights Activists Take Part in Lebanon Protests'. *Al Bawaba*. Available at: https://www.albawaba.com/node/gays-revolution-lgbt-rights-activist-take-part-lebanon-protests (accessed 10 July 2020).

Butler, J. (2004). *Precarious Life: The Powers of Mourning and Violence*. London: Verso.

Byrne, S. (2020). 'Feminist Reflections on Discourses of (Power)+(Sharing) in Power-Sharing Theory'. *International Political Science Review*, 41(1): 58–72.

Cammett, M. (2014). *Compassionate Communalism: Welfare and Sectarianism in Lebanon*. Ithaca, NY: Cornell University Press.

Caprioli, M. (2005). 'Primed for Violence: The Role of Gender Inequality in Predicting Internal Conflict'. *International Studies Quarterly*, 49 (2): 161–78.

Carabelli, G. (2018). *The Divided City and the Grassroots: The (Un)making of Ethnic Divisions in Mostar*. Basingstoke: Springer.

Carpi, E. (2019). 'Winking at Humanitarian Neutrality: The Liminal Politics of the State in Lebanon'. *Anthropologica*, 61(1): 83–96.

Chaaban, J., Haidar, D., Ismail, R., Khoury, R., and Shidrawi, M. (2016). 'Beirut's 2016 Municipal Elections: Did *Beirut Madinati* Permanently Change Lebanon's Electoral Scene?' *Arab Centre for Research and Policy Studies*. Available at: https://www.dohainstitute.org/en/lists/ACRPS-PDFDocumentLibrary/Case_Analysis_on_Beirut_Madinati_by_Chaaban_et_al_October_2016.pdf (accessed 10 July 2020).

Chamas, S. (2015). 'The Fight Goes on for Lebanon's LGBT Community'. *Al-Monitor*. Available at: https://www.al-monitor.com/pulse/originals/2015/06/lebanon-lgbt-gay-rights-article-534-helem-legal-agenda.html (accessed 10 July 2020).

Cho, S., Crenshaw, K. W., and McCall, L. (2013). 'Toward a Field of Intersectionality Studies: Theory, Applications, and Praxis'. *Signs: Journal of Women in Culture and Society*, 38 (4): 785–810.

Choudry, A., and Kapoor, D. (2013). *NGOization: Complicity, Contradictions and Prospects*. London: Zed Books.

Choukeir, C., and Poladoghly, J. (2019). 'Pride Week in Beirut: IDAHOTB 2019'. *An-Nahar*. Available at: https://en.annahar.com/article/975283-pride-week-in-beirut-idahotb-2019 (accessed 10 January 2020).

Clark, J. A., and Salloukh, B. F. (2013). 'Elite Strategies, Civil Society, and Sectarian Identities in Postwar Lebanon'. *International Journal of Middle East Studies*, 45 (4): 731–49.

Cohen, L. Anthem. (1992). *The Future*. New York: Columbia Records.

Collins, P. H., and Bilge, S. (2020). *Intersectionality*. Oxford: John Wiley.

Council of the European Union. (2013). 'Guidelines to Promote and Protect the Enjoyment of all Human Rights by Lesbian, Gay, Bisexual, Transgender and Intersex (LGBTI) Persons'. Available at: https://eeas.europa.eu/sites/eeas/files/137584.pdf (accessed 6 March 2020).

CrimethInc. (2019). 'Lebanon: A Revolution against Sectarianism'. *CrimethInc*. Available at: https://crimethinc.com/2019/11/13/lebanon-a-revolution-against-sectarianism-chronicling-the-first-month-of-the-uprising (accessed 10 October 2020).

Dalacoura, K. (2014). 'Homosexuality as Cultural Battleground in the Middle East: Culture and Postcolonial International Theory'. *Third World Quarterly*, 35 (7): 1290–1306.

Dammeh Coop. (n.d.). Available at: https://www.facebook.com/DammehCOOP/ (accessed 10 July 2020).

Darwich, M., and Fakhoury, T. (2017). 'Casting the Other as a Threat: The Securitization of Sectarianism in the International Relations of the Syria Crisis'. *Global Discourse*, 6 (4): 712–32.

Darwich, L., and Maikey, H. (2011). 'From the Belly of Arab Queer Activism: Challenges and Opportunities'. *AlQaws*, 12 October. Available at: http://www.alqaws.org/articles/From-the-Belly-of-Arab-Queer-Activism-Challenges-and-Opportunities?category_id=0 (accessed 10 July 2020).

Deeb, L., and Harb, M. (2013). *Leisurely Islam: Negotiating Geography and Morality in Shi'ite South Beirut*. Princeton, NJ: Princeton University Press.

De la Dehesa, R. (2010). *Queering the Public Sphere in Mexico and Brazil: Sexual Rights Movements in Emerging Democracies*. Chapel Hill, NC: Duke University Press.

D'Emilio J (1983). *Sexual Politics, Sexual Communities: The Making of a Homosexual Minority in the United States, 1940–1970*. Chicago, IL: University of Chicago Press.

Díez, J. (2015). *The Politics of Gay Marriage in Latin America: Argentina, Chile, and Mexico*. Cambridge: Cambridge University Press.

Duggan, L. (2012). *The Twilight of Equality? Neoliberalism, Cultural Politics, and the Attack on Democracy*. Boston, MA: Beacon Press.

Duran, K. (1993). 'Homosexuality in Islam'. In *Homosexuality and World Religions*, ed. A. Swidler. Harrisburg, PA: Trinity Press International, pp. 181–97.

Duriesmith, D. (2016). *Masculinity and New War: The Gendered Dynamics of Contemporary Armed Conflict*. Abingdon: London.

El Feki, S. (2014). *Sex and the Citadel: Intimate Life in a Changing Arab World*. New York: Random House.

El Hage, S. (2012). 'Nasawiya: A New Faction in the Women's Movement'. *Al-Raida Journal*, 138: 46–57.

EIDHR. (2017). 'Annual Report 2017 on the List of Actions to Advance LGBTI Equality'. Available at: https://ec.europa.eu/info/sites/info/files/2017annualreportonlgbtilistofactions.pdf (accessed 10 July 2020).

El-Shenawi, E. (2013). 'Are the Lebanese Becoming More Tolerant to Homosexuality?' *Al Araby*. Available at: https://english.alarabiya.net/en/perspective/features/2013/07/20/Are-the-Lebanese-becoming-more-tolerant-to-homosexuality- (accessed 10 July 2020).

Encarnación, O. G. (2016). 'The Troubled Rise of Gay Rights Diplomacy'. *Current History*, 115 (777) (January): 17–22.

Enloe, C. (2000). *Maneuvers: The International Politics of Militarizing Women's Lives*. Berkeley, CA: University of California Press.

Epprecht, M. (2013). *Sexuality and Social Justice in Africa: Rethinking Homophobia and Forging Resistance*. London: Zed Books.

EU Commission. (2015). 'Action Plan on Human Rights and Democracy (2015–2019)'. Available at: https://www.consilium.europa.eu/en/documents-publications/publications/eu-action-plan-on-human-rights-democracy/ (accessed 6 March 2020).

Fakhoury, T. (2014). 'Do Power-Sharing Systems Behave Differently amid Regional Uprisings? Lebanon in the Arab Protest Wave'. *Middle East Journal*, 68 (4): 505–20.

Fakhoury, T. (2015). 'Lebanon's Perilous Balancing Act'. *Current History*, 114 (776): 349–54.

Fakhoury, T. (2019). 'Power-Sharing after the Arab Spring? Insights from Lebanon's Political Transition'. *Nationalism and Ethnic Politics*, 25 (1): 9–26.

Fakhoury, T. (2020). 'Refugee Return and Fragmented Governance in the Host State: Displaced Syrians in the Face of Lebanon's Divided Politics'. *Third World Quarterly*, 1–19 (Online First).

Farah, R. (2012). 'AUB Faculty Statement on Hate Speech and Bigotry'. *Ohmyhappiness*. Available at: https://ohmyhappiness.com/2012/05/30/aub-faculty-statement-on-hate-speech-and-bigotry/ (accessed 10 July 2020).

Farha, M. (2019). *Lebanon*. Cambridge: Cambridge University Press.

Freedom House. (2020). 'Lebanon'. *Freedom House*. Available at: https://freedomhouse.org/country/lebanon (accessed 10 July 2020).

Foucault, M. (1980). *The History of Sexuality Vol.1*. New York, NY: Vintage Books.

France Diplomatie. (2019). 'Sexual Orientation and Gender Identity'. *France Diplomatie*. Available at: https://www.diplomatie.gouv.fr/en/french–foreign–policy/human–rights/sexual–orientation–and–gender–identity/ (accessed 6 March 2020).

Friedman, E. J. (2012). 'Constructing "the Same Rights with the Same Names": The Impact of Spanish Norm Diffusion on Marriage Equality in Argentina'. *Latin American Politics and Society*, 54 (4): 29–59.

Ganz, M. (2000). 'Resources and Resourcefulness: Strategic Capacity in the Unionization of California Agriculture 1959–1966'. *American Journal of Sociology*, 105 (4): 1003–62.

Garretson, J. J. (2018). *The Path to Gay Rights: How Activism and Coming Out Changed Public Opinion*. New York: New York University Press.

Geha, C. (2015). *Citizens' Perceptions of Security Institutions in Lebanon*. Beirut: International Alert.

Geha, C. (2018). 'Politics of a Garbage Crisis: Social Networks, Narratives, and Frames of Lebanon's 2015 Protests and Their Aftermath'. *Social Movement Studies*, 18 (1): 78–92.

Geha, C. (2019a). 'The Myth of Women's Political Empowerment within Lebanon's Sectarian Power-Sharing System'. *Journal of Women, Politics & Policy*, 40 (4): 498–521.

Geha, C. (2019b). 'Resilience through Learning and Adaptation: Lebanon's Power-Sharing System and the Syrian Refugee Crisis'. *Middle East Law and Governance*, 11(1): 65–90.

Geha, C. (2020). 'How Does the Political System Deal with Revolutionary Protest Movements?' Talk at *Aaaliya's Book*, Beirut, 3 February.

Gender and Sexuality Club – AUB. (2017). 'Statement on the Cancellation of the Insight Club's Event'. *Gender and Sexuality Club – AUB Facebook Page*. Available at: https://www.facebook.com/gscaub/posts/aub-students-following-days-of-hard-work-and-effort-from-concerned-members-of-th/711348105704680/ (accessed 10 July 2020).

Gender & Sexuality Resource Centre. (2015). *Lebanese Attitudes towards Sexualities and Gender Identities*. Beirut: Arab Foundation for Freedoms and Equality.

Ghaziani, A. (2015). *There Goes the Gayborhood?* Princeton, NJ: Princeton University Press.

Gorman-Murray, A., and Waitt, G. (2009). 'Queer-Friendly Neighbourhoods: Interrogating Social Cohesion across Sexual Difference in Two Australian Neighbourhoods'. *Environment and Planning A*, 41(12): 2855–73.

Haddad, F. (2011). *Sectarianism in Iraq: Antagonistic Visions of Unity*. Oxford: Oxford University Press, USA.

Hall, R. (2019). 'Lebanon Blocks Grindr in Latest Attack on LGBT+ Community'. *The Independent*. Available at: https://www.independent.co.uk/news/world/middle-east/ grindr-lebanon-ban-lgbt-rights-dating-app-gay-a8933556.html (accessed 4 July 2020).

Halperin, D. M. (2012). *How to Be Gay*. Cambridge, MA: Harvard University Press.

Hage, G. (2018). 'Inside and Outside the Law: Negotiated Being and Urban Jouissance in the Streets of Beirut'. *Social Analysis*, 62 (3): 88–108.

Hanf, T. (2015). *Coexistence in Wartime Lebanon: Decline of a State and Rise of a Nation*. London: I. B. Tauris.

Harb, A. (2019). 'This Revolution Has Raised the Bar: How Lebanon's Protests Have Created a Surprising Space for LGBT Rights'. *Time*. Available at: https://time. com/5726465/lgbt-issues-lebanon-protests/ (accessed 10 July 2020).

Hashemi, N., and Postel, D. (2017). 'Sectarianization: Mapping the New Politics of the Middle East'. *The Review of Faith & International Affairs*, 15 (3): 1–13.

Haugbolle, S. (2012). 'The (Little) Militia Man: Memory and Militarized Masculinity in Lebanon'. *Journal of Middle East Women's Studies*, 8 (1): 115–39.

Haven for Artists. (2019a). 'The Way Back'. *Haven for Artists Facebook Page*. Available at: https://www.facebook.com/events/529643451188224/ (accessed 10 July 2020).

Haven for Artists. (2019b). 'Design for Social Change'. *Haven for Artists Facebook Page*. Available at: https://www.facebook.com/havenforartists/photos/ pcb.2966622446746486/2966622110079853/?type=3&theater (accessed 10 July 2020).

Haven for Artists. (2019c). 'The Sisterhood Salon V.5'. *Haven for Artists Facebook Page*. Available at: https://www.facebook.com/events/514989739245509/ (accessed 10 July 2020).

Haven for Artists. (2019d). 'Face to Face: An Exhibition by Rama Duwaji'. *Haven for Artists Facebook Page*. Available at: https://www.facebook.com/ events/499803147491680/ (accessed 10 July 2020).

Haven For Artists. (2020a). 'Contact Us'. *Haven for Artists*. Available at: https:// havenforartists.org/ (accessed 10 July 2020).

Haven for Artists. (2020b). 'Strategic Report for the Year 2020'. Beirut: Haven for Artists.

Haven for Artists. (2020c). 'Artist Residencies'. *Haven for Artists*. Available at: https:// havenforartists.org/artist-residency/ (accessed 10 July 2020).

Hayes, B. C., and McAllister, I. (2013). 'Gender and Consociational Power-Sharing in Northern Ireland'. *International Political Science Review*, 34 (2): 123–39.

Hayes, B. C., and Nagle, J. (2016). 'Ethnonationalism and Attitudes towards Gay and Lesbian Rights in Northern Ireland'. *Nations and Nationalism*, 22 (1): 20–41.

Hayes, B. C., and Nagle, J. (2019). 'Shifting Public Attitudes? Power-Sharing and Intergroup Tolerance'. In *Power-Sharing and Power Relations after Civil War*, ed. A. Mehler and C. Hartzell. Boulder, CO: Lynne Rienner, pp. 169–90.

Healy, P. (2009). 'Beirut, the Provincetown of the Middle East'. *New York Times*. Available at: www.nytimes.com/2009/08/02/travel/02gaybeirut.html (accessed 4 July 2020).

Heartland Alliance. (2014). 'No Place for People Like You: An Analysis of the Needs, Vulnerabilities, and Experiences of LGBT Syrian Refugees in Lebanon'. Available at: https://www.heartlandalliance.org/wp-content/uploads/sites/13/2016/02/no-place-for-people-like-you_hai_2014.pdf (accessed 10 July 2020).

Helem (2008). 'HELEM: A Case Study of the First Legal, Above-Ground LGBT Organization in the MENA Region'. Available at: www.moph.gov.lb/userfiles/files/Prevention/NationalAIDSControlProgram/Helem.pdf (accessed 10 July 2020).

Helem. (2010). 'Am I Queer? Ana shaz?' Available at: https://queeramnesty.ch/docs/Helem_Infos_DEU_ENG_Soli_20110115.pdf (accessed 10 July 2020).

Helem. (2017a). 'Human Rights Violations against Lesbian, Gay, Bisexual, Transgender, and Queer (LGBTQ) Individuals in Lebanon'. Available at: https://www.ecoi.net/en/file/local/1398874/1930_1493282102_int-ccpr-ico-lbn-27152-e.pdf (accessed 10 July 2020).

Helem. (2017b). 'Homophobia Is Terrorism'. *Helem Facebook Page*. Available at: https://www.facebook.com/watch/?v=1366367466733193 (accessed 10 July 2020).

Helem. (2018). 'Queer, Trans and Intersex Storytelling Night'. *Helem Facebook Page*. Available at: https://www.facebook.com/133916233311662/photos/a.4956304404735 71.1073741825.133916233311662/1716715138365089/?type=3&theater (accessed 10 July 2020).

Helem. (2019a). 'Unleash Your Talent: Creating Slime with Colors and Glitter'. *Helem Facebook Page*. Available at: https://www.facebook.com/helemlebanon/photos/a.49563 0440473571/2442713655765230/?type=3&theater (accessed 10 July 2020).

Helem. (2019b). 'Lebanese Independence 2019: Independent from Your Patriarchal System'. *Helem Facebook Page*. Available at: www.facebook.com/helemlebanon/photos/a.177397855630166/2598846383485289/?type=3&theater (accessed 9 March 2020).

Helem. (2019c). 'Gay Is Not an Insult'. *Helem Facebook Page*. Available at: https://www.facebook.com/helemlebanon/photos/a.495630440473571/2544546015581993/?type=3 (accessed 10 July 2020).

Helem. (2020a). 'The Ultimate Closure (on Breakups)'. *Helem Facebook Page*. Available at: https://www.facebook.com/helemlebanon/photos/a.495630440473571/2770397132 996879/?type=3&theater (accessed 10 July 2020).

Helem. (2020b). 'Lady Bird'. *Helem Facebook Page*. Available at: https://www.facebook.com/helemlebanon/photos/a.495630440473571/2826767974026461/?type=3&theater (accessed 10 July 2020).

Helem. (2020c). 'Girl, Woman, Other'. *Helem Facebook Page*. Available at: https://www.facebook.com/helemlebanon/photos/a.495630440473571/2784669231569669/?type=3 &theater (accessed 10 July 2020).

Helem. (2020d). 'Storytelling Night: Stories of Revolution'. *Helem Facebook Page*, 24 February. Available at: https://www.facebook.com/helemlebanon/photos/a.1773978556 30166/2796948283675097/?type=3&theater (accessed 9 March 2020).

Henley, A. D. (2016). *Religious Authority and Sectarianism in Lebanon*. New York: Carnegie Endowment for International Peace.

Hinnebusch, R. (2016). 'The Sectarian Revolution in the Middle East'. *R/evolutions: Global Trends & Regional Issues*, 4 (1): 120–52.

Hirschman, A. O. (1970). *Exit, Voice, and Loyalty: Responses to Decline in Firms, Organizations, and States*. Cambridge, MA: Harvard University Press.

Horowitz, D. L. (2014). 'Ethnic Power Sharing: Three Big Problems'. *Journal of Democracy*, 25 (2): 5–20.

Human Dignity Trust. (2020). 'Lebanon'. Available at: www.humandignitytrust.org/country-profile/lebanon/ (accessed 7 July 2020).

Human Rights Watch. (2012). 'Lebanon: Stop "Tests of Shame"'. Available at: https://www.hrw.org/news/2012/08/10/lebanon-stop-tests-shame (accessed 10 July 2020).

Human Rights Watch. (2015). 'Unequal and Unprotected: Women's Rights under Lebanese Personal Status Laws'. Available at: https://www.hrw.org/report/2015/01/19/unequal-and-unprotected/womens-rights-under-lebanese-personal-status-laws (accessed 10 July 2020).

Human Rights Watch. (2016). 'Twin Threats: How the Politics of Fear and the Crushing of Civil Society Imperil Global Rights'. Available at: https://www.hrw.org/world-report/2016/country-chapters/global-0 (accessed 7 July 2020).

Human Rights Watch. (2018a). 'Audacity in Adversity: LGBT Activism in the Middle East and North Africa'. Available at: https://www.hrw.org/report/2018/04/16/audacity-adversity/lgbt-activism-middle-east-and-north-africa (accessed 7 July 2020).

Human Rights Watch. (2018b). 'Lebanon: Same-Sex Relations Not Illegal'. Available at: https://www.hrw.org/news/2018/07/19/lebanon-same-sex-relations-not-illegal (accessed 10 July 2020).

Human Rights Watch. (2019). '"Don't Punish Me for Who I Am": Systemic Discrimination against Transgender Women in Lebanon'. Available at: https://www.hrw.org/report/2019/09/03/dont-punish-me-who-i-am/systemic-discrimination-against-transgender-women-lebanon (accessed 10 July 2020).

Human Rights Watch. (2020). 'Brutal Crackdown on Protesters'. Available at: www.hrw.org/blog-feed/lebanon-protests#blog-338073 (accessed 10 July 2020).

International Commission of Jurists. (2012). 'Criminal Court of al-Bitroun'. Available at: www.icj.org/wp-content/uploads/2012/07/In-Re-Article-534-Criminal-Court-of-Al-Bitroun-English (accessed 10 January 2020).

The Invisible Committee. (2017). 'Now'. *Autonomies*. Available at: https://autonomies.org/2017/06/now-and-the-anarchy-of-destituent-power-reading-politics-with-the-invisible-committee/ (accessed 10 January 2020).

Ismail, K., Wilson, C., and Cohen-Fournier, N. (2017). 'Syrian Refugees in Tripoli, Lebanon'. Refugees in Towns Case Study Series, *Feinstein International Centre, Tufts University*. Available at: https://fic.tufts.edu/assets/Tripoli-FINAL-5-July.pdf (accessed 10 July 2020).

Issa, A. (2017). 'In Lebanon, Gay Activism Is Fueling a New Conversation about Democracy and Civil Rights'. *The Washington Post*. Available at: www.washingtonpost.com/news/democracy-post/wp/2017/05/20/in-lebanon-gay-activism-is-fueling-a-new-conversation-about-democracy-and-civil-rights (accessed 10 July 2020).

Jolly, S. (2000). '"Queering" Development: Exploring the Links between Same-Sex Sexualities, Gender, and Development'. *Gender & Development*, 8 (1): 78–88.

Jones, L. (2015). *Societies under Siege: Exploring How International Economic Sanctions (Do Not) Work*. Oxford: Oxford University Press.

Joseph, S. (1997). 'The Public/Private – The Imagined Boundary in the Imagined Nation/State/Community: The Lebanese Case'. *Feminist Review*, 57 (1): 73–92.

Joseph, S. (1999). 'Descent of the Nation: Kinship and Citizenship in Lebanon'. *Citizenship Studies*, 3 (3): 295–318.

Joseph, S. (ed.). (2000). *Gender and Citizenship in the Middle East*. Syracuse, NY: Syracuse University Press.

Joseph, S. (2011). 'Political Familism in Lebanon'. *The Annals of the American Academy of Political and Social Science*, 636 (1): 150–63.

Karame, L. (2016). 'Lebanese Article 534 Struck Down: Homosexuality No Longer 'Contrary to Nature'. *Legal Agenda*. Available at: https://legal-agenda.com/en/article. php?id=3149 (accessed 10 January 2020).

Khatib, L. (2007). 'Violence and Masculinity in Maroun Baghdadi's Lebanese War Films'. *Critical Arts: A Journal of South-North Cultural Studies*, 21(1): 68–85.

Kingston, P. (2013). *Reproducing Sectarianism: Advocacy Networks and the Politics of Civil Society in Postwar Lebanon*. Albany, NY: Suny Press.

Klapeer, C. M. (2018). 'Dangerous Liaisons?: (Homo) Developmentalism, Sexual Modernization and LGBTIQ Rights in Europe'. In *Routledge Handbook of Queer Development Studies*, ed. C. L. Mason. Abingdon: Routledge, pp. 102–18.

Knio, K. (2005). 'Lebanon: Cedar Revolution or Neo-Sectarian Partition?' *Mediterranean Politics*, 10 (2): 225–31.

Kohl: A Journal of Body and Gender Research. (2019). 'Feminist Revolutionaries'. *Kohl: A Journal of Body and Gender Research*, 5(3): https://kohljournal.press/issue-5-3 (accessed 10 July 2020).

Kohl: A Journal for Body and Gender Research. (2020). 'Current issue: Feminist Revolutionaries'. *Kohl: A Journal for Body and Gender Research*. Available at: https:// kohljournal.press/ (accessed 10 July 2020).

Koopmans, R. (2004). 'Protest in Time and Space: The Evolution of Waves of Contention'. In *The Blackwell Companion on Social Movements*, ed. D. A.Snow, S. A. Soule and H. Kriesi. Oxford: John Wiley & Sons, p. 40.

Kraidy, M. M. (2016). 'Trashing the Sectarian System? Lebanon's "You Stink" Movement and the Making of Affective Publics'. *Communication and the Public*, 1(1): 19–26.

Kriesi, H. (2004). 'Political Context and Opportunity'. In *The Blackwell Companion on Social Movements*, ed. D. A. Snow, S. A. Soule and H. Kriesi. Oxford: John Wiley & Sons, p. 72.

Laruni, E., Maydaa, C., and Myrttinen, H. (2018). 'Engaging with the Gender, Peace and Security Agenda in Research and Activism in Lebanon'. *LSE Centre for Women, Peace and Security*, LSE Women, Peace and Security Working Paper Series, Paper 17/2018. Available at: http://www.lse.ac.uk/women-peace-security/assets/documents/2018/ WPS17LaruniMaydaaMyrttinen.pdf (accessed 10 July 2020).

Lawson, G. (2019). *The Anatomies of Revolution*. Cambridge: Cambridge University Press.

LebMASH. (2014a). '27 Men Arrested in Agha Hammam, Beirut'. Available at: https:// lebmash.wordpress.com/2014/08/17/27-men-agha-hammam/ (accessed 4 July 2020).

LebMASH.. (2014b). 'Homosexuality Is Not an Illness, Lebanese Scientists Decide'. Available at: http://blogs.nature.com/houseofwisdom/2013/08/homosexuality-not-a-disease-says-lebanese-psychiatric-society.html (accessed 10 January 2021).

LebMASH. (2016). 'Statement from the Lebanese Psychiatric Society'. Available at: https:// www.lebmash.org/statement-lebanese-psychiatric-society/ (accessed 10 January 2020).

LebMASH. (2017). 'Homepage'. *LEBMASH*. Available at: https://www.lebmash.org/ (accessed 10 July 2020).

LSE Middle East Centre. (2020). 'Coronavirus: The Coup de Grace for Lebanon?' *LSE Middle East Centre*. Available at: https://soundcloud.com/lsemiddleeastcentre/ coronavirus-the-coup-de-grace-for-lebanon-webinar (accessed 10 July 2020).

Maginn, P. J., and Ellison, G. (2015). '"Sextarianism" Is Drawing New Battle Lines in Northern Ireland'. The *Conversation*, Available at: https://theconversation.com/ sextarianism-is-drawing-new-battle-lines-in-northern-ireland-42209 (accessed 20 May 2021).

Maginn, P. J., and Ellison, G. (2017). '"Ulster Says No": Regulating the Consumption of Commercial Sex Spaces and Services in Northern Ireland'. *Urban Studies*, 54(3): 806–21.

Majed, R. and Salman, L. (2019). 'Lebanon's Thawra'. *Middle East Research and Information Project: Middle East Report 292/3*. Available at: https://merip.org/2019/12/lebanons-thawra/ (accessed 10 July 2020).

Makarem G. (2011). 'The Story of Helem'. *Journal of Middle East Women's Studies*, 7 (3): 98–112.

Makdisi, U. (2000). *The Culture of Sectarianism: Community, History, and Violence in Nineteenth-Century Ottoman Lebanon*. Berkeley, CA: University of California Press.

Makhlouf, I. (1988). *Beyrouth, ou, La Fascination de la Mort: Essai*. Paris: Editions de La Passion.

Malmvig, H., and Fakhoury, T. (2020). 'Tales of the Unexpected: Will the Lebanese Uprising Stay Clear of Attempts at Geopolitization?' *POMEPS Studies*, 38. Available at: Project on Middle East Political Science (pomeps.org) (accessed 10 July 2020).

Mandour, S. (2013). *Potential Change in Media Discourse on Sexuality in Lebanon: Cinema Plaza and Beyond*. Oxford: Reuters Institute for the Study of Journalism.

MARSA Sexual Health Centre. (2018). 'Trans*'. *MARSA Sexual Health Centre*. Available at: http://trans.marsa.me/ (accessed 10 July 2020).

Massad, J. (2007). *Desiring Arabs*. Chicago, IL: University of Chicago Press.

Massena, F. (2020). 'A Lebanese Couple's Secular Marriage Triggered "Death Fatwas". But Now, Sweden Wants to Deport Them'. *The New Arab*. Available at: https://english.alaraby.co.uk/english/news/2020/2/5/sweden-deporting-lebanese-couple-despite-death-fatwas-back-home-1 (accessed 10 July 2020).

McAdam, D. (2010). *Political Process and the Development of Black Insurgency, 1930–1970*. Chicago, IL: University of Chicago Press.

McAdam, D., McCarthy, J. D., and Zald, M. N. (eds.) (2008). *Comparative Perspectives on Social Movements Political Opportunities, Mobilizing Structures, and Cultural Framings*. Cambridge: Cambridge University Press.

McCulloch, A. (2014). 'Consociational Settlements in Deeply Divided Societies: The Liberal-Corporate Distinction'. *Democratization*, 21(3): 501–18.

McGarry, A. (2016). 'Pride Parades and Prejudice: Visibility of Roma and LGBTI Communities in Post-Socialist Europe'. *Communist and Post-Communist Studies*, 49 (3): 269–77.

McGarry, J., and O'Leary, B. (2006). 'Consociational Theory, Northern Ireland's Conflict, and Its Agreement. Part 1: What Consociationalists Can Learn from Northern Ireland'. *Government and Opposition*, 41(1): 43–63.

McWilliams, M. (1997). 'Violence against Women and Political Conflict: The Northern Ireland Experience'. *Critical Criminology*, 8 (1): 78–92.

Meaker M. (2017). 'Despite Allegedly Torturing Gay People, UK Still Funds Lebanese Police Force'. *Middle East Eye*. Available at: www.middleeasteye.net/news/despite-allegedly-torturing-gay-people-uk-still-funds-lebanese-police-force (accessed 4 July 2020).

Medina, D. A., and Chehayeb, K. (2020). 'As the Lebanon Uprising Hits 100-Day Mark, Protesters Allege Torture by Security Forces'. *The Intercept*. Available at: https://theintercept.com/2020/01/25/lebanon-protests-torture/ (accessed 4 July 2020).

Meem. (2009). *Bareed Mista3jil*. Beirut: Meem.

Meem. (2010a). *Arab Queer Women and Transgenders Confronting Diverse Religious Fundamentalisms: The Case of Meem in Lebanon*. Meem: Beirut.

Meem. (2010b). 'Framing Invisibility: Coming Out and the International LGBT Spectrum of Progress'. Available at: http://thebridgebrant.com/wp-content/uploads/2014/03/Queer-Women-Framing-Visibility-and-Coming-Out.pdf (accessed 4 July 2020).

Melander, E. (2005). 'Gender Equality and Intrastate Armed Conflict'. *International Studies Quarterly*, 49 (4): 695–714.

Melucci, A. (1996). *Challenging Codes: Collective Action in the Information Age.* Cambridge: Cambridge University Press.

Merry, M. (2006). *Human Rights and Gender Violence: Translating International Law into Local Justice.* Chicago, IL: University of Chicago Press.

Michelson, M. R. (2019). 'The Power of Visibility: Advances in LGBT Rights in the United States and Europe'. *Journal of Politics*, 81(1): e1–e5

Mikdashi, M. (2014). 'Sex and Sectarianism: The Legal Architecture of Lebanese Citizenship'. *Comparative Studies of South Asia, Africa and the Middle East*, 34(2): 279–93.

Mikdashi, M. (2018). 'Sextarianism: Notes on Studying the Lebanese State'. In *The Oxford Handbook of Contemporary Middle-Eastern and North African History*, ed. A. Ghazal and J. Hanssen. Oxford: Oxford University Press.

Milan, C. (2019). *Social Mobilization beyond Ethnicity: Civic Activism and Grassroots Movements in Bosnia and Herzegovina.* Abingdon: Routledge.

Milk, H. (2013). *An Archive of Hope: Harvey Milk's Speeches and Writings.* Berkeley, CA: University of California Press.

Ministry of Information. (2020). 'Berri from Geneva Warns of Attempts to Liquidate Palestinian Cause'. Available at: http://nna-leb.gov.lb/en/show-news/96201/Hasbani-calls-for-national-strategy-to-fight-childhood-obesity (accessed 10 July 2020).

Mordecai, M. (2019). 'Protests in Lebanon Highlight Ubiquity of WhatsApp, Dissatisfaction with Government'. *Pew Research Centre*. Available at: https://www.pewresearch.org/fact-tank/2019/11/19/protests-in-lebanon-highlight-ubiquity-of-whatsapp-dissatisfaction-with-government/ (accessed 10 July 2020).

Mosaic MENA. (2020a). 'Homepage'. *Mosaic MENA*. Available at: https://www.mosaicmena.org (accessed 10 July 2020).

Mosaic MENA. (2020b). 'Activities'. *Mosaic MENA*. Available at: https://www.mosaicmena.org/activities (accessed 10 July 2020).

Mouawad, J. (2015). 'Lebanon's Rubbish Crisis Is a Chance to Clean Up the Polluted Political System'. *The Guardian*. Available at: https://www.theguardian.com/commentisfree/2015/sep/02/lebanon-rubbish-crisis-clean-up-political-system (accessed 10 July 2020).

Mouawad, N. (2019). 'Episode 62 – Changing Tactics & Demographics'. Interview in *The Lebanese Politics Podcast*. Available at: https://soundcloud.com/lebpoliticspodcast/episode-62-changing-tactics-demographics (accessed 10 July 2020).

Mouffe, C. (2000). *The Democratic Paradox.* London: Verso.

Mounzer, Lina. (2020). 'Waste Away: Notes on Beirut's Broken Sewage System'. Available at: https://thebaffler.com/latest/waste-away-mounzer (accessed 10 July 2020).

Moussawi, G. (2015). '(Un)critically Queer Organizing: Towards a More Complex Analysis of LGBTQ Organizing in Lebanon'. *Sexualities*, 18 (5/6): 593–617.

Moussawi, G. (2018). 'Queer Exceptionalism and Exclusion: Cosmopolitanism and Inequalities in "Gay-Friendly" Beirut'. *The Sociological Review*, 66 (1): 174–90.

Moussawi, G. (2020). *Disruptive Situations: Fractal Orientalism and Queer Strategies in Beirut.* Pennsylvania: Temple University Press.

Muñoz, J. E. (2009). *Cruising Utopia: The Then and There of Queer Futurity*.
    New York: New York University Press.

Myrttinen, H. (2019). 'Stabilizing or Challenging Patriarchy? Sketches of Selected "New"
    Political Masculinities'. *Men and Masculinities*, 22 (3): 563–81.

Myrttinen, H., Khattab, L., and Naujoks, J. (2017). 'Re-Thinking Hegemonic Masculinities
    in Conflict-Affected Contexts'. *Critical Military Studies*, 3 (2): 103–19.

Naber, N., and Zaatari, Z. (2014). 'Reframing the War on Terror: Feminist and Lesbian,
    Gay, Bisexual, Transgender, and Queer (LGBTQ) Activism in the Context of the 2006
    Israeli Invasion of Lebanon'. *Cultural Dynamics*, 26 (1): 91–111.

Nadeem, M. (2019). 'LGBTQ, Women's Rights Part of Uprising Conversation'. *The Daily
    Star Lebanon*. Available at: www.dailystar.com.lb/News/Lebanon-News/2019/Nov-
    14/495548-lgbtq-womens-rights-part-of-uprising-conversation.ashx (accessed 10
    July 2020).

Najib. (2020). 'Thawra Is Not Dead, Thawra Is Now a Lifestyle!' *Blog Baladi*.
    Available at: https://blogbaladi.com/thawra-is-not-dead-thawra-is-now-
    a-lifestyle/?fbclid=IwAR1osb5i1u0t_yV9xfc1khLwGt2XGBPPRfyhg-
    cgbgU_25KphzpoilQNPB4 (accessed 10 July 2020).

Nagle, J. (2003). *Race, Ethnicity, and Sexuality: Intimate Intersections, Forbidden Frontiers*.
    New York: Oxford University Press.

Nagle, J., and Clancy, M. A. C. (2010). *Shared Society or Benign Apartheid? Understanding
    Peacebuilding in Divided Societies*. Basingstoke: Palgrave Macmillan.

Nagle, J. (2016a). 'Between Entrenchment, Reform and Transformation: Ethnicity and
    Lebanon's Consociational Democracy'. *Democratization*, 23 (7): 1144–61.

Nagle, J. (2016b). *Social Movements in Violently Divided Societies: Constructing Conflict
    and Peacebuilding*. Abingdon: Routledge.

Nagle, J. (2018a). 'Beyond Ethnic Entrenchment and Amelioration: An Analysis of Non-
    Sectarian Social Movements and Lebanon's Consociationalism'. *Ethnic and Racial
    Studies*, 41 (7): 1370–89.

Nagle, J. (2018b). 'Crafting Radical Opposition or Reproducing Homonormativity?
    Consociationalism and LGBT Rights Activism in Lebanon'. *Journal of Human Rights*,
    17 (1): 75–88.

Nardi, P. M. (1998). 'The Globalization of the Gay & Lesbian Socio-Political
    Movement: Some Observations about Europe with a Focus on Italy'. *Sociological
    Perspectives*, 41 (3): 567–86.

Nasawiya. (2012). 'Nasawiya a Feminist Collective'. Available at: https://www.nasawiya.
    org/about-us/ (accessed 10 July 2013).

Nash, Jennifer C. (2008). 'Re-Thinking Intersectionality'. *Feminist Review*, 89 (1): 1–15.

Nasser, A. (2003). 'Fadlallah Puts Case for Death Penalty'. *The Daily Star Lebanon*.
    Available at: www.dailystar.com.lb/News/Lebanon-News/2003/Aug-30/25551-
    fadlallah-puts-case-for-death-penalty.ashx (accessed 10 July 2020).

Nasser-Eddin, N., Abu-Assab, N., and Greatrick, A. (2018). 'Reconceptualising and
    Contextualising Sexual Rights in the MENA Region: Beyond LGBTQI Categories'.
    Gender & Development, 26 (1): 173–89.

Nassif, G. (2020). 'Women's Political Participation in Lebanon and the Limits of Aid-
    Driven Empowerment'. Available at: https://civilsociety-centre.org/sites/default/files/
    resources/ls-womensassessmentreport_en-online_1.pdf (accessed 10 July 2020).

Nasr, N., and Zeidan, T. (2015). *As Long as They Stay Away: Exploring Lebanese Attitudes towards Sexualities and Gender Identities*. Beirut: Arab Foundation for Freedoms and Equality.

The New Arab. (2016). 'Lebanon's Controversial Foreign Minister in "Misogyny and Racism" Row'. Available at: https://english.alaraby.co.uk/english/blog/2016/9/19/the-lebanese-foreign-ministers-misogyny-and-racism-double-whammy (accessed 10 July 2020).

Nichols, R. (2012). 'Empire and the Dispositif of Queerness'. *Foucault Studies*, 14: 41–60.

Nogueira, M. B. B. (2017). 'The Promotion of LGBT Rights as International Human Rights Norms: Explaining Brazil's Diplomatic Leadership'. *Global Governance: A Review of Multilateralism and International Organizations*, 23 (4): 545–63.

Nucho, J. R. (2016). *Everyday Sectarianism in Urban Lebanon: Infrastructures, Public Services, and Power*. Princeton, NJ: Princeton University Press.

Nuñez-Mietz, F. G. (2019). 'Resisting Human Rights through Securitization: Russia and Hungary against LGBT Rights'. *Journal of Human Rights*, 18 (5): 543–63.

Obama, B. (2016). 'Remarks of President Barack Obama – State of the Union Address'. *The White House*, 12. Available at: https://obamawhitehouse.archives.gov/the-press-office/2016/01/12/remarks- president-barack-obama-%E2%80%93-prepared-delivery-state-union-address (accessed 15 March 2021).

Obeid, G. (2019). 'Megaphone, Megaresponsibility: Emcees Talk Protest Slogans'. *The Daily Star Lebanon*. Available at: www.dailystar.com.lb/News/Lebanon-News/2019/Oct-31/494675-megaphone-megaresponsibility-emcees-talk-protest-slogans.ashx (accessed 10 July 2020).

Office of the High Commission for Human Rights. (2015). 'Ending Violence and Discrimination against Lesbian, Gay, Bisexual, Transgender and Intersex People'. Available at: www.ohchr.org/Documents/Issues/Discrimination/Joint_LGBTI_Statement_ENG.PDF (accessed 6 March 2020).

Öztop, N. (2013). 'Mayor Shakhtoura: Responsible for Sexual and Racial Violations in Lebanon'. *Kaos GL*. Available at: https://www.kaosgl.org/en/single-news/mayor-shakhtoura-responsible-for-sexual-and-racial-violations-in-lebanon (accessed 11 July 2020).

Payne, W. J. (2016). 'Death-Squads Contemplating Queers as Citizens: What Colombian Paramilitaries Are Saying'. *Gender, Place & Culture*, 23 (3): 328–44.

Peale, F. (2015). 'Pursuing Equality: Western Response to Gay Rights Abroad'. *Harvard Political Review*. Available at: http://harvardpolitics.com/world/gay-rights-western-response/ (accessed 6 March 2020).

Picard, E. (2002). *Lebanon, a Shattered Country: Myths and Realities of the Wars in Lebanon*. New York: Holmes & Meier.

Poushter, J., and Kent, N. (2020). 'The Global Divide on Homosexuality Persists'. *Pew Centre*. Available at: www.pewresearch.org/global/2020/06/25/global-divide-on-homosexuality-persists/ (accessed 10 July 2020).

The A Project. (2019). 'Sex & Society Reading Retreat Nov 2019!' *The A Project*. Available at: https://www.theaproject.org/content/sex-society-reading-retreat-nov-2019 (accessed 10 July 2020).

The A Project. (2020a). 'Home'. *The A Project*. Available at: https://www.theaproject.org/ (accessed 10 July 2020).

The A Project. (2020b). 'About'. *The A Project*. Available at: https://www.theaproject.org/content/what-theaproject (accessed 10 July 2020).

Puar, J. K. (2018). *Terrorist Assemblages: Homonationalism in Queer Times*. Chapel Hill, NC: Duke University Press.

Purcell, M. (2009). 'Resisting Neoliberalization: Communicative Planning or Counter-Hegemonic Movements?' *Planning Theory*, 8 (2): 140–65.

Qiblawi, T. (2018). 'Gay Rights Come to the Fore as Lebanon Prepares to Vote'. *CNN Middle East*. Available at: https://edition.cnn.com/2018/05/04/middleeast/lebanon-elections-lgbt-rights-intl/index.html (accessed 10 July 2020).

Qiblawi, T., Wedeman, B., and Balkiz, G. (2019). 'Lebanon Is at a Crossroads between a New Start or a Return to Unrest'. *CNN Middle East*. Available at: https://edition.cnn.com/2019/10/26/middleeast/lebanon-protests-crossroads-intl/index.html (accessed 10 July 2020).

Rahman, M. (2014). *Homosexualities, Muslim Cultures and Modernity*. Basingstoke: Palgrave Macmillan.

Rao, R. (2014). 'The Locations of Homophobia'. *London Review of International Law*, 2 (2): 169–99.

Rebellious Lebanon. (2019). 'Gay Revolution'. *YouTube*, 6 November. Available at: https://www.youtube.com/watch?v=xk5GjIEA_jI (accessed 10 July 2020).

Reid-Smith, T. (2012). 'Beirut and Lebanon: The Gay Paradise of the Arab World'. *Gay Star News*. Available at: www.gaystarnews.com/article/beirut-and-lebanon-gay-paradise-arab-world080612/ (accessed 4 July 2020).

Reporters Sans Frontières. (2020). 'Classement RSF 2020: Le mirage de l'accalmie au moyen-orient'. *Reporters Sans Frontières #RSFIndex 2020*. Available at: https://rsf.org/fr/classement-rsf-2020-le-mirage-de-laccalmie-au-moyen-orient (accessed 10 July 2020).

Rexhepi, P. (2016). 'From Orientalism to Homonationalism: Queer Politics, Islamophobia and Europeanization in Kosovo'. *Southeastern Europe*, 40 (1): 32–53.

Richardson, D. (2017). *Sexuality and Citizenship*. Oxford: Wiley.

Rights in Exile Programme. (2020). 'Lebanon LGBTI Resources'. Available at: http://www.refugeelegalaidinformation.org/lebanon-lgbti-resources (accessed 10 July 2020).

Rizk, A., and Makarem, G. (2015). '"Masculinity-under-Threat": Sexual Rights Organizations and the Masculinist State in Lebanon'. *Civil Society Review*, 1: 97–108.

Rizkallah, A. (2017). 'The Paradox of Power-Sharing: Stability and Fragility in Postwar Lebanon'. *Ethnic and Racial Studies*, 40 (12): 2058–76.

Rønn, A. K. (2020). 'The Development and Negotiation of Frames during Non-Sectarian Mobilizations in Lebanon'. *The Review of Faith and International Affairs*, 18 (1): 87–96.

Rosenfeld, D. (2009). 'Heteronormativity and Homonormativity as Practical and Moral Resources: The Case of Lesbian and Gay Elders'. *Gender & Society*, 23 (5): 617–38.

Rowell, A. (2018). 'Lebanon's Elections: Independents' Day?' *Al Jumhuriya*. Available at: https://www.aljumhuriya.net/en/content/lebanon%E2%80%99s-elections-independents%E2%80%99-day (accessed 10 July 2020).

Saab, B. Y. (2015). 'Trashy Politics in Beirut: The Garbage Crisis and Lebanon's Political Future'. *Foreign Affairs*. Available at: https://www.foreignaffairs.com/articles/lebanon/2015-08-31/trashy-politics-beirut (accessed 10 July 2020).

Salibi, K. (1990). *A House of Many Mansions: The History of Lebanon Reconsidered*. Berkeley, CA: University of California Press.

Salloukh, B. F., Barakat, R., Al-Habbal, J. S., Khattab, L. W., and Mikaelian, S. (2015). *Politics of Sectarianism in Postwar Lebanon*. London: Pluto Press.

Salloukh, B. F. (2019). 'Taif and the Lebanese State: The Political Economy of a Very Sectarian Public Sector'. *Nationalism and Ethnic Politics*, 25 (1): 43–60.

Salloukh, B. F. (2020). 'Consociational Power-Sharing in the Arab World: A Critical Stocktaking'. *Studies in Ethnicity and Nationalism*, 20 (2): 100–8.

Sandels, A. (2013). 'Lebanese Medical Group Says Being Gay Is Not a Disease'. *LA Times*. https://www.latimes.com/world/la-xpm-2013-jul-12-la-fg-wn-lebanon-homosexuality-20130712-story.html (accessed 10 January 2020).

Sayegh, G. (2019). 'We Raise Fists, They Shake Fingers: Remembering Feminist Revolutions'. *Kohl: A Journal for Body and Gender Research*, 5 (3): http://kohljournal. press/we-raise-fists. (accessed 15 February 2021).

Seidman, S. (2004). *Beyond the Closet: The Transformation of Gay and Lesbian Life.* Hove: Psychology Press.

Seidman, S. (2012). 'The Politics of Cosmopolitan Beirut: From the Stranger to the Other'. *Theory, Culture & Society*, 29 (2): 3–36.

Semerene, G. (2019). '*Mithliyy, mithlak*: Language and LGBTQ Activism in Lebanon and Palestine'. In *Queer Asia: Decolonising and Reimagining Sexuality and Gender*, ed. L. J. Daniel and J. Ung Loh. London: Zed, pp. 85–108.

Shamma, M. (2017). 'The A Project: Spreading Awareness and Establishing Agency for Lebanese Sexuality'. *Beirut*. Available at: https://www.beirut.com/l/51263 (accessed 15 February 2021).

Sharp, J. (2011). 'Subaltern Geopolitics: Introduction'. *Geoforum*, 42 (3): 271–3.

Siraj, A. (2009). 'The Construction of the Homosexual "Other" by British Muslim Heterosexuals'. *Contemporary Islam*, 3 (1): 41–57.

Stel, N., and El-Husseini, R. (2015). 'Lebanon's Massive Garbage Crisis Isn't Its First. Here's What That Teaches Us'. *The Washington Post*. Available at: https://www. washingtonpost.com/news/monkey-cage/wp/2015/09/18/this-isnt-lebanons-first-garbage-crisis-and-what-that-should-teach-us/ (accessed 10 July 2020).

Stryker, S. (2008). *Transgender History*. Berkeley, CA: Seal Press.

Thayer, M. (2009). *Movement or Market? Rural Women, NGO Activists, and Northern Donors in Brazil*. Abingdon: Routledge.

Thomas, B-B. (2019). 'Mashrou' Leila Concert Cancelled after "Homophobic" Pressure from Christian Groups'. *The Guardian*. Available at: https://www.theguardian.com/music/2019/jul/31/mashrou-leila-byblos-festival-concert-cancelled-after-pressure-from-christian-groups (accessed 10 July 2020).

Tilly, C., and Tarrow, S. (2006). *Contentious Politics*. Oxford: Oxford University Press.

Traboulsi, F. (2012). *A History of Modern Lebanon*. London: Pluto Press.

Tria Kerkvliet, B. J. (2009). 'Everyday Politics in Peasant Societies (and Ours)'. *The Journal of Peasant Studies*, 36 (1): 227–43. DOI: 10.1080/03066150902820487.

UK Lebanon. (2019). IDAHOT. Available at: https://www.facebook.com/ukinlebanon/videos/vb.110637838979258/2352690655007940/?type=2&theater (accessed 10 July 2020).

UN High Commissioner for Refugees (UNHCR). (2016). 'Submission to the United Nations Committee against Torture on Tunisia'. Available at: https://www.refworld.org/docid/5703732f4.html (accessed 10 July 2020).

UN High Commissioner for Refugees (UNHCR). (2017). 'UNHCR: LGBTI Youth Group – Lebanon'. Available at: https://www.refworld.org/pdfid/5a38e08e4.pdf (accessed 10 July 2020).

UN Women. (2019). 'Understanding the Role of Women and Other Feminist Actors in the 2019 Lebanese Protests'. *UN Women Arab States*. Available at: https://arabstates. unwomen.org/en/digital-library/publications/2019/12/gendering-lebanons-2019-protests (accessed 10 July 2020).

Van de Sande, M. (2013). 'The Prefigurative Politics of Tahrir Square – An Alternative Perspective on the 2011 Revolutions'. *Res Publica*, 19 (3): 223–39.

Van Laer, J., and Van Aelst, P. (2010). 'Internet and Social Movement Action Repertoires'. *Information, Communication and Society*, 13 (8): 1146–71.

Vatican. (2020). 'Catechism of the Catholic Church'. Available at: https://www.vatican.va/archive/ccc_css/archive/catechism/p3s2c2a6.htm (accessed 10 July 2020).

Waites, M. (2017). 'LGBTI Organizations Navigating Imperial Contexts: The Kaleidoscope Trust, the Commonwealth and the Need for a Decolonizing, Intersectional Politics'. *Sociological Review*, 65 (4): 644–62.

Weeks, J. (2015). 'Gay Liberation and Its Legacies'. In *The Ashgate Research Companion to Lesbian and Gay Activism*, ed. M. Tremblay and D. Paternotte. Farnham: Ashgate, pp. 45–57.

Whitaker, B. (2011). *Unspeakable Love: Gay and Lesbian Life in the Middle East*. London: Saqi.

Whittier, N. E. (2001). 'Emotional Strategies: The Collective Reconstruction and Display of Oppositional Emotions in the Movement against Child Sexual Abuse'. In *Passionate Politics: Emotions and Social Movements*, ed. J. Goodwin, J. M. Jasper and F. Polletta. Chicago, IL: University of Chicago Press, pp. 233–50.

Wright, H., and Welsh, P. (2014). *Masculinities, Conflict and Peacebuilding: Perspectives on Men through a Gender Lens*. London: Saferworld.

X. (2017). 'Beirut, a History'. *Kohl: A Journal of Body and Gender Research*, 3 (2): kohljournal.press/beirut-a-history (accessed 15 February 2021).

Yan, V. (2016). 'Helem Opens New Community Centre in Mar Mikhael after Two-Year Hiatus'. *The Daily Star Lebanon*. Available at: www.dailystar.com.lb/News/Lebanon-News/2016/Oct-18/376944-helem-opens-new-community-centre-in-mar-mikhael-after-two-year-hiatus.ashx (accessed 10 July 2020).

Younes, R., and Bailly, A. (2020). ' "If Not Now, When?" Queer and Trans People Reclaim Their Power in Lebanon's Revolution'. Human Rights Watch. Available at: www.hrw.org/video-photos/interactive/2020/05/07/if-not-now-when-queer-and-trans-people-reclaim-their-power (accessed 10 July 2020).

Zeidan, T. (2019). 'For LGBTI People in Lebanon, They Go through Their Own Stonewall Everyday'. Available at: www.gaystarnews.com/article/for-lgbti-people-in-lebanon-they-go-through-their-own-stonewall-everyday/ (accessed 7 July 2020).

INDEX